LOYALISM AND RADICALISM IN LANCASHIRE, 1798–1815

OXFORD HISTORICAL MONOGRAPHS

Loyalism and Radicalism in Lancashire, 1798–1815

KATRINA NAVICKAS

OXFORD
UNIVERSITY PRESS

OXFORD
UNIVERSITY PRESS

Great Clarendon Street, Oxford OX2 6DP

Oxford University Press is a department of the University of Oxford.
It furthers the University's objective of excellence in research, scholarship,
and education by publishing worldwide in

Oxford New York

Auckland Cape Town Dar es Salaam Hong Kong Karachi
Kuala Lumpur Madrid Melbourne Mexico City Nairobi
New Delhi Shanghai Taipei Toronto

With offices in

Argentina Austria Brazil Chile Czech Republic France Greece
Guatemala Hungary Italy Japan Poland Portugal Singapore
South Korea Switzerland Thailand Turkey Ukraine Vietnam

Published in the United States
by Oxford University Press Inc., New York

First published 2009

British Library Cataloguing in Publication Data
Data available

Library of Congress Cataloging in Publication Data
Data available

Typeset by Laserwords Private Limited, Chennai, India
Printed in Great Britain
on acid-free paper by
the MPG Books Group

ISBN 978–0–19–955967–1

1 3 5 7 9 10 8 6 4 2

The book is dedicated to Simon.

Acknowledgements

The author wishes to thank Joanna Innes for her skilful editing, Mark Philp, John Stevenson, Kathryn Gleadle, and Perry Gauci for their advice, and St John's College, Oxford, for its support. John Walton, Robert Glen, Alan Crosby, Mark Smith, and John Walsh have also provided useful information. Thanks also to Jane and Michael at Chetham's, gems amidst the archives. The Arts and Humanities Research Board (now Council) funded the thesis upon which this book is based.

Permission has been graciously granted by: Chetham's Library, for the reproduction of extracts of Michael Weatherley's diary, Manchester Local Studies for the reproduction of maps from John Aikin's *A Description of the Country from Thirty to Forty Miles Round Manchester*, and Oldham Local Studies and Archives, for reproduction of Edwin Butterworth's map of Tandle Hill, and extracts from William Rowbottom's 'Annals of Oldham'.

K. N.

Contents

List of Maps

List of Abbreviations

BL	British Library
Cheshire RO	Cheshire Record Office
Cumbria RO	Cumbria Record Office, Barrow-in-Furness
Greater Manchester RO	Greater Manchester Record Office
House of Lords RO	House of Lords Record Office
JRLUM	John Rylands Library, University of Manchester
Lancashire CRO	Lancashire County Record Office
Liverpool RO	Liverpool Record Office
MCL	Manchester Archives, Manchester Central Library
NA	National Archives, Public Record Office, Kew
West Yorkshire RO	West Yorkshire Record Office, Leeds
CMG	*Cowdroy's Manchester Gazette*
Hansard	*Hansard's Parliamentary Debates* (Baldwin & Cradock, 1832)
Holden diaries	Bolton Archives, ZZ 530/1, diaries of John Holden
MM	*Manchester Mercury*
NA, HO	National Archives, Home Office, Domestic Correspondence, George III
PP	Parliamentary Papers
Rowbottom diaries	Oldham Local Studies, typescript, William Rowbottom, 'Annals of Oldham', 1787–1823
EHR	*English Historical Review*
HJ	*Historical Journal*
JBS	*Journal of British Studies*
JORALS	*Journal of Regional and Local Studies*
MRHR	*Manchester Region Historical Review*
NH	*Northern History*

P & P	*Past & Present*
SH	*Social History*
THSLC	*Transactions of the Historic Society of Lancashire and Cheshire*
TLCAS	*Transactions of the Lancashire and Cheshire Antiquarian Society*

Place of publication is London unless otherwise stated.

Introduction

This book surveys radicalism, loyalism, and patriotism in Lancashire during the Napoleonic wars. It follows the inner workings of popular political activity in response to a multitude of external and internal challenges, including the threat of French invasion, economic crisis, food scarcities, Irish immigration, and serious social unrest. Lancashire's distinctive political culture and status at the heart of the industrial revolution affords the region a central place in this story, one which previous historians have not fully explained. Lancashire was unique or at least distinctive in many respects. As E. P. Thompson and other historians of radicalism recognized, the region witnessed some of the most intense, disruptive, and violent popular politics in this period and beyond.[i] Particularly active groups emerged, including not only extreme republicans, more moderate radicals, Luddites, and early trade unions, but also strong networks of 'Church-and-King' loyalists and Orange lodges. This book explains how this heady mix combined to produce such a politically charged region during the French and Napoleonic wars. If the 'Peterloo massacre' in Manchester in 1819 was not inevitable, the conditions for it had nevertheless been created during the Napoleonic wars.

The historiography of popular politics during the French wars is plentiful but unbalanced. Many studies surreptitiously gloss over the Napoleonic era, which has received less attention in proportionality and depth than the popular and elite reaction in Britain to the French Revolution. There are of course notable exceptions. A. J. Hone and Mark Philp are among the few who have analysed radicalism during the French wars in their entirety.[ii] Roger Wells and Marianne Elliott make a bold case for republicanism between 1797 and 1802. Michael Turner, J.

[i] E. P. Thompson, *The Making of the English Working Class*, 2nd edn (Harmondsworth, 1968), p. 208.

[ii] M. Philp, ed., *Resisting Napoleon: the British Response to the Threat of Invasion, 1797–1815* (Basingstoke, 2006); A. J. Hone, *For the Cause of Truth: Radicalism in London, 1796–1821* (Oxford, 1982).

E. Cookson, and Peter Spence discuss the revival of moderate radicalism from 1806.[III] Radicalism in the 1800s nevertheless receives most attention from literary historians, who look less at the politics of action than on the language of literary and intellectual debate.[IV] Loyalism is still more poorly served. It seems static, if not unchanged, in descriptions of Britain during the Napoleonic wars, or it is conflated with patriotism. Following Linda Colley's enormously influential *Britons: Forging the Nation*, works abound concerning the patriotism of the British public.[V] Of course, what J. E. Cookson has termed 'national defence patriotism' enjoyed a swell of popular interest during the invasion scares.[VI] Yet loyalism did not amalgamate totally with patriotism, even if it may have gained hegemony over its expression in this period. This book redresses these imbalances in the historiography and provides a richer local context for the complexities of popular politics.

Loyalism and radicalism were redefined in more centrist terms, retreating from the extremes that they had been forced into by the immediate reaction to the French Revolution. The superficial unity Lancashire had attained in the face of the Napoleonic threat had reduced the need for such polarities between political positions. The actions of the government after the threat had passed, combined with an increasingly attritional war, played their part in enabling the schism between loyalism and radicalism to soften. Elements among loyalists adopted previously radical criticisms of government and monarchy, and radicalism came to encompass a wider section of a generally loyally disposed population. Radicalism in effect had to make terms with loyalism to claim a mass following. Patriotism was at the heart of these changes. The process was, however, no mere xenophobic or defensive reaction against the French.

[III] R. Wells, *Insurrection: the British Experience, 1795–1803* (Gloucester, 1983); M. Elliott, *Partners in Revolution, The United Irishmen and France* (New Haven, 1982); P. Spence, *The Birth of Romantic Radicalism: War, Popular Politics and English Reformism, 1800–1815* (Aldershot, 1996); M. J. Turner, *Reform and Respectability, the Making of a Middle-Class Liberalism in Early Nineteenth Century Manchester*, Chetham Society, 3rd ser., 40 (Manchester, 1995); J. E. Cookson, *The Friends of Peace: Anti-War Liberalism in England, 1793–1815* (Cambridge, 1982).

[IV] S. C. Behrendt, ed., *Romanticism, Radicalism and the Press* (Detroit, 1997); K. Gilmartin, *Print Politics: The Press and Radical Opposition in Early Nineteenth Century England* (Cambridge, 1996).

[V] L. Colley, *Britons: Forging the Nation, 1707–1837* (New Haven, 1992). See A. Gee, *The British Volunteer Movement, 1794–1814* (Oxford, 2003); J. Mori, 'Languages of Loyalism: Patriotism, Nationhood and the State in the 1790s', *EHR* 118 (2003), 33–58.

[VI] J. E. Cookson, *The British Armed Nation, 1793–1815* (Oxford, 1997).

It is evident, as Colley has shown, that the experience of the wars 'forged' a sense of 'Britishness' among the inhabitants of Lancashire. Yet this feeling of attachment to king and country differed from the Britishness of other regions. It was coloured by the filters of regional identity and local prejudices: in effect, a Lancashire Britishness. This regional Britishness could incorporate suspicion of intrusion in local affairs from the metropolis and parliament, a provincial or 'country' attitude common to both radicals and loyalists. Lancashire, as a region, had been at the forefront of popular political action during the 1790s and the latter years of the Napoleonic War. It would achieve leadership of the new radical movement in the 1810s and beyond.

The French Revolution changed the way in which popular politics was defined and conducted in Britain. It shaped the language of political expression and opportunities for political action, both in the short term during the Napoleonic wars, and in the long term, to the 1832 Reform Act and Chartism. The main consequences were the popularization of new forms of radicalism and a concurrent reaction by loyalists and local authorities. Lancashire experienced the effects of these political changes in particular and often unusual ways, which reflected both its longer political heritage and the new circumstances induced by industrialization. Though radical pockets remained in the West Riding, it was in Lancashire that artisanal and plebeian radicalism flourished. It was in Lancashire that 'mass platform' radicalism emerged, and the Blanketeers and the 'Peterloo' massacre became the great landmarks of the nineteenth-century reform movement.

The political and social peculiarities of Lancashire contributed to the shift northwards of the centre of gravity of extra-parliamentary agitation. The region was marked out by its contrasts: it was relatively acquiescent or loyal during the American revolutionary period by comparison with Yorkshire, but some inhabitants warmly received the much more radical and egalitarian message of Thomas Paine's *Rights of Man* from 1792. The towns where Paineite radicalism thrived in Lancashire were also renowned for vicious loyalist repression. Though the reaction to the French Revolution will be discussed briefly here, because it created the framework for much of the later political activity, it will not be allowed to overshadow the impact of the 1798 Irish Rebellion and the Napoleonic War. Two changes came to the fore in response to the French invasion scares from 1798: firstly, vivid manifestations of patriotism and 'Britishness' emanated from every town and village across the country; and secondly, this ebullition of patriotism altered the context for public political expression. Even in these respects, Lancashire evinced unique qualities. Inhabitants filtered a national sense of Britishness through distinctly regional identities, as expressed in local propaganda and the formation of volunteer regiments.

'Loyalism', 'patriotism', and 'radicalism' have always been mutable political categories. Prior to the upheavals of 1789–93, British inhabitants chose their political opinions from a spectrum that gave room for manoeuvre and offered some scope for independence of action. A country gentleman could, and often did, for example, profess loyalty to the king and Established Church, while concurrently calling for reform of the electoral system or an end to parliamentary corruption. The French Revolution altered these parameters of political adherence. The British government was drawn into an ideological war against the republicanism and atheism of Jacobin France. This development contributed to a process whereby loyalism and radicalism polarized to the extreme ends of the political spectrum. The two stances—'stance' being a preferable term to 'ideology' because of the intellectual rigidity that it implies—were portrayed as diametrically opposite in the propaganda. Loyalist elites nurtured suspicion of any form of political or religious deviance that they believed would disturb public order and social hierarchy. No longer was it safe to inhabit a middle ground of moderate, constitutionalist reformism such as had been marked out by Yorkshire gentry in the heyday of the Association movement of the 1780s. Edmund Burke and even William Pitt were impelled to shore up the conservative cause and hide their reforming pasts.[vii] Through royal proclamations and legislation against sedition, loyalists ensured that those who were not for them were at least perceived to be against them. Any form of radicalism was proscribed as sedition. Church-and-King magistrates, clergy and other provincial notables took this new attitude on board wholeheartedly, and used the new atmosphere of repression to legitimate their efforts to maintain order and their authority in the provinces.

British radicals of the 1790s and 1800s drew inspiration from two main sources: the 'constitutional' radicalism of the eighteenth century and the republican egalitarianism of Thomas Paine's *Rights of Man* of 1792. Constitutional radicalism encompassed a tradition inherited from John Wilkes and Reverend Christopher Wyvill. It employed as common tropes old Country Whig tenets, including appeals to

[vii] J. J. Sack, *From Jacobite to Conservative: Reaction and Orthodoxy in Britain, c.1760–1832* (Cambridge, 1993), pp. 88–9.

precedent based on Magna Charta, Hampden, Commonwealth, and the restoration of liberties lost to a Norman 'yoke'. Constitutional demands usually centred on a moderate reform in parliament, particularly the removal of pocket boroughs and parliamentary corruption, reasonable extension of franchise, and freedom of the press. 'Paineite' radicalism by contrast was initially inspired by the French Revolution and then by Paine's *Rights of Man*. It moved away from appeals to historical precedent and instead deployed ideas of inherent rights with a basis in political economy. It was infused with elements of republicanism and egalitarianism, and was suspicious of social, political, and ecclesiastical hierarchies. 'Paineite' demands were more likely to centre upon the redistribution of representation into equal electoral districts, purity of elections, secret ballot, and universal suffrage by right, though this right was rarely attributed to women. More extreme republicans maintained their Francophilia even after the general reaction on the part of many radicals against the Terror in revolutionary France from 1793.[VIII]

Though there clearly was a spectrum of radical thought, in practice radicalism was much more mutable than loyalists allowed. Radicals employed both constitutionalist and Paineite tenets in parallel or in combination from the 1790s. In 1792, the Manchester Constitutional Society called for an end to parliamentary corruption through the passage of measures traditionally demanded, including an end to placemen in parliament and more frequent elections. Yet they also admitted in their propaganda that the French Revolution had inspired them to call for an equal representation of all men and to appeal to a much larger section of the population with political information.[IX] As E. P. Thompson argued, this combination proved particularly appealing in Lancashire, where the traditional message of anti-corruption and a larger representation were reinterpreted and extended in the context of the social welfare rhetoric of the second part of Paine's *Rights of Man*. Opinion and political conduct could also be ambiguous and fluctuating. Radical tenets did not determine political behaviour, as their variety allowed individuals to opt in and out of different campaigns. With the exception of the egalitarianism nurtured by isolated groups such as the radical Taylor family of Royton, near Oldham, there is little evidence

[VIII] M. Philp, *The French Revolution and British Popular Politics* (Cambridge, 1991), p. 84.

[IX] T. Walker, *A Review of the Political Events which have Occurred in Manchester during the Last Five Years*. . . (1794), pp. 26–30.

of any clear ideological argument that the artisan and labouring classes produced the wealth of society and thereby earned a right to vote. Radicalism involved not dogged subscription to concrete ideologies but political stances, to be adopted selectively according to the situation or to the nature of challenges offered by loyalist opposition. Especially after the government's suppression of the corresponding societies in 1797–8, radical identities were amorphous and responsive to specific circumstances. Radicals were not as institutionalized as the loyalist elites with their formal and informal networks of local government and association. What united all radicals was a desire for political change, although they differed as to ends and means.

Popular politics, particularly after 1798, was more nuanced than historians have recognized. Loyalism did not merge all its original principles or organization into patriotism, however incoherent or disparate those loyalist tenets may have been. 'Church-and-King' principles were sustained by magistrates and middle classes in contradistinction to the 'vulgar conservatism' of the ordinary populace that these same loyalist elites had ironically encouraged during the 1790s. An increasingly exclusive attitude emerged among local authorities, many of whom were attracted to the Orange movement that had transferred over the Irish Sea. This subtle shift occurred as a result of the British reaction to the Napoleonic invasion scares. Patriotism itself was not definitively the preserve of the loyalist elites. Kevin Gilmartin has applied Mark Philp's definition of 'vulgar conservatism' to the loyalist propaganda of the 1800s, showing that British governing elites continued to risk appealing to the populace in the hope of maintaining their hegemony and social stability.[x] Church-and-King magistrates, clergy, gentry, and manufacturers encouraged a loyalist form of patriotism among the working classes through membership of local volunteer corps. J. E.Cookson had argued persuasively for the predominance of a 'national defence patriotism' among the British population from 1798. Yet this urge for defence was complicated by political changes in revolutionary France. Stuart Semmel argues that the rise of Napoleon Bonaparte confused the dichotomies between republican France and the constitutional monarchy of Britain that loyalist propaganda had established in the 1790s. Bonaparte represented a system Britons were supposed to abhor, yet paradoxically also aroused admiration for qualities associated with Britain, primarily

[x] K. Gilmartin, *Writing Against Revolution: Literary Conservatism in Britain, 1790–1832* (Cambridge, 2007), p. 12.

for his military and imperial prowess.[xi] Church-and-King members of local elites were left searching for political and social certainties they believed were being eroded by their promotion of 'vulgar conservatism' among the working classes. Many magistrates and clergy in Lancashire therefore attempted to maintain their social and political exclusivity and identity through Orange lodges or High Anglican clubs.

Two phases of political change provide the context to which popular politics responded and evolved. The year 1806 marked the point when the first phase gave way to the next. Internationally, the first phase began in 1798, when the French threatened to invade Britain, until the battle of Trafalgar in October 1805 ensured British naval dominance. The second phase saw the invasion scares replaced by economic blockade on both sides and a war of attrition against Napoleonic 'imperial' dominance on the Continent. Popular opinion about the way in which the war was being fought, loyalist and radical alike, was altered and became more pessimistic from 1806, in contrast to the exuberant patriotism that had been prompted by the invasion scares a few years previously. In part this change of mood resulted from war-weariness and discontent with George Canning's 'gunboat diplomacy' against Britain's former allies. Wellington's victories on the Continent only made their mark from 1813; before then, few were able to sustain hopes that Britain could achieve a successful peace swiftly. The battle of Waterloo halted only temporarily the demands for change that had been stirred by the economic distress caused by the government's Orders in Council, policy blunders in Copenhagen, Cintra, and Walcheren, and aristocratic corruption at home manifested especially by Lord Melville and the Duke of York.[xii]

Domestically, politics followed a similar chronology. The defeat of the Irish Rebellion of 1798 provided a major fillip to the government's sense of security, and as such was perhaps a more significant event than historians have recognized. From 1799 to 1805, however, William Pitt the Younger and Henry Addington maintained a certain level of stability in parliament and continued the policy of checking radicalism inside and outside Westminster. Charles James Fox, leader of the Whig opposition, absented himself from parliament and the more radically leaning of his followers were quietened. The patriotism of the invasion

[xi] Cookson, *British Armed Nation*; S. Semmel, *Napoleon and the British* (New Haven, 2004), p. 16.

[xii] P. Harling, 'The Duke of York Affair and the Complexities of Wartime Patriotism', *HJ* 39 (1996), 963.

scares contributed to a superficial sense of political unity in the face of the threat. The death of Pitt in 1806, however, left the political ground unstable. The brief interlude of a Whig coalition, the 'Ministry of All the Talents', reopened opportunities for wider political debate that had not been encouraged since the passing of the anti-seditious proclamations and legislation in 1792–5. The Whig sojourn in power proved illusory and the Duke of Portland and later Spencer Perceval took the reins. Nevertheless the political interruption of 1806–7 had been enough to ensure that the renewed anti-corruption campaign had too firm a hold to be silenced. War and popular revolt against Napoleon in Spain and Portugal made it possible for government to revise its attitudes towards the population's role in politics. The assassination of Perceval by a disgruntled merchant in May 1812 created a brief period of crisis, especially since it occurred in the midst of the Luddite disturbances in the north and Midlands, and a brewing war with America over the economic blockade. The situation was eased more quickly than expected, as Lord Liverpool began his steady premiership which would take Britain up to and beyond Wellington's victory at Waterloo.[xiii]

Popular politics in Lancashire mirrored national patterns of activity, though often the region exhibited the more extreme ends of the political spectrum, which ran from Orange loyalism to republican radicalism. What distinguished Lancashire popular politics in this period from other regions was that radicals began to break away from following the trends from the metropolis. Though Burdett, Cartwright, and Henry 'Orator' Hunt still mattered as 'national' figures, they were not the sole leaders of protest. Lancashire began to decide its own agenda. The wars may have made Lancastrians feel more British, but they also strengthened their sense of regional identity. The region came of age as a political as well as an economic entity towards the end of the war. Through the 'mass platform' radicalism of the post-war era, agitation shifted north; by 1819, politicians had to look towards the politics of the north of England, over Spa Fields to St Peter's Fields, to gauge the direction and influence of popular protest and radicalism.[xiv] This is the key to the importance of the region during the Napoleonic wars.

[xiii] M. J. Turner, *The Age of Unease: Government and Reform in Britain, 1782–1832* (Stroud, 2000), pp. 138–9.

[xiv] J. Belchem, 'Henry Hunt and the Evolution of the Mass Platform', *EHR* 93 (1978), 739–73.

Radicalism and loyalism were constituted as political positions by terms, phrases, and words which formed the rhetoric of political discourse. It was within this discourse that debates were conducted and identities were constructed. Radicals continued to challenge loyalists in the 1800s, but they employed more subtle means of protest than before. They attempted to subvert elite ownership of the addresses and rituals that demonstrated the meanings of 'loyalism' and patriotism to the nation. This formed the basis for the success of the 'mass platform' after the end of the war. It must be confessed that the term 'radical' did not frequently occur within this language, and those seeking change regarded themselves either as 'reformers' or indeed as the true loyalists. Reform in itself encompassed a wide range of goals, including educational, religious, and welfare causes.[xv] Though many 'reformers' in this period subscribed to one or more of these other goals, 'radical' will be used here to distinguish those who sought constitutional change. In any case, analysis of popular politics in this period cannot be confined to debate in speeches and texts alone. Popular culture was conducted not just through words but also through symbols, signs, and rituals. The calendar was punctuated by celebrations and remembrances; the ordinariness of the week could be disrupted by a multitude of displays and protests: the processions of notables through the town, the toasts at a dinner, displays of banners and sashes by friendly societies, meetings of guilds and political clubs, election hustings, and the 'rough music' and effigy burning at demonstrations outside prisons or at marketplaces. James Epstein and Nicholas Rogers are among the few historians who have explored ways in which symbols were integral to popular political understanding and expression.[xvi] This book highlights the importance of the wider culture of politics during the Napoleonic wars and shows that contesting the symbols of power often meant contesting power itself.

This book is also consciously regional rather than national; it focuses on the politics of ordinary inhabitants of Lancashire rather than 'high' or philosophical debates. For over thirty years, J. D. Marshall continued to argue for the primacy of the region as a unit of historical study. He pointed to the importance of regional dynamism, captured in early

[xv] J. Innes and A. Burns (eds.), *Rethinking the Age of Reform: Britain 1780–1850* (Cambridge, 2003).

[xvi] J. Epstein, *In Practice: Studies in the Language and Culture of Popular Politics in Modern Britain* (Stanford, 2003); N. Rogers, *Crowds, Culture, and Politics in Georgian Britain* (Oxford, 1998).

twentieth-century regional studies and the work of historical geographers in the late 1970s.[xvii] Some studies of northern regions have followed, but they are often presented as case studies rather than as integrated explorations of social, political, and economic change in their own right. John Walton's masterful survey of Lancashire from the early modern to Victorian eras touches on the social significance of some of the political themes that this book discusses, but of course because of its scope and purpose, remains general.[xviii] The considerable influence of Linda Colley's work on the formation of British identity has overshadowed Marshall's call for more integrative regional history.[xix] The influence of *Britons: Forging the Nation* lies in its argument that British identity was able to overlay or incorporate itself into existing identities and prejudices in a particularly resonant and lasting way during the French Wars, primarily through Britons' strong attachment to Protestantism and the monarchy. The question of national identity is still very much at the core of many new studies of the period 1688–1914. In recent studies, national identity is no longer seen as organic or inherent but as a constructed cultural concept, often formed in reaction to a foreign 'other'.[xx] Yet, like the old Whig scholars, many historians still generalize about British identity; if they acknowledge regional or local differences, they regard them as subservient to an all-encompassing, coherent, and indeed forward-marching Britishness, contested only by the Irish and to a lesser degree the Scots and the Welsh.

This book shows that Britishness was undoubtedly an important identity shared by most inhabitants in this period and that it was brought into sharp focus by the Napoleonic invasion scares. Yet national identity was a complex entity. It was never a monolithic or homogeneous concept. Nor did it progress from confusion and localism to embody clear, national principles shared by all. Geographical identities have always been multiple, changing, overlapping, and contested. Britishness was a conglomeration of local and regional affiliations, which could be transcended or connected by the supra-national allegiances of religious,

[xvii] J. D. Marshall, *The Tyranny of the Discrete: a Discussion of the Problems of Local History in England* (Aldershot, 1997), p. 84.

[xviii] J. K. Walton, *Lancashire, A Social History, 1558–1939* (Manchester, 1987); C. Aspin, *The First Industrial Society: Lancashire* (Preston, rev. edn., 1995); C. B. Phillips and J. H. Smith, *Lancashire and Cheshire from AD 1540* (1994).

[xix] L. Colley, *Britons: Forging the Nation, 1707–1837* (New Haven, 1992).

[xx] B. Anderson, *Imagined Communities: Reflections on the Origin and Spread of Nationalism* (London, 1983).

philosophical, or political beliefs. Popular politics in Lancashire revealed aspects of all these adherences, expressed within the form of a 'Lancashire Britishness' shared by loyalists and radicals alike.

Certain difficulties arise when one attempts to cover such a diverse region as Lancashire. The county prior to 1974 encompassed the region from what is now south Cumbria down to north Cheshire. Balancing the narrative of events and personalities between north and south of the county is problematic. Jon Stobart's analysis of the North West has demonstrated how north Lancashire was increasingly left out of the frame in the eighteenth century because Manchester, Liverpool, and Chester were the centres of urban trade and transport systems. [xxi] Peter Borwick's study of society in north Lancashire conceded that most of the popular political action in this period occurred in Lancashire 'below the Sands'.[xxii] The huge significance of Manchester and its textile satellite towns, and of Liverpool with its mining and engineering hinterland, therefore overshadows the daily lives and politics of the more rural parts of the region. This does not imply that radicalism or strikes did not feature in north Lancashire, rather that little may have been recorded.

Furthermore, some sections of Lancashire society have left little surviving evidence of political activity, particularly the very highest and very lowest echelons, and rural dwellers. The highest are absent partly because Lancashire was not aristocratically dominated compared with its surrounding regions. This in itself is indicative of the distinctive nature of its social relations, wherein an industrial 'squirearchy' presided over rapidly increasing working and middle-class populations. Though not destroyed, the rural yeomanry were far less visible and prominent than they had been two hundred years previously. The political views and actions of domestic servants and agricultural labourers remain largely undiscovered.[xxiii] There are also many groups of individuals within the region who may have had their own distinctive perspectives but who generate only a few lines of enquiry: miners, the immigrant Welsh and Scottish, Jews and Africans, attorneys, doctors, and fishermen, amongst

[xxi] J. Stobart, *The First Industrial Region: North West England, c.1700–60* (Manchester, 2004), p. 89.

[xxii] P. D. R. Borwick, 'An English Provincial Society: North Lancashire 1770–1820', Ph.D. thesis (Lancaster, 1994).

[xxiii] See K. Navickas, 'The Cragg Memorandum Book: Society, Politics and Religion in North Lancashire During the 1790s', *NH* 42 (2005), 151–62. The only study of rural labourers is A. Gritt, 'The Survival of Service in the English Agricultural Labour Force: Lessons from Lancashire, c.1650–1851', *Agricultural History Review*, 50 (2002), 35–56.

other specialised trades and occupations.[xxiv] Women in their own right are not a focus. Although the views of Mary Rathbone, Elizabeth Aikin, and other women among the Liverpool 'Friends of Peace' circle are accounted for, there is much women's correspondence that could not be included, principally that of the Wigan circles of Joanna Holt Leigh and the Standish family. Amanda Vickery's study of the latter families illuminates their participation behind the political scenes in the earlier part of the eighteenth century.[xxv]

The economic, social, and political structures of the region are surveyed in Chapter 1. Chapter 2 looks at aspects of patriotism, particularly at the volunteers and at patriotic propaganda which influenced the daily lives of local inhabitants. Civic patriotism provided another arena within which social and political tensions manifested themselves. Chapter 3 discusses the effects of the Napoleonic War upon loyalist ideologies and forms of loyalist government, the development of a Church-and-King hegemony over public life with an accompanying undercurrent of Orangeism among the magistracy. Chapter 4 highlights how committed individuals and isolated circles in Lancashire towns and villages kept radicalism alive during the radical 'silence' of 1795–1806. Chapter 5 charts the bitter conflicts between manufacturers and their employees, when a shared discourse of legality and common narratives of action made it possible for workers to overcome the physical limitations of unionised action. The revival of political agitation from 1806 is charted in Chapter 6. It was a revival on a scale not seen since the early 1790s and much earlier than historians of the post-war 'mass platform' have recognized. In this period, a new generation of radical activists emerged, who found inspiration in witnessing the conflicts of 1806–12, just as the writings of Paine had inspired their predecessors. This period formed the crucible for the personalities and ideas which would shape radical history at Peterloo and in Chartism.[xxvi]

[xxiv] J. Langton, *Geographical Change and Industrial Revolution: Coalmining in South West Lancashire, 1590–1799* (Cambridge, 1979); B. Williams, *The Making of Manchester Jewry* (Manchester, 1976).

[xxv] Wigan RO, D/D Lei C, Leigh correspondence, 1796–1811; D/D St C, Standish correspondence, 1793–1812. A. Vickery, *The Gentleman's Daughter: Women's Lives in Georgian England* (New Haven, 1998).

[xxvi] The personalities and politics of the post-war radicals have been extensively discussed in Turner, *Reform and Respectability*, and L. Edwards, 'Popular Politics in the North West of England, 1815-21', Ph.D. thesis (Manchester, 1998).

1

Defining the Region

Samuel Bamford (1788–1872), post-war radical activist and writer, wrote a lyrical paean to the landscape of south-east Lancashire in the 1840s. He described a view from the summit of the road through Thornham near his native town of Middleton:

> To the west are the hills and moors of Crompton, the green pastures year by year, cutting further up into the hills; the ridge of Blackstone Edge, with Robin Hood's bed, darkened as usual by shadow; whilst the moors, sweeping round to the left (the hills of Caldermoor, Whitworth and Wuerdle) bend somewhat in the form of a shepherd's crook around a fair and sunny vale, through which the Roche flows past cottages, farms and manufactories. [1]

Bamford manifested a vivid awareness of the changes affecting place, particularly the spread of manufactories and enclosure. In his description, the reader witnessed a physical representation of how industry and rurality evolved in the early nineteenth century, perhaps not harmoniously, but certainly not in isolation from each other. The region was composed of a network of economic and communication links, but, as Bamford's recollections intimate, it was also formed by its inhabitants' sense of the geographical context of their daily lives. Though both national and local politics were convulsed by the reaction to the French Revolution and Napoleonic wars, longer-term forces were concurrently affecting the quotidian lives of the inhabitants of Lancashire, principally industrialization and urbanization.

The county of Lancashire was defined by administrative and juridical borders which were delineated on three sides by the coast, the Pennines, and the plains south of the river Mersey. The effects of the Industrial

[1] S. Bamford, *Walks in South Lancashire* (Blackley, 1844), pp. 25–6.

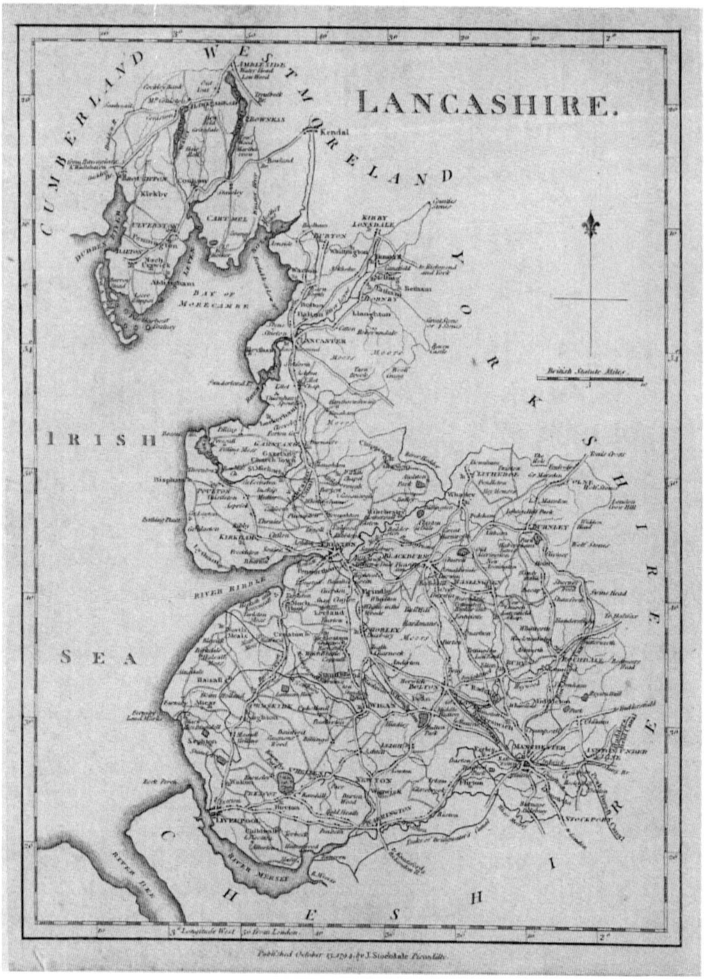

Map 1. 'Lancashire', in J. Aikin, *A Description of the Country from Thirty to Forty Miles Around Manchester* (Manchester, 1794).

Revolution created alternative frameworks of economic and political power. Trade links and socio-familial relationships often crossed county boundaries and thereby created a wider region. This region encompassed the county (including Lonsdale hundred 'over the Sands'), together with its immediate environs of north Cheshire and the Pennine part of the West Riding of Yorkshire. It was often in these boundary areas that the most virulent political activity took place. Border districts, centred in the river valleys of the Pennines, meant ambiguous jurisdiction; when combined with the largest rise in population and industrialization, they opened more possibilities for vigorous and vocal political agitation. Regionalism must be therefore taken into account in the study of popular politics in this period. This chapter charts the social and economic changes affecting Lancashire at this time, understandings of class, and tensions between local and national government.

INDUSTRIALIZATION AND THE REGION

The Lancashire region was central to the economic and social development of Britain in this period. It was in many ways unique. The rise in population of its urban areas was unprecedented; vivid changes to the physical landscape were rapid and lasting. Its most prominent association with cotton manufacture masked intra-regional specializations, each with its own economic character and identity. Textile production of all kinds was concentrated in the south-east Pennines stretching over to the West Riding of Yorkshire towards Huddersfield, and into north-east Cheshire. The south-west of the region was dominated by mining and coal-based heavy industries, while the fertile agricultural plains of central and west Lancashire provided arable and dairy produce. Pastoral agriculture still marked the character and landscape of north Lancashire and Westmorland, especially as the port of Lancaster was losing business to Liverpool. As the major commercial port hub, Liverpool stood somewhat above the other ports and towns.[2] This differentiation was not an immediate result of industrialization, but had already been established by the early eighteenth century. This was reflected in the network of turnpikes, which focused on Manchester and left Liverpool relatively isolated from its hinterland, while Chester was oriented away from the northern parts of the region towards western Cheshire and north Wales. The notion of an economic region and intra-regional differentiation thus had a longer, pre-industrial history.[3]

2 S. King and G. Timmins, *Making Sense of the Industrial Revolution* (Manchester, 2001), p. 36; J. K. Walton, *Lancashire: A Social History, 1558–1939* (Manchester, 1987), p. 121.

3 J. Stobart, 'The Spatial Organization of a Regional Economy: Central Places in North-West England in the Early Eighteenth Century', *Journal of Historical Geography*, 22 (1996), 152.

Lancashire interacted with the ever-expanding dominance of London but developed its own provincial character and connections in response. The lessening of mailcoach times from the metropolis to provincial towns was one manifestation of the altered pace of communications. In 1770 there was only one bi-weekly stagecoach from Manchester to London and one to Liverpool; by 1816 there were seventy distinct coaches.[4] From the 1770s, canals brought coal-producing areas of the west within easier reach of the factories of the east, and connected the region to food supplies and markets in Yorkshire and the Midlands. Individual gentry and manufacturers made huge investments in canals not solely out of a spirit of financial speculation; they also expressed local pride and regional vision. The lavish celebrations and ceremony that greeted canal openings were testimony to the easing of trade, communications, and travel that the system offered. Huddersfield Canal, for example, was opened in April 1811; about 500 investors sailed from Ashton-under-Lyne to Marsden in the West Riding: 'attended by a band of music playing Rule Britannia and entered the tunnel loudly cheered by at least 10,000 spectators'.[5]

Although the region was becoming more integrated as a whole within itself through trade and manufacture, south-east Lancashire was the most distinctive and most rapidly growing in terms of population, industry, and communications. Manchester and its burgeoning 'satellite' towns were cohering together and developing a distinct sub-regional identity. Contemporary awareness of this coherence was exemplified with the publication of *A Description of the Country from Thirty to Forty Miles Around Manchester* in 1795 by Dr John Aikin (1747–1822). The title in itself was significant. His magnificent survey marked another departure from conceiving Lancashire as a county towards a perception of Lancashire as a greater region. In the seventeenth and eighteenth centuries, antiquarians had delighted in producing traditional county histories which meticulously detailed the aristocratic seats and endowed parishes which signified their county's heritage.[6] Aikin's work reflected the changes that industry and commerce had wrought upon the society and the interests of the inhabitants within its remits. It illustrated that at least some Manchester merchants and manufacturers envisaged their

[4] D. Gregory, 'The Friction of Distance: Information Circulation and the Mails in Early Nineteenth Century England', *Journal of Historical Geography*, 13 (1987), 134.

[5] *CMG*, 13 April 1811.

[6] C. R. J. Currie and C. R. Elrington, *English County Histories, A Guide* (Stroud, 1994), pp. 219–20.

surroundings in terms of an alternative, forward-oriented identity. It was also a product of the analytic and scientific thinking that Aikin had imbibed from Warrington Dissenting Academy in the 1770s, together with his fellow scholars the physician Thomas Percival and the population theorist Thomas R. Malthus.[7] Aikin was primarily concerned with delineating markets, urban institutions and housing, a progressive farming landscape, and economic conditions. He was perhaps guilty of Mancuno-centricity, but was nevertheless observant of the main changes affecting his part of the region. Manchester was at the heart of economic as well as political activity in this period.

Dr Aikin branded the cotton trade as the region's defining characteristic, both economically and in terms of identity:

> Manchester is . . . the heart of this vast system, the circulating branches of which spread all around it, though to different distances. To the north-western and western points it is most widely diffused, having in those parts established various headquarters, which are each the centres to their lesser circles. Bolton, Blackburn, Wigan and several other Lancashire towns are stations of this kind; and the whole interesting country takes its character from them. Stockport to the south, and Ashton to the east, of Manchester, are similar appendages of this trade; and its influence is spread, more or less, over the greatest part of Lancashire.[8]

The French economist Léon Faucher made a tour of parts of England in 1844, and his famous analysis of Manchester presented a developed version of Aikin's earlier description. The city was 'like an industrious spider', at the centre of a web of roads and railways 'towards its auxiliaries, formerly villages but now towns, which serve as outposts to the grand centre of industry'. He described the whole regional process of the textile industry, whereby an order sent from Liverpool to the Manchester Exchange would be spun at Manchester, Bolton, Oldham, or Ashton, 'woven in the sheds of Bolton, Stalybridge or Stockport; dyed and printed at Blackburn, Chorley or Preston and finished, measured and packed at Manchester'.[9] This of course simplified the complex economic processes occurring in industrializing Lancashire, but in essence it still indicated contemporary awareness of the centrality of Manchester to the infrastructure of the region.

[7] B. Smith (ed.), *Truth, Liberty, Religion: Essays Celebrating Two Hundred Years of Manchester College* (Oxford, 1986).

[8] J. Aikin, *A Description of the Country from Thirty to Forty Miles Around Manchester* (Manchester, 1795), p. 3.

[9] L. Faucher, *Manchester in 1844* (Manchester, 1844), pp. 15–16.

According to the 1801 census, Lancashire had over 670,000 inhabitants. The population underwent rapid expansion during the French and Napoleonic wars. Old market towns thickened along their main roads as did their surrounding hill villages. This was associated with the spread of water-powered mills in the Pennines and (latterly) large mills in the city centres. Manchester's population apparently trebled in fifty years. The 1811 census recorded 91,130 inhabitants in the city, including 9,000 spinners and 12,000 weavers. The 'principal inhabitants', mostly involved in manufacture, numbered more than 5,000 in the mid-1790s. Many towns saw their population double during the twenty years between the 1801 and 1821 censuses. Notable among these were Stockport (from 17,000 in 1801 to 27,000 in 1821), Liverpool town (83,250 to 141,500), Bolton (24,000 to 41,200), and Preston (11,900 to 24,600).[10] These figures of course do not include all the villages and 'neighbourhoods' in these towns' hinterlands, where much growth took place. For example, the Court Leet and Vestry of Ashton-under-Lyne found it hard to control the expansion around their town. Industrial villages sprouted during the American War, and notably bore the names of contemporary imperial places or battles: Quebec, Boston, Botany Bay, Charlestown, and Bengal. The area that increased most rapidly during the French wars was the overcrowded corner in the Hartshead division of the town. This became the major part of a new town, Stalybridge, formed by the building of mills along the banks of the river Tame.[11] Agricultural areas also experienced socio-economic change, though not on the same scale as urban industrial districts. Leases were also becoming increasingly commercialized as they shifted from customary inheritance to a general limit of three lives, thereby encouraging mobility between districts, and from village to town.[12]

Momentous among these changes was enclosure. The period 1789–1815 was the most eventful for parliamentary enclosure across the country; in Lancashire more than forty acts, public and private, were passed from 1789 to 1815. Indeed, the parliamentary enclosure of north Lancashire was more concentrated in the first two decades of the nineteenth century than in most other regions: nearly 58 per cent,

[10] W. H. Thomson, *History of Manchester to 1852* (Altrincham, 1967), p. 277; C. B. Phillips and J. H. Smith, *Lancashire and Cheshire from AD1540* (1994), pp. 134, 136.

[11] W. M. Bowman, *England in Ashton-under-Lyne* (Altrincham, 1960), p. 433.

[12] Aikin, *A Description of the Country*, p. 326.

comprising a total area of 30,000 statute acres. Extensive areas of common were reclaimed on either side of the Lune above Lancaster and on the fringes of Bowland. Further north, nearly all the Lonsdale commons and wastes had been enclosed by 1800.[13] As Samuel Bamford witnessed, the enclosure of moors opened up land opportunities for urban development on the outskirts of manufacturing towns as well as in traditional agricultural areas. In some manufacturing towns, the main purpose or consequence was urbanization and the development of working-class colonies on the outskirts of towns. Hundreds of established landowners, speculators, and manufacturers took up plots during the private enclosure of the moors around Oldham in 1810 and Bolton expanded its residential and manufacturing areas on land from the moor to the south of the town, enclosed in 1793.[14] The effects were visually striking yet blurred the boundaries between urban and rural areas.

Industrialization and enclosure did not create an urban proletariat isolated from their 'rural' past and customs. On the contrary, the location of water-powered mills and the 'bearing home' of cotton weft by weavers strengthened urban–rural connections. The meeting of urban and rural life in the neighbourhood was a key feature of quotidian life in the Lancashire region in the late eighteenth and early nineteenth centuries. 'Neighbourhood' was a key geographical descriptor commonly used in reports in newspapers, examinations in court, magistrates' descriptions of unrest, personal correspondence, and written sources. It was understood to mean an area within a day's walk, being not too far from home but with larger horizons than the parochial. The prevalence of the concept of 'neighbourhood' demonstrates that industrialization did not cause an irrevocable urban–rural divide. Methodist and other Dissenting itinerant circuits, camp meetings, and chapels flourished in semi-rural 'neighbourhoods' as well as among the more concentrated industrial populations of Lancashire towns.[15] These semi-rural neighbourhoods were important because, as is illustrated in the following chapters, they often hosted protests and other forms of popular politics.

13 R. H. Adcock, *A Handlist of Lancashire Enclosure Acts and Awards* (Preston, 1946); I. Whyte, *Transforming Fell and Valley: Landscape and Parliamentary Enclosure in North West England* (Lancaster, 2003), p. 24.

14 Lancashire CRO, AE 5/7, Oldham enclosure map, 1810; Bolton Archives, ZAL/1, Enclosure Plan of Bolton Moor, 1793.

15 P. Stigant, 'Wesleyan Methodism and Working-Class Radicalism in the North, 1792–1821', *NH* 6 (1971), 98–116.

LANDOWNING AND CLASS

Class is a major preoccupation in studies of this period and especially in histories of popular politics in industrializing regions. Forty years after its publication, *The Making of the English Working Class* by E. P. Thompson still resonates with unresolved issues about the formation of class identities in response to industrialization and the French Revolution. It is well known that during the eighteenth century, a variety of conceptions of occupations or economic and social positions existed, usually in parallel rather than in contest with each other. David Cannadine posits three basic models of society that were entertained in parallel: firstly, it was conceived as an ordered hierarchy of 'ranks', 'orders', 'sorts', or 'classes'; secondly, as a triad of upper, middle, and lower groups; and thirdly, as an antagonistic dichotomy between 'patricians' and 'plebs'.[16] Models of class involve problematic assumptions based upon individuals' occupations. It is difficult to determine a person's identity by his or her occupation (even when their status within the occupational group is clear) because many did not follow a single activity. More often they derived a composite livelihood from several sources. This was especially the case with women and small farmers. The category of 'weavers' must be qualified by the recognition that many wove only casually or at desperate times in their lives, and perhaps would only call themselves weavers at these times. Furthermore, changes of trade following apprenticeship were far from uncommon.[17] Even where workers' occupations fell within a single category, this very fact often blocked rather than facilitated a wider class identity. As will be seen later, vigorous activity by early trade unions and combinations in this period demonstrated that most trades remained very much separate in organization and identity, even when expounding common grievances against employers or political figures.

These caveats and complications do not negate the existence of class consciousness, but rather suggest that workers and indeed all different 'classes' had recourse to other means of collective expression and organization. The formation of a shared class identity, like that of British

16 B. Lewis, *The Middlemost and the Milltowns, Bourgeois Culture and Politics in Early Industrial England* (Stanford, 2001), p. 5, citing D. Cannadine, *The Rise and Fall of Class in Britain* (New York, 1999).

17 D. Bythell, *The Handloom Weavers: A Study in the English Cotton Industry During the Industrial Revolution* (Cambridge, 1969), p. 60; P. Glennie, *Distinguishing Men's Trades, Occupational Sources and Debates for Pre-Census England* (Bristol, 1990), p. 103.

identity, was not necessarily a teleological evolution. It did not begin in the handloom weaving colonies in the Pennines nor in the gigantic spinning mills of McConnel and Kennedy in Ancoats, Manchester. Notions of class did exist, but they offered only one among many conceptions of collective belonging, and like geographical identities were used according to circumstances. Individuals and 'communities' usually made their own choices about shared identities. Choosing an identity was not, however, entirely a matter of free will: identities of all kinds were shaped by social regulation through cultural norms and the power of some groups to define the identity of others.[18] This became especially obvious when the 'principal inhabitants', as they termed themselves, claimed to represent the political opinions of the towns or communities over which they presided.

The balance between classes was changing in Lancashire, and in a way that contrasted with patterns in other counties. South-east Lancashire was not dominated by the aristocracy. Rather, the region was essentially a land of squirearchy. This was in part a cause and in part a product of its economic and political development. Many contemporaries, including Dr Aikin, economists, and writers of trade directories, charted how the old gentry and yeomanry lineages were dying out and how landownership was fragmenting in the east of the region. For example, Aikin noted that the surroundings of Mottram-in-Longdendale, on the border of Lancashire and Cheshire, 'was formerly famous of the number of halls occupied by their owners, who resided on their own estates, most of which are now in the possession of farmers'.[19] In 1815, W. R. Dickson, the economic investigator, reported to the Board of Agriculture that only a few large landed estates existed in the county.[20] Revd T. D. Whitaker's nostalgic 'Country' lament about the decline of the old gentry, in his history of Whalley, was published in 1801.[21] His pessimism was reflected by other Anglican clergy across the diocese. A revealing question concerning the number of 'families of note' was asked in the questionnaire sent out by the Bishop of Chester as part of his visitation in 1804. Many clerics reported their dismay about the decline of the old names and their manors. The curate of Milnrow near Rochdale, for example, reported that there were none 'since Richard

18 C. Brace, 'Landscape and Identity', in I. Robertson and P. Richards (eds.), *Studying Cultural Landscapes* (Arnold, 2003), p. 122.

19 Aikin, *A Description of the Country*, p. 468.

20 R. W. Dickson, *General View of the Agriculture of Lancashire* (1815), p. 91.

21 T. D. Whitaker, *An History of the Original Parish of Whalley* (Blackburn, 1801).

Towneley left Belfield about fifteen years ago'.[22] Even in areas with a resident landowner, influence was declining. The Earls of Bradford, the Bridgemans, possessed much property around Bolton and Wigan, but although their agent figured prominently in local affairs, they remained aloof from the governing elite of Bolton. Orlando Bridgeman was an MP for Wigan, but preferred to stay at his other seat in Staffordshire.[23]

The pessimism of the clergy about the state of social hierarchy in the county owed a lot to conservative reactions to visible change on the horizons of towns. It also stemmed from a suspicion of a dislocating, commercial ethos, identified with Dissent, an opinion which must have been strengthened by John Aikin's survey, the author being a prominent Dissenter.[24] This pessimism did not take into account that landowning had always been in a process of flux, especially so after confiscations followed the Jacobite rebellions. Moreover, the small estates and mansion-villas springing up could never match the prominence of old aristocratic estates. There may have been numerically more landowners holding small estates and various other forms of property, but the weight of the surviving aristocracy and old gentry, though small in relation to other counties, still prevailed. The distribution of titled estates was uneven in the rest of Lancashire, but they especially congregated in the fertile plains of the south-west and the Fylde, where economic gains from agriculture and mining could still support their way of life. In 1815, Dickson listed eleven 'noblemen who possess landed property in this county', who included Edward Smith Stanley (1752–1834), the twelfth Earl of Derby and the Lord Lieutenant of Lancashire, who resided at Knowsley Hall; Thomas Egerton, the Earl of Wilton of Heaton Hall near Manchester; the Earl of Sefton of Sefton Park near Liverpool; Thomas Powys, Lord Lilford of Bewsey Hall near Warrington; and Sir Henry Houghton of Houghton, near Carlisle.[25] George Harry Grey (1737–1819), fifth Earl of Stamford and Warrington, Derby's counterpart in Cheshire, held large agricultural estates and almost 10,000 acres around Ashton-under-Lyne.[26] Sefton owned a large estate less than seven miles from the Stanleys' Knowsley estate. Much of the land extending from Southport to the river Wyre in

[22] Cheshire RO, EDV7/3, Bishop of Chester Visitation Returns, 1804.

[23] B. Lewis, *The Middlemost and the Milltowns: Bourgeois Culture and Politics in Early Industrial England* (Stanford, 2001), p. 11.

[24] N. Murray, 'The Influence of the French Revolution on the Church of England and its Rivals, 1789–1802', D.Phil. thesis (Oxford, 1975), pp. 371–2.

[25] Dickson, *General View*, p. 91.

[26] M. Nevell, *Tameside, 1700-1930* (Ashton-under-Lyne, 1993), p. 93.

central north Lancashire was shared between branches of the Hesketh and the Cliftons of Lytham, who owned an estate of 16,000 acres.[27] Derby's annual income from Lancashire rents was over £26,000 net in 1797, with his largest gross rents arising from Preston, his Knowsley seat, Bury, and Pilkington.[28]

Lancashire was thus a landscape of squires and gentry with the aristocracy standing above them in some areas but certainly not having dominance everywhere. This patchwork of authority was important in relation to the popular politics of the Lancashire region. The situation of the Derbys in Lancashire contrasted with that prevailing in Cumberland, where the lords Lowther, headed in this period by Sir James Lowther, first Earl of Lonsdale (1736–1802), made conscious efforts to increase their landowning and Tory political influence. The Earl of Derby was no Lord Lowther, in terms of either political or even landed influence. Although the equation between popular unrest and a lack of a dominant landowner or aristocratic patron is far from direct or determinate, the confusion of authority that proliferated in the south of the region must have had some impact in providing opportunities to act without major restraint.

The position of the aristocracy in Lancashire furthermore had an effect on the nature of class relations and identities in this period. The wealth generated by commerce and industrialization tipped the cultural and social balance towards a base of middling gentry values rather than encouraging a strict hierarchy of deference controlled from the top. The middle classes aspired to the gentry level of estates through wealth or marriage, while the gentry and aristocracy for their part eagerly participated in commercial ventures such as mines, turnpikes, and canals. This negotiation and cooperation between the values of property and commerce brought with it an increasing conservatism in an uncertain economic world, and at least for the long-established merchants and manufacturers, whatever may have been the case with the *nouveaux riches*, a desire to preserve the status quo often came before loyalty to the middle class and led to them adopting overtly loyalist, if not Tory, values.[29] This integration was never complete, however, and conspicuous consumption made the urban bourgeoisie appear a

27 B. Lewis, 'Bourgeois Ideology and Order: Middle-Class Culture and Politics in Lancashire, 1789–1851', Ph.D. thesis (Harvard, 1994), p. 29.

28 Lancashire CRO, DDK 27/11, Derby MS, Statement of Annual Income, 1797.

29 M. Billinge, 'Hegemony, Class and Power in Late Georgian and Early Victorian England: Towards a Cultural Geography', in A. R. H. Baker and D. Gregory (eds.), *Explorations in Historical Geography, Interpretative Essays* (Cambridge, 1984), p. 31.

separate class. Samuel Renshaw and R. H. Roughsedge, rector and curate of Liverpool respectively, reflected on their sense that merchants were a class apart in their visitation return of 1804 about the rise in population in the port:

> Many of the inhabitants have acquired affluent fortunes by a commercial intercourse with each other, as well as with many distant Nations. There are few or no Persons who have derived their wealth from their ancestors or who can assume to themselves the credit of an illustrious origin or a remote antiquity. They are more deservedly conspicuous for their general benevolence and social dispositions, their loyalty to the King and reverence for the Constitution of their Country.[30]

The gentry also marvelled at the changes in economic roles that industrialization offered the working classes. In 1799, John Singleton, magistrate of Wigan, wrote to the Home Office about the proliferation of handloom weavers in his town despite the war. He attributed this to increasing female employment in such roles: 'Altho' numbers of our people are gone for soldiers and sailors there is still an increase of Looms for if a man enlists, his Wife turns Weaver (for here the women are weavers as well as the men) and instruct her children in the art of weaving'.[31]Duncan Bythell's quantification of the fortunes of handloom weavers shows that their numbers experienced a short spurt of massive growth during the French wars before their well-documented decline in the early nineteenth century. Most of the rapid rise in population in southern Lancashire was spurred by the new opportunities that industry offered semi- and unskilled workers, both native and immigrant.[32]

The increasing civic pride and identity of the major urban centres was another notable feature of this period. The fabric and appearance of most towns in Lancashire was being transformed by urban development. Fashionable townhouses, public squares, and civic buildings sprang up in response to the needs of the 'polite and commercial' middle classes and their desire to express civic identity. The effects were immediate. New civic buildings in Manchester included: the Assembly Rooms on Mosley St (1792); the Portico Library opposite designed by Thomas Harrison (1802); the Literary and Philosophical Society building behind it on George Street; and another Harrison creation, the Theatre Royal on the corner of Fountain Street (1807). These were surrounded by merchants'

30 Cheshire RO, EDV 7/3, visitation returns, 1804.
31 NA, HO 42/41/1, Singleton to King, 27 May 1799.
32 Bythell, *The Handloom Weavers*, p. 50.

townhouses on St Ann's Square, St John Street and King Street.[33] Fashionable suburbia was one result of the economic activities of their merchants and manufacturers. Dr Aikin commented on Manchester's 'many excellent houses, very elegant fitted up, chiefly occupied by the merchants of the town, which may in some measure be considered as their country residences, being one or two miles from their respective warehouses'. He highlighted Ardwick Green, an old village transformed by its middle-class influx, as being 'particularly distinguished by the neatness and elegance of its buildings'.[34] In Liverpool, the Earl of Sefton developed Toxteth Park as a desirable residence to the south of the town, although its social character was soon altered by the encroachment of working-class housing in the early nineteenth century. Williamson Square and Everton were also becoming areas à la mode.[35] The development of Preston befitted its status as a guild town, with the new streets and civic buildings built on the land of the Earl of Derby ensuring that it maintained its reputation for having 'always taken the lead in point of gentility'.[36] It was still common for many merchants, manufacturers, and attorneys to remain in the centre of towns, as was the case in Bolton, which gradually expanded its centre southwards with a mixture of townhouses, working-class terraces, and factories constructed on the new streets. Improvement commissions began to have an impact upon the paving, sewage, and market facilities of the major towns. A survey of Lord Bradford's estates in 1810 included land rented by Bolton Township's Improvement trustees 'allotted for the intended Town Hall and Market Place', though these were not completed until the 1820s.[37] These changes were to influence the nature of popular protest in towns, particularly towards the end of this period.

LOCAL GOVERNMENT

The character and nature of local government also had to change in response to the effects of industrialization and regionalization. The county

33 C. Hartwell, M. Hyde, and N. Pevsner, *Lancashire: Manchester and the South-East* (New Haven, 2004), p. 257.

34 Aikin, *A Description of the Country*, p. 205.

35 F. Vigier, *Change and Apathy: Liverpool and Manchester During the Industrial Revolution* (1970), p. 52.

36 Aikin, *A Description of the Country*, p. 283.

37 Bolton Archives, DDBM 1/34, 'Survey of Lancashire estates of Lord Bradford, 1810'.

of Lancashire was traditionally divided into six hundreds: Salford, West Derby, Leyland, Blackburn, Amounderness, and Lonsdale (North and South). The traditional system of county government, headed by the Lord Lieutenant, the Earl of Derby, and his deputy lieutenants was beginning to sit uneasily with the new realities of governing the industrial region. The outer edges of the region were under a confused or intermittent jurisdiction at the very time when they were rapidly populating and industrializing. This affected the control of popular politics in these areas. In practice, the sole source of authority in many places was the magistracy, backed up by special constables and local militia. Though the large urban centres and their middle-class inhabitants were ostensibly self-governed by their corporations, headed by a mayor or court leets headed by a boroughreeve (and civic pride was more visible as a result of the building of conspicuous public buildings in this period), it was the active members of the county magistracy who made the real decisions on the ground and had the most influence over the quotidian lives of the working classes. This was amplified during the wars by the operation of what John Foster termed 'a three-cornered dialogue between the Home Office, the local military command and the local Home Office intelligence network (operated by the Stipendiary Magistrate Act at Manchester and for a time by Colonel Fletcher from Bolton)'.[38] The magistrates' decisions about how to deal with disorder and suspected 'sedition' among the working classes, and the latter's reaction to their actions, formed a constant theme in the history of radicalism and loyalism in the region.

Traditional notions of county government and the new requirements of the region began to diverge. This was exemplified in a conflict among magistrates over the physical and symbolic location of the Lancashire quarter sessions. The disagreement surfaced in 1798 at a time of distress and threat of French invasion, when the war was straining magistrates' capabilities to administer the rising population and threats of disorder in the south-east of the region. The magistrates from the southern hundreds wanted to meet in a location nearer to areas of more concentrated population. They therefore proposed a parliamentary bill to move the quarter sessions from its traditional county centre of Lancaster to the genteel yet more industrial town of Preston. This caused a protracted wrangle between the magistrates of the two Lonsdale

[38] J. Foster, *Class Struggle in the Industrial Revolution, Early Industrial Capitalism in Three English Towns* (London, 1974), pp. 64–5.

hundreds north of Lancaster and the southern magistrates. The records of the quarter sessions from 1797 to 1808 are filled with acrimonious debate over the relative importance of both sites for the county. The Lonsdale magistrates effectively seceded in 1798 by refusing to attend sessions south of Lancaster, apart from one delegate whom they sent to argue their case and keep track of decisions made.[39]

Individual town and general county petitions to parliament were drawn up about the siting of quarter sessions. They gathered thousands of signatures on both sides, from freeholders of all political stances as well as from the magistrates and major landowners. This indicated the great importance attached to the issue of whether the political centre of the county should reflect historical precedent or the changed economic landscape. The petitions against the parliamentary bill suggested that the dividing line in terms of who did and did not support administrative tradition rested along the Wyresdale district around Lancaster and not solely those in Lonsdale north of the Sands. The county petition against the bill stressed the inconvenience of travelling to Preston from this area. By contrast, the individual petition from Lancaster focused on the civic identity of the port as the 'capital town of the County' and the potential loss in value to the newly built townhouses which signatories believed would ensue from the move. The historic and aristocratic connotations of the county town still meant much to north Lancashire inhabitants. Petitions in favour of the bill were less numerously signed, although there were individual petitions from Preston, Rochdale, Manchester and Salford, Bolton, Wigan, Blackburn, Liverpool, and Warrington.[40] This was the last attempt by Lancashire north of the Sands to save the vestiges of an old Lancastrian county identity. When the bill passed, inhabitants of northern Lancashire were pushed into a growing identification with the more rural and aristocratic-dominated culture and customs of Cumberland and Westmorland, gradually consolidating under the forceful influence of the Lowthers.[41] Hence although one eye will be kept upon Lancashire 'north of the Sands', the main focus of this book will be from Lancaster southwards, a focus further legitimized by the contrasting nature of landholding and power in the two regions.

39 R. Sharpe-France, 'The Lancashire Sessions Act, 1798', *THSLC* 96 (1944), 1–57.

40 House of Lords RO, HL/PO/JO/10/3/292/48, petitions for and against the Lancashire Sessions Bill, 31 May 1798.

41 P. D. R. Borwick, 'An English Provincial Society: North Lancashire 1770–1820', Ph.D. thesis (Lancaster, 1994) p. 278.

PARLIAMENT AND REPRESENTATION

The relationship between the provinces and metropolitan government has always been a concern of popular politics. During the eighteenth century, many political and economic interests within Lancashire maintained a 'Country' suspicion of centralization and intrusion from parliamentary legislation that was not of their own asking. Radicals and loyalists shared this critique of parliamentary interference or obstruction of local needs. This sustained a regional sense of Britishness and influenced the nature of popular politics, both radicalism and the forces bent on suppressing it. The 'independence' of both candidates and voters was a standard theme running through most squibs and speeches of borough elections.[42] For other towns, particularly those without parliamentary representation, enclosure and turnpike bills took up much attention. These concerns still evinced similar feelings of independence and identity, and this suggests why the anti-corruption campaign was able to take root so successfully later in the decade: it was able to build upon provincial suspicion of parliament.

Liverpool was particularly active in relation to parliament. Liverpudlian merchants, both West Indian and American, recognized the need for state policies to back successful enterprise, but were keen to stress their distinctive economic identity. The strength of the various special interest groups in the town had no counterpart in the region. The Liverpool Corporation minute book contains frequent votes of thanks and financial gifts to merchants for their activities defending the slave trade in London. Liverpool Corporation, together with various other groups of merchants and inhabitants, petitioned the Commons 825 times from 1775 to 1835, with the two most popular topics of petitions being economic regulation and civic improvement. This activity was so regular that it became formalized when the Liverpool American Chamber of Commerce, after initial reluctance, set up a London office to coordinate its lobbying of parliament.[43]

[42] R. Sweet, 'Freemen and Independence in English Borough Politics, *c.*1770–1830', *P&P* 161 (1998), 88; F. O'Gorman, *Voters, Patrons and Parties: the Unreformed Electoral System of Hanoverian England* (Oxford, 1989), p. 300.

[43] Liverpool RO, 252 MIN/COU I, Liverpool Corporation minute book; J. Civin, 'Slaves, Sati and Sugar, Constructing Imperial Identity through Liverpool Petition Struggles', in J. Hoppit (ed.), *Parliaments, Nations and Identities in Britain and Ireland, 1660–1850* (Manchester, 2003), pp. 187–8.

The representation of Lancashire by its members of parliament also perpetuated feelings of provincial opposition and identity. Their conduct demonstrated how members saw the role of parliament in relation to the provinces and their own role within that link. Lancashire county and borough MPs spoke over sixty times on military issues between 1798 and 1812.[44] This was expected because of their military role within the county during the wars. The MPs for Liverpool, Generals Isaac Gascoyne (1763–1841) and Banastre Tarleton, baronet (1754–1833), were by far the most vocal on issues of pay for the army, the raising and organization of the volunteers, and military victories or failures on the Peninsula. The second subject that persuaded Lancashire members to raise their voices in parliament was commerce: between 1798 and 1812, twenty-seven speeches concerned the slave trade alongside thirty-six on other issues of interest to merchants, particularly the Orders in Council and the East India Company monopoly. These latter two issues which attracted many petitions nationally also saw the highest number of petitions presented to parliament from Lancashire towns. The two Generals and John Dent (1761–1826) of Cockerham, MP for Lancaster (who married Gascoyne's former sister-in-law), were the most vocal members from Lancashire boroughs, a consequence of the pressure placed on them by the corporations and merchant associations of their boroughs. General Tarleton, who might have voted for abolition if he had represented a borough other than Liverpool, felt it his duty to oppose it in May 1804, though he explained that this was because of the need to defend the colonies against Napoleon.[45] The activity of Liverpool and Lancaster MPs was however counterbalanced by the relative inactivity of other members. John Cust, MP for Clitheroe in 1802–7, 'made no mark in the House and is not known to have spoken in debate'. He was often away on duty as captain of the north Lincolnshire militia and in 1807 was a defaulter ordered to attend the House.[46] The borough of Newton-le-Willows produced a string of inactive MPs, including Thomas Brooke, MP from 1786 to 1807. He did not speak in the House after 1790 and the only known votes he

44 *Cobbett's Parliamentary Debates, 1798–1804* and *Hansard*, vols I–XXII, 1804–1812: analysis of 191 speeches, 28 votes and 20 petitions by MPs from Lancashire boroughs and county, excluding Sir Robert Peel.

45 *Cobbett's Parliamentary Debates,* XXXVII, 469, 30 May 1804.

46 R. G. Thorne, *The House of Commons, 1780–1820* (Cambridge, 1986), p. 555; see BL, Additional MS 35646, f. 70, Cust to Hardwicke, 1806.

cast were against slave trade abolition and for a motion condemning the ministerial pledge on Catholic relief on 9 April 1807.[47]

Even allowing for the inconsistencies of reporting in *Cobbett's Parliamentary Debates* and *Hansard*, speeches and voting in parliament do not indicate how Lancashire (or most other counties) were most importantly represented. In fact, MPs were most active in select committees, which reflected much more about their view of their role. These also provided an important context for involving the non-electorate, especially unionized artisans, in the national legislative process. County members Colonel Stanley and the manufacturer John Blackburne, quiescent in the Commons, were intimately involved in the workings of many committees. Many investigated the grievances of the working classes in Lancashire, for example the 1810 select committee examining petitions for relief from Bolton handloom weavers. Their investigations and judgements were on the whole sympathetic, with Stanley's careful questioning of weavers seemingly showing understanding of their plight. The committee represented a cross-party Lancashire interest, including: John Blackburne and chair Colonel Stanley; Lord Archibald Hamilton (1770–1827), Foxite Scottish MP for Lancaster; Sir Robert Peel the elder (1750–1830); and Edward Wilbraham Bootle (1771–1853), Baron Skelmersdale and MP for Clitheroe from 1812.[48]

As parliament extended its reach into Britons' daily lives, it thus paradoxically provided fuel for regional identities and enhanced local sources of power.[49] That expansion was a negative as well as positive process. Taxes were a source of tension amongst most avowed loyalist local elites. Wigan magistrate John Singleton wrote to William Pitt on 22 April 1799 about himself and his brother: 'We shall this year pay the Govt for our Estates and for our profits in trade and manufacture—more than the whole of what my Brother hath received from Govt half pay as 2*nd* Lt of marines and he was put on that list at the end of the American Warr and thank God we pay it cheerfully and freely'.[50] Restrictions which affected Lancashire merchants directly roused mistrust, which motivated successful campaigns to the House of Commons against them on the part of loyalists as well as radicals. In April 1812, Revd Thomas Wilson of Clitheroe cynically expressed to a friend in Liverpool

47 Thorne, *House of Commons*, p. 264.

48 PP 1810–11, II, *Select Committee into the Petitions for Economic Relief*. . .

49 R. Sweet, 'Local Identities and a National Parliament c. 1688–1835', in J. Hoppit (ed.), *Parliaments, Nations and Identities in Britain and Ireland, 1660–1850*, (Manchester, 2003) pp. 48–9.

50 NA, PRO 30/8/178/2/235, Singleton to Pitt, 22 April 1799.

his relief that at least the petition against the East India Company monopoly would 'give us an opportunity of communicating with our representatives and making them of some use to us'.[51]

THE ECONOMIC EFFECTS OF THE WARS

Three major economic crises in this period resulted in major incidents of food rioting and disturbances: the winters of 1799–1800, 1800–1, and 1811–12. William Rowbottom intimated that 1799 was a particularly bad year. Rowbottom's 'annals of Oldham' is one of the key sources for the region in this period. He was probably a handloom weaver or small artisan, and it appears that he wrote his entries contemporaneously with the 1780s to 1820s, though this does not preclude his having undertaken some editing after the events. The annals are rich with detail about local life and the impact of national events and the economy upon local politics. His personal view of the situation in Oldham was occasionally overstated but his impressions were reflective of popular reactions to wider patterns in wages and prices. He was sympathetic towards the weavers' plight; on New Year's Day 1799, he moaned: 'Roast beef, Pies and Ale are not to be seen in the poor mans table on the contrary it is grazed with Misery and Want and a universal lowness of spirits and dejected countenance appear in every one'. He was well aware of the wider regional conditions exacerbating distress; on 28 February 1799, he wrote: 'Never in the memory of the oldest person living was weaving at a lower Eb than at present especially Fustians for it is an absolute fact that Goods within this last fortnight have lowered in Manchester Market astonishingly so that the Masters have lowered the wages at least 5s a piece'.[52]

Fourteen of the twenty-two harvests between 1793 and 1814 were deficient. Combined with fluctuating international trade, this strained most sections of the economy, forcing traders to widen their search for markets and goods. Reports commissioned by the Board of Agriculture in 1795 and 1812 revealed how grain shortages in the rapidly populating towns caused 'badgers' or middlemen dealers to travel further in search of supplies.[53] During near-famine conditions in many parts of Britain

51 F. R. Raines, *Miscellanies*, Chetham's Society, 45 (1897), p. 211.

52 Rowbottom diaries.

53 Dickson, *General View*; see R. Scola, *Feeding the Victorian City: the Food Supply of Manchester, 1770–1870* (Manchester, 1992), p. 38.

in the winter of 1800–1, the Anglican cleric of each parish made returns to the Home Office about the state of the market. Many reported that prices for grain had doubled since winter 1798. The vicar of Stockport, for example, claimed that wheat was being sold for nineteen shillings a bushel, compared with seven shillings and ninepence two years previously, while oats and potatoes had both doubled in price.[54] The labouring poor normally subsisted on oats but in many areas were living on imported rice. Wheat prices reached their highest wartime level in April 1801. The reaction of local landowners and notables was traditional paternalism, reflecting both charity and desperation. Soup shops set up by clergy and charities were a common sight in the major towns, while lords of the manor often offered some form of relief to their tenants. In September 1800, Lord Lilford of Lilford Hall attempted to alleviate the situation by sending the grain produced on his estate to Atherton market at a 'respectable price'. By March 1801, his steward indicated the sense of unease afflicting districts not as yet troubled by the food rioting that blighted public order across the region:

> If the explosion do take place it will be dreadful and I confess I do not at present see how it will be avoided—The poor are absolutely starving for want of food and clothing . . . The manufacturers are already beginning to reduce their work people and I look forward with the most alarming apprehensions to the moment when the Port of Hamburgh will be against us.[55]

The minister of Colne commented that the 'labouring people' were to be commended for 'bearing their privations with exemplary patience', but he warned, 'I now very much fear their patience will soon be exhausted'.[56] Riots over the high prices of food indeed occurred in marketplaces across the region, though most were localized and formed the last major outbreaks of popular disturbance until 1812.

A deep suspicion of 'badgers', the middlemen who hawked produce around the region, was prevalent in many clerical responses. The vicar of Preston suspected that middlemen 'keep up the Price by purchasing the farmers' stock of grain, cheese, etc, at their houses and by a variety of their manoeuvres it is supposed that the Price is kept up far above such prices as might be proportionate to the real state of the grain'.[57] This was a common conspiracy theory among all classes during times of

54 NA, HO 42/54/109, crop returns, 1801.

55 Lancashire CRO, DDLi, box 57, Lilford to Hodgkinson, 27 September 1800; Hodgkinson to Lilford, 22 March 1801.

56 NA, HO 42/54/109, crop returns, 1801.

57 Ibid.

shortage. Broadside ballads reflected and perpetuated the rumours. 'The Badger's Downfall or Good News for the Poor' was a broadside ballad published around the time of the food riots of 1800. It lamented:

> There's a gang of hucksters that ride up and down
> Forestalling the markets in capital towns,
> They buy all the butter, potatoes and greens . . .[58]

The clerical returns were perhaps exaggerated because of their fear of the effects of industrialization and of the disruptive effects of war upon social order. The vicar of Alderley listed his suspicions as to why grain was so scarce in his part of north-east Cheshire. He complained of the 'enlargement of Gentlemen's Deer Parks and Pleasure Grounds', which he believed had decreased cultivable land for their tenants, together with the 'astonishing increase of Manufactures' and an increase in consumption of wheat flour, as a result of the newly urbanized workers rejecting their 'traditional' diet of rye for the sake of fashion and social emulation.[59] Of course these fears were exaggerated, but they intimated his traditional way of thought, common to many clergy witnessing rapid development and wartime distress. Contemporary demonizing of 'badger' middlemen indicated the economic changes occurring within the wider region. Lancaster market increased its importance as the crossing point between north and south grain currents. In 1796, Cragg, a diarist from Wyresdale, the agricultural district east of Lancaster, reported 'badgers, or traders in corn and meal going from Preston, Chipping and other parts and buying up all the meal they can from Kendal, Penrith and the North Country all of which passes through Lancaster and goes to Blackburn, Burnley, Bolton and other parts'. Lancaster remained the market for local farmers, but carts were increasingly conveying local grain to the 'South'.[60] The returns to the Home Office suggest that even the more rural areas had long relied upon fairly distant sources for the greatest part of their arable produce. Haslingden, for instance, was said to be 'almost wholly dependent upon Yorkshire and Cheshire for meal, flour and potatoes', whilst the incumbent of Burnley believed that 'both flour and meal are brought to our market from the eastern and northern Ridings of Yorkshire chiefly by the Leeds and Liverpool canal'. The new canals had enabled and

58 MCL, BR f. 824.04, BA 1, ballads, vol. 2, p. 165.
59 NA, HO 42/54/100, crop returns, 1801.
60 Lancashire CRO, DDX 760/1, Cragg family memorandum book.

indeed created reliance on cross-Pennine traffic for market provisions.[61] The clerical crop returns and the conclusions of the Board of Agriculture reports again showed county boundaries no longer applying with regard to trade, if they ever did. The eastern areas' dependence upon cross-Pennine trade was obvious, though it is notable that they, like the western parts of the region, also relied on Liverpool as a major source of supply. The clerical returns furthermore indicated their acute awareness of the effects of the war upon a fragile regional economy. The vicar of Winwick, near Warrington, noted the farmers' dependence upon the Bolton market for trade and, with an eye on the food riots and distress of 1799, warned, 'regular supply to Bolton is a circumstance of the greatest importance to the preservation of the peace and security and property in the south west district of the county of Lancaster as well as in the immediate vicinity of the town of Bolton'.[62]

The war heightened manufacturers', merchants', and farmers' dependence on a wider network of business connections; consequently, when London markets were affected by Napoleon's economic sanctions, the Lancashire region suffered. Rowbottom recorded on 14 August 1810: 'At Manchester this day trade very slack on account of so many failures in London, Manchester and other places, the House of Messrs Longsden as stoped [sic] this day for a very large sum and it will materially affect the Manufacturers in Royton'.[63] The ballad writer was well aware of the international market sustaining local supplies:

> Our wants to supply, foreign corn's coming in,
> Which makes these black badgers a little to grin.[64]

The increasingly intricate pan-regional market was complicated by the growing reliance of industrializing areas upon grain imported from America and the Baltic; clergy in some areas reported that virtually all the supplies were foreign.[65] Underneath the patriotism and calls for unanimity during the wars, therefore, lay a tense unease about the threat of starvation, bankruptcy, and the dissolution of social order.

All these elements of the society and government impacted upon popular politics in Lancashire: the regional economy and communications, the dominance of the squirearchy over the aristocracy, the civic

[61] NA, HO 42/53-54; Scola, *Feeding the Victorian City*, pp. 100–1.
[62] NA, HO 42/54. [63] Rowbottom diaries.
[64] MCL, BR f. 824.04, BA 1, ballads, vol. 2, p. 165.
[65] NA, HO 42/54; see A. Booth, 'Food Riots in the North West of England, 1790–1801', *P & P* 77 (1977), 84–107.

pride of the middle classes, the multiplying working classes in the 'neighbourhoods' of rapidly expanding manufacturing towns, the role of the magistracy in maintaining social order, and a somewhat taut relationship with parliament. The short-term economic strains that the wars placed on food supplies, commerce, and manufacturing overlay the longer-term tensions that industrialization placed on society in the region. This complex mix of forces shaped the development of loyalism, radicalism, and patriotism in this period.

LANCASHIRE POPULAR POLITICS IN THE 1790s

Campaigns for parliamentary reform only took off in Lancashire after 1789. It is significant that in the 1770s and 1780s, the Revd Christopher Wyvill's Association movement did not successfully branch out across the Pennines. Radicals in Lancashire were outnumbered by vocal and powerful loyalists during the American Revolution and well into the French wars.[66] The French Revolution and reform, as that concept was interpreted by Thomas Paine's *Rights of Man,* by contrast offered the discontented artisans and traders of Lancashire something more directly appealing. Parts of industrializing Lancashire and Cheshire became hotspots of radical activism after 1792 and remained active in various ways during the waves of discontent that surfaced in the 1790s, the Napoleonic and post-war periods, and right through to Chartism. Paine gave them the confidence to speak out, though Lancashire radicals, as elsewhere, usually based their principles upon the older heritage of Cartwright and constitutionalism rather than upon outright republicanism.

The most prominent radical figures in Lancashire included the organizers of the Manchester Constitutional Society: the cotton merchants Thomas Walker (1749–1817), Thomas Cooper (1759–1839), and George Philips (1766–1847), and manufacturers James Watt Jnr (1769–1848), George Duckworth, Samuel Greg (1758–1834), George Lloyd (d. 1805), and Dr Thomas Percival, amongst other bourgeois Dissenters and artisans with broad interests in philosophy and science.[67] Middle-class and artisanal debating and corresponding clubs formed

66 P. Marshall, 'Manchester and the American Revolution', *Bulletin of the JRLUM* 62 (1979), 168–86.

67 M. Turner, 'The Making of a Middle Class Liberalism in Manchester, c.1815–32: A Study of Politics and the Press', D.Phil. thesis (Oxford, 1991), pp. 44–5.

in the larger towns, Paineite radical principles were propagated in the *Manchester Herald* from 1792 and numerous pamphlets were published, one of the most notable being *The Necessity of a Speedy and Effective Reform in Parliament* by George Philips in 1794. It is likely that in most towns could be found at least one circle of intellectual artisans and middle-class sympathisers. Samuel Bamford recalled his father's small group of radical friends, who were called 'Jacobins' and 'Paineites' by their loyalist neighbours in Middleton near Manchester. One of the group, Samuel Ogden, a shoemaker, was attacked by a 'Church-and-King' mob, whom Bamford identified as coming from the nearby villages of Ringley and Radcliffe. His description of the circle suggests a situation that probably applied in most towns and villages, with known radicals forming distinct but minor parts of working communities, while the rest of the inhabitants were either hostile or indifferent to spending their time discussing politics and philosophy in an intellectual setting. Most radicals remained unknown outside their local neighbourhoods, though the Taylor family of Royton gained a wider reputation for Paineite republicanism. They were commonly mentioned by Lancashire magistrates in their reports to the Home Office. Samuel Bamford commented that Royton was 'looked upon as the chief resort of Jacobins on that side of Manchester'.[68] A 'Jacobin library' was run by shopkeepers and small manufacturers at the Light Horseman on Sandy Lane, Thorpe, near Royton. Although the Inn was nearly destroyed during the 'Royton races' Church-and-King riot in 1794, the library moved to the Hope and Anchor Inn and later provided the basis for the circulating library.[69]

The loyalist response to the French Revolution and its ideologies was also significant in the region. The governing elites and aspirant middle classes formed loyalist clubs on the model of the society set up by John Reeves in London. The most prominent societies in Lancashire were of course established in its largest cities. Most vocal amongst these was the Association for the Protection of Constitutional Order and Liberty against Republicans and Levellers (APCOL) formed in Manchester in 1792 from members of the Tory Bull's Head Association. The association's purpose and outlook is indicated in its very name. APCOL functioned as part of gentlemanly civic sociability, but with an explicitly propagandic purpose, publishing hundreds of copies of pamphlets for

[68] S. Bamford, *The Autobiography of Samuel Bamford: Early Days*, new edn, ed. W. H. Chaloner (London, 1967), pp. 43–4.

[69] E. Butterworth, *Historical Sketches of Oldham* (Oldham, 1856), p. 202.

distribution.[70] It had corresponding members among the satellite towns, but virtually every town and village formed their own loyalist society in the early 1790s. For example, the Church Loyal and Constitutional Society in Saddleworth, nestled among the Pennines near Oldham, was reported to have had 700 people (out of a population of about 12,000) present at a meeting on 3 January 1793, with Revd Charles Zouch in the chair. The object of the meeting was to express abhorrence of sedition and attachment to the existing constitution, so the audience may have of course included opponents, those wishing to appear loyal in public, and the simply curious.[71] Most of the committed loyalists who joined clubs such as these would at least initially describe their stance as Church-and-King, implying defence of the political and religious status quo against the Paineite radicals, whom they regarded as seditious or 'Jacobin'. The ideological response was translated given practical effect by narrowing the opportunities for radical individuals to meet. Most notably, in 1792 a long list of publicans and innkeepers in Manchester and most of its satellite towns signed a testimony that they would ban from their pubs 'all authors, publishers and distributors of Treasonable and Seditious Writings', and 'prevent in our Houses any Conversation, Songs or Toasts . . . by such wicked designing men'.[72] This did not of course preclude radical activity from occurring elsewhere, but it did demonstrate the strength of loyalist feeling on the part of many local inhabitants, and how the political atmosphere had polarized, at least in terms of inhabitants' public stances.

The politics of the period 1789–93 created much of the atmosphere within which radicalism and loyalism were conducted during the Napoleonic wars and beyond. Three key political clashes occurred in Lancashire in this period: the St Ann's Square riot, the attacks on the Manchester Constitutional Society and *Manchester Herald* (and the subsequent trial of Thomas Walker), and the 'Royton Races', all described below. Though perhaps not as well known among historians as the Priestley riots in Birmingham, these events remained in popular political memory and were alluded to in later events and annals in Lancashire. For loyalist elites, they served as evidence of the political instability of the masses that needed to be controlled; radicals lauded

70 Chetham's Library, Mun A 6.45, Minutes of the Association for the Protection of Constitutional Order and Liberty, 1792–7.

71 G. Shaw, *Annals of Oldham*, vol. 3 (Oldham, 1906), p. 181.

72 Butterworth, *Historical Sketches of Oldham*, p. 171.

them as examples of popular bravery against loyalist repression. There were over twenty-five recorded disturbances in the North West in the 1790s, the majority occurring in 1792–3, 'the apogee of militant Toryism'.[73] It is significant that many occurred in Manchester. This was in part because more evidence exists and it does not preclude there having been similar events on a smaller scale in towns and villages across the region.

Liverpool presented a different case and continued to contrast with Manchester throughout this period. The most active radicals, the 'Friends of Peace', were a circle of Rational Dissenters, headed by the bourgeois intellectuals William Roscoe (1753–1831) and William Rathbone IV (1757–1809). The Roscoe circle had been involved in Francophile radicalism in the Liverpool Constitutional Society.[74] One of their members, the Scottish physician Dr James Currie (1756–1805), wrote in an autobiographical account how a combination of revulsion at the Terror and the increased fear of loyalist repression dampened their activity: 'The War of 1793 came, a fearful crisis to the lovers of freedom and the friends of their species'.[75] They clashed with the Tory-Anglican Corporation and a supporting mob at a town's meeting in 1795.[76] Currie's colleagues were equally quiet during this period. A scrapbook compiled by William Rathbone contains many records of meetings and dinners during the early years following the French Revolution. It contains no more political or reform material, however, between 1795 and January 1807. Most of William Roscoe's voluminous correspondence is apolitical between 1796 and 1805, with little or nothing on the events of 1798, the peace of 1801–2, or the invasion scare of 1803. He began to comment on political affairs again from 1806, but this was mainly concerned with wider economic and religious campaigns and elections. This perhaps intimated a continued fear of his letters being read by spies, such that he confined his more radical ideas to private conversation.[77]

[73] A. Booth, 'Popular Loyalism and Public Violence in the North-West of England, 1790–1800', *Social History* 8 (1983), 297.

[74] Liverpool RO, 900 MD 16-18, Currie papers, Liverpool Constitutional Society, 1791–3.

[75] W. W. Currie, *Memoir of the Life, Writings and Correspondence of James Currie of Liverpool*, vol. 1 (1831), pp. 500–1.

[76] W. R. Ward, *Religion and Society in England, 1790–1850* (Batsford, 1972), p. 24.

[77] Liverpool University Special Collections, RP.II.4.16, Rathbone papers, Scrapbook 1; Liverpool RO, 920 ROS, Roscoe correspondence.

On 4 June 1792, a Church-and-King riot occurred in St Ann's Square, at the heart of the Georgian-built area of Manchester. William Rowbottom, the diarist from Oldham, thought the trouble was connected with the royal proclamation against 'seditious publications' which was read out in Anglican churches across the country in that month. A 'Church-and-King mob' pulled up the trees in the square and used them to attack the Unitarian chapels on Cross Street and Mosley Street.[78] The anti-Dissenting motive on the part of its organizers was clear, though the rest of the 'mob' were probably inspired more by the general political atmosphere at the time. The riot might have remained an isolated incident were it not for the three nights of rioting that broke out from 11 December 1792. The focus of the attack upon the chapels suggests a more coherent organization, most likely directed behind the scenes by the notables of the loyalist societies, who had held a meeting at the Bull's Head Inn to draw up an address to the king congratulating him on his proclamation against sedition. Crowds laid siege to the houses of the prominent radical reformers, Matthew Faulkner, Thomas Walker, Joseph Collier, and William Gorse. The office of Faulkner's radical newspaper the *Manchester Herald* was ransacked, leading to its collapse.[79] Walker was tried unsuccessfully for treason at the Lancaster Assizes in 1794. He made sure to publicize widely the sense of injustice he felt at both events, especially in a book that established a place in the radical canon, *The Political Events which have Occurred in Manchester During the last Five Years*.[80] The polemic solidified the impression among radicals that the Manchester authorities were arrayed against them and that new directions had to be undertaken if they were to survive. The 'Royton Races' were a similar attack by a 'mob' of up to four thousand on a reformers' meeting on 21 April 1794. It was immortalized in Samuel Bamford's memoirs as a scene of 'Church-and-King' irrationality and violence. Six reformers were arrested for riotous assembly and assault, though only one was convicted.[81]

78 Rowbottom diaries, 1792.

79 P. Handforth, 'Manchester Radical Politics, 1789–94', *TLCAS* 66 (1956), 87–106; See also G. Philips, *The Necessity for a Speedy and Effectual Reform in Parliament* (Manchester, 1793).

80 T. Walker, *A Review of the Political Events*; *The Whole Proceedings on a trial of an action brought by Mr Thomas Walker, Merchant, against William Roberts, Barrister. . .* (Manchester, 1791).

81 Butterworth, *Historical Sketches of Oldham*, p. 204; Booth, 'Popular Loyalism and Public Violence', 301.

After 1795, as loyalist suspicion of sedition intensified, radicals were forced into more separatist modes of operation. Committed Paineite radicals did not cease aspiring towards the ideal of republicanism, but had to accept the more practical ideas of constitutionalism, or at least speak publicly in constitutionalist terminology. Thomas Cooper, former Manchester Reformation Society secretary, George McCallum, and John Smith amongst others exiled themselves to America in 1793–4 and established an anti-slavery movement there. Similarly, in March 1793, Priestley wrote of the flight from England of the Manchester printers Faulkner and Birch; they were, he hoped, 'safe in America'.[82] Some were quieted by other means. William Rowbottom reported that former MCS member John Clegg had died in Manchester in November 1800, 'a Gentleman of fine abilities, a True Patriot, a firm friend to the Cause of Freedom'.[83] Most radicals shifted their focus from active to personal or private radicalism. Silence would indeed represent a means of protest in itself. A 'Thinking Club' met at the Coopers' Arms in Manchester, at which the members sat in silence in protest against the Two Acts of 1795.[84] A pamphlet 'An Appeal to the Inhabitants of Manchester and its Neighbourhood', signed by 'a friend to my country and the liberties and happiness of the people', was published by the radical printer William Cowdroy on behalf of former MCS members and as a last-gasp remonstration against the government legislation.[85]

These political clashes mirrored general patterns in the nation as a whole, particularly following the burning of effigies of Thomas Paine that occurred in most towns and villages across the country over New Year 1793.[86] Rowbottom commented on the psychological mood surrounding these events, almost a flare-up of pent-up energy and rage. They perhaps had less to do with genuine loyalist beliefs than with fervour for any form of political expression in a time of rapid political change which could only be conceptualized through stereotypes or manifested in anger:

1793–January 4th—peoples' minds far from temperate for a kind of frenzy [h]as burst out amongst the people of this land under the cover of loyalty and shielded by the crys of Church and King and Constitution have burst out

[82] J. Graham, *The Nation, the Law and the King: Reform Politics in England, 1789–1799*, vol. 2 (Oxford, 2000), p. 516.

[83] Rowbottom diaries, 10 November 1800.

[84] Turner, 'Making of Middle-Class Liberalism', p. 56.

[85] W. E. A. Axon, *Annals of Manchester* (Manchester, 1886), p. 22; Chetham's Library, Cambrics broadsides 98 (3).

[86] F. O'Gorman, 'The Paine Burnings of 1792–3', *P & P* 193 (2006), 114.

their disgust against the people that have countenanced the opinion of Thomas Pain.[87]

The effigy burnings resulted from a mixture of motives. They were expressions of popular frustration, loyalism, and 'customs in common', and were either sponsored or at least acquiesced in by the local notables. Benjamin Shaw, a machinemaker in central Lancashire, commented on the planned ritual of the event which distilled popular emotion into some form of order:

> We in Dolphinholme were as loyal as any etc. We made an Image, and got a cart, and set off with the Image to Scorton, and then to Golgate, with such a crowd with it, shouting and laughing, etc. – at last the Image was tried, cast and executed on a gallows while the Cannon roared and the mob shouted etc.[88]

Rowbottom noted the solemn ritual and show of the event in Oldham and highlighted the expense and organization involved in the Failsworth effigy burning. A pole was erected, with a costly crown placed on top, at the culmination of an afternoon's rituals involving a procession of local notables wearing blue scarves and sashes.[89] This illustrated how the ceremony was firmly part of civic loyalist ritual, perhaps being intended to control the crowd rather than endorse it.

The significance of these events in the longer term was, as Nicholas Rogers has pointed out, not that they indicated any deep strength of Church-and-King feeling among the populace, but rather that the loyalist elites witnessed the potential volatility of the local inhabitants they ruled. In future they would control carefully not just popular radicalism and social unrest, but the exuberance of popular loyalism.[90] They sustained if not increased their suspicion of the 'mob' when the Church-and-King riots faded and were replaced by food riots and mass peace meetings in 1795. Rowbottom recorded riots in Manchester and all its main satellite towns in July of that year. The reaction to William Pitt's 'Two Acts', which prohibited seditious meetings and publications, quickly filtered into the provinces, with loyalist elites wishing to uphold

[87] Rowbottom diaries.

[88] *The Family Records of Benjamin Shaw, Mechanic of Dent, Dolphinholme and Preston, 1772–1841*, ed. A. G. Crosby, Record Society of Lancashire and Cheshire, 130 (Chester, 1991), p. 27. See K. Navickas, 'The Cragg family memorandum book: Society, Politics, and Religion in North Lancashire During the 1790s', *NH* 42 (2005), 151–62.

[89] Rowbottom diaries, 1793.

[90] N. Rogers, *Crowds, Culture, and Politics in Georgian Britain* (Oxford, 1998), pp. 202–9.

them and radicals reacting against their restrictions on the freedom of speech that they posed. On 7 December 1795, Rowbottom noted that two petitions had been drawn up in Bolton, Stockport, Oldham, and Royton regarding the Two Acts and calling for peace, but were opposed by a party 'under their old shield of Church and King'.[91]

The political upheavals of the 1790s had three important consequences for popular politics in the 1800s. Firstly, radicals had a history of struggle and a legacy to carry forwards, together with a widened range of radical viewpoints and a more complex language combining constitutionalism and Paineite tenets. Secondly, loyalist attitudes were crystallized not only towards radicals but also towards any form of collective action or gathering, now automatically assumed to be seditious or aggravated by 'seditious leaders'. Finally, the economic and social impact of almost a decade of war combined with industrialization and urbanization created extra pressures upon the enforcement of law and order in the provinces. The combination of these factors and the altered circumstances challenged the political stances and behaviours of all sections of Lancashire society. The Napoleonic wars witnessed more than the continuance of old ideological battles; rather, the wartime conditions fostered new political movements and bitter conflicts over changed political grounds.

[91] Rowbottom diaries, 1795.

2

Patriotism

John Bull defiantly raising his fists against Napoleon 'Boney' Bonaparte, is a classic image of British patriotism. John Bull had the solid, stubborn, no nonsense, masculine outlook of a Country gent or yeoman, while his counterpart, Britannia, encapsulated values of justice, free speech, and Protestantism, and was a courageous defender of 'liberty'. Broadside ballads, caricatures, pamphlets, and sermons extolled the courage of John Bull, particularly his confidence in his own masculine identity against the effeminate and deranged Jacobins of revolutionary France. This portrayal, popularized in cartoons and ballads, caricatured both national character and popular patriotism. It nevertheless struck a chord with a majority of the English population at least, otherwise the character would not have survived and been adopted enthusiastically by the Victorians. Many historians argue that though Britishness may not have overridden local or political attachments, in essence, it was embodied in Britannia or John Bull.[1]

Although it is clear that inhabitants of the provinces received these images and tropes with interest, they did not translate what they read wholly into practice in their everyday lives. Nor did they fulfil the stereotypes of John Bull that they digested from the press. Patriotism was never instinctive, but often included motivations of self-interest and ostentation. Just as John Bull was only a simple caricature of a more complex set of national identities, volunteering and patriotic activity were manifestations of an ideal more than a reality of selflessness and unanimity in the name of 'Britain'. Patriotism was composed of a fluctuating mixture of negative and positive emotions: xenophobia

[1] M. Taylor, 'John Bull, the Iconography of Public Opinion in England, 1712–1929', *P&P* 134 (1992), 93–128.

combined with attachment to certain distinct qualities of the nation. Both radicals and loyalists contributed to patriotic culture. This certainly was the case in Lancashire.

This chapter analyzes patriotism as expressed through the volunteer regiments, civic celebrations, and propaganda. Ambiguity about the nature of both patriotism and national identity abounded in Lancashire. Patriotism was not always transmitted as a top-down process from centre to periphery; on the contrary, as the mass participation in volunteering illustrated, enthusiasm for defence of the country was shaped and defined by local and regional priorities. William Wordsworth recognized that 'Local attachment . . . is the tap-root of the tree of patriotism', a theme common to the Romantics.[2] Regional populations often accepted national propaganda about the importance of Britishness only through the filter of local and regional structures of communication. Local propaganda and civic ritual demonstrated that the inhabitants of Lancashire faced Napoleon in similar ways to other regions, but adapted their practice to the region's own identity. This culminated in a 'Lancastrian Britishness', shared by all classes and political persuasions. The idea of Britain versus the 'other' of France represented a dichotomous model of patriotism. This dichotomy could also apply within British identity itself. Lancashire Britons occasionally defined themselves against the 'other' of metropolitan Britons as well as against the French. 'Lancastrian Britishness' demonstrates the permeability of the persona of John Bull. National elements of British identity may indeed have been accepted by regional inhabitants, but these represented the overall fabric through which existing allegiances shone.

POPULAR PATRIOTISM AND THE VOLUNTEERS

The invasion scares of 1798 and 1803–5 stimulated serious determination more than they did ebullient patriotism. The government's *levée en masse*, in imitation of the French, called upon all Britons to serve in defence of the nation. The year 1803 represented a much more serious invasion threat than Britain had faced during the American War of Independence and gave rise to the mass mobilization of the male population on a scale never before seen. As J. E. Cookson and Austin Gee have

[2] K. D. M. Snell, *The Regional Novel in Britain and Ireland, 1800–1990* (Cambridge, 1998), p. 46.

demonstrated, all sections of society in Britain focused their energies on 'national defence patriotism'.[3] Government and loyalist propaganda in multifarious forms stressed the absolute necessity for complete dedication to the defence of Britain. Responses ranged from vast enlistment in the ranks of newly created volunteer corps across the country to the support from female patriots in raising money and sewing uniforms. If not already signed up to the armed forces or militia, inhabitants were encouraged to form and join volunteer corps or drive livestock and carts away from invading forces. On 15 July 1803, Bolton clerk John Holden recorded in his diary how the process translated to the localities:

> The Constables of G[rea]t Bolton whent to every house to take down the names of every Man that was able to bear arms and in what Company he meant to serve in case of necessity of the French landing. Henry [at the] Union Buildings was to bake 100 [loaves] in one day. Tho[ma]s Mason in Bradshawgate was to bake 500 in one day and one night and to have four men to assist him.[4]

The direction of the emergency preparations came from the authorities and the situation called more for a matter-of-fact assessment of resources than the showy posturing prompted by the previous invasion scare of 1798. A general lieutenancy meeting was held in Wigan on 8 August, where the Earl of Derby and his forty-nine deputy lieutenants compiled their manpower capabilities and responsibilities.[5] This greater sense of determination was a feature of the volunteer corps that materialized in their hundreds in response to the government's call.

The difficulty for the government and social elites lay, on the one hand, in the novelty of the situation, and on the other, in the response of the British population. The government usually relied on county-based and aristocratically controlled militia regiments and fencible units, raised by large landowners and paid by the Treasury. Unpaid volunteer corps were not new, most memorably having been raised during the American War of Independence, but the scale of the mobilization from 1803 was novel. The raising of volunteer regiments involved almost a fifth of adult males and the auxiliary efforts of their families.[6] It entailed a militarization of the middle and working classes that was rapid and a product of necessity in face of the immediate threat. Yet a disconcerting sense that the masses might use their new military skills and arms against their rulers

[3] J. E. Cookson, *The British Armed Nation, 1793–1815* (Oxford, 1997); A. Gee, *The British Volunteer Movement, 1794–1814* (Oxford, 2003).

[4] Bolton Archives, Holden diaries.

[5] *CMG*, 20 August 1803.

[6] Cookson, *British Armed Nation*, p. 101.

underlay much of the official correspondence on the volunteers. Charles Yorke, Home Secretary, agreed that although arming the masses might be dangerous, the danger of invasion was greater. William Pitt believed that mixing the disaffected with the loyal would infuse the former with the submission to authority that characterized the latter.[7] Government's lack of enthusiasm contrasted with the 'national defence' patriotism of the nation. The difference can most clearly be seen in wavering attempts by the Home Office to restrict the huge numbers of regiments given permission to form in August 1803. Another indication of the government's ambivalent attitude to popular patriotism is evident in 1807, with Lord Castlereagh's demobilization of the volunteers in favour of a national militia that could be more easily and centrally controlled by the government in tandem with local supervision by the aristocracy.

The government's call for troops, and the language of the sermons, speeches, broadsides, and ballads that enveloped such activity from 1803 all emphasized the common identity of Britons (or at least Englishmen) against the French. Yet in practice, the volunteers could not have been anything but decentralized and highly individualized. The volunteers were not intended to be a homogeneous, nationally controlled force and, as J. E. Cookson has argued, certainly were not so by result.[8] However much draped in patriotic British rhetoric, volunteering encouraged identification with the locality. Regiments were independent of each other, initially electing their own officers and selecting their own rank and file. According to the December 1803 returns, Lancashire raised a total of 53 volunteer regiments, with 61 field officers commanding 14,000 rank and file. 'Independent' companies of volunteers were either accepted under the 'June allowances', under which the government required them to serve for twenty days in a neighbouring town or district, or they were raised by commanders at their own expense.[9] The Home Office was not prepared to accept all the regiments offered in the largest towns; this was partly because they had restricted funds, and partly out of fear of the consequences of arming a large portion of the industrial working classes. It therefore delayed the acceptance of offers for almost two months and eventually limited the volunteers to six times

[7] A. Gee, 'The British Volunteer Movement, 1793–1807', D.Phil. thesis (Oxford, 1989), p. 59.

[8] J. E. Cookson, 'The English Volunteer Movement of the French Wars, 1793–1815', *HJ* 32 (1989), 875.

[9] PP, 1803–4, 10 (XI), *Returns of Yeomanry and Volunteer Corps*; NA, HO 50/76, Internal Defence, Lancaster, volunteer lists, 3 September 1803.

the number of the militia. Manchester was allowed nine regiments, composed of over 4,000 rank and file, and Liverpool eight regiments, of over 2,000. All served under varying conditions and levels of pay. To the Home Office and to some historians this represented inefficiency, but it is doubtful that such manpower could have been raised in any other way at this time.[10]

Volunteering became an exercise in self-advertisement. The officers who created the corps used them to reflect their own wealth and position in local society. This was the main feature of the 1798 corps and continued in 1803, but the more serious level of threat produced some other unintended consequences relating to identity. Firstly, the rank and file found in the corps an opportunity to express their own need for a perhaps lost communality as well as preserving what communality they had left. Secondly, regions employed their volunteer regiments to express their collective identity to the nation; the volunteers confirmed what was distinctive and special about the local particular version of patriotism and Britishness.

The magnitude of enrolment furthermore meant that the volunteer corps of 1803 contained a wider spread of religious and political views than had those that had originally responded in 1798. Indeed, the 'original' and more gentrified corps of 1798 in some places regarded the new more socially mixed corps of 1803 with some *hauteur*. In Warrington, for example, the more 'respectable' regiment of 1798, nicknamed the 'Bluebacks', derided their successors of 1803 as 'Robin Redbreasts'.[11] The wider mobilization was momentarily surrounded by patriotic rhetoric that portrayed an ideal of social harmony, though perhaps not reality. The editorial of the *Manchester Mercury* declared on 2 August 1803:

> We shall soon behold the rich and the poor harmoniously blended and mixed together in the same corps in the same line —We shall see the labourer and the mechanic, after the day's business is over, assembling with their fellow citizens, to learn the use of arms.[12]

Such mixing was indeed a reality in many regiments as a consequence of manufacturers recruiting their workmen, or whole villages forming one corps. Some existing fissures could therefore be bridged through volunteering. This was particularly a feature of smaller towns where the

[10] J. Fortescue, *County Lieutenancies and the Army, 1803–14* (1909), pp. 66, 79.
[11] J. Kendrick, *Some Account of the Warrington Volunteers* (Warrington, 1856), p. 3.
[12] *MM*, 2 August 1803.

inhabitants were all known to each other. Different religious denominations could be accommodated, as in Ulverston, where non-Anglican volunteers were allowed to fall out of church parades to attend their own chapels (though this could also be testimony to religious tolerance in the town or the numerical dominance of Dissent).[13] Politically also, the rank and file were more varied than their officers. So in Preston, although the officers of the town's two volunteer regiments were segregated strictly along Whig–Tory lines, the rank and file were not bound by political allegiance: at the contested election of 1807, at least twenty privates from each regiment voted for the independent radical Joseph Hanson. Similarly, in the Liverpool election of 1806, although volunteer officers voted overwhelmingly for the two sitting military members, the voting of the privates was more mixed, some voting for the Whig-radical contender, William Roscoe.[14] Yet the social and political inclusiveness of volunteering remained only a transient ideal for the officers. For the rank and file, it is similarly doubtful whether existing political and religious frictions would have remained quiescent for so long.

SELF-IDENTIFICATION OF THE OFFICERS

The loyalist elites initially attempted to accommodate their more socially exclusive loyalism to the inclusive patriotism of the volunteer corps and mass meetings. Members of local social elites donated huge sums to the voluntary subscriptions of 1798 and 1803. The voluntary subscription of 1798 was instigated by William Pitt and represented his attempt to capture the instinctive response of patriotism for national government.[15] In 1803, like the volunteer corps, subscriptions for defence were much less centralized. The accounts of the committee for General Defence for Manchester in 1803 totalled over £21,500 from over 1,300 subscribers. These included manufacturers and merchants, such as the Gould brothers who gave £315, and Lawrence Peel, £300.[16] Ostentation, exclusivity, and social status were interwoven with the genuine patriotism

[13] P. D. R. Borwick, 'An English Provincial Society: North Lancashire 1770–1820', Ph.D. thesis (Lancaster, 1994), p. 275.

[14] *The Whole of the Addresses, Squibs, Songs. . .* (Preston, 1807); *A Collection of Addresses, Songs, Squibs etc. . .* (Liverpool, 1807).

[15] Cookson, *British Armed Nation*, p. 216.

[16] MCL, BR 356 M12, Accounts of the Treasurers to the Committee for General Defence, Manchester, 1803.

of these donations of the local notables. Wealthy members of the middle classes contributed most to patriotic activity during the war and arguably gained the most from it in terms of prestige and enhanced involvement in local government.[17] This was conspicuously the case in the towns of Lancashire, where the increasingly wealthy bourgeoisie commonly took full advantage of any opportunity for aggrandisement or imitation of the county gentry that they could find. The war gave them the ideal opportunity. Their ostentation and involvement in civic institutions raised their profile, making the urban bourgeoisie firmly part of the loyalist establishment. Being an officer and especially a commandant became a prestigious honour in the associational world in which local elites mixed. A volunteer officer could flaunt the trappings of a military career but did not need to participate in it full time. Lieutenant-Colonel John Leigh Philips wrote to the poet Anna Seward about the Prince of Gloucester's upcoming review of the volunteer regiments in September 1803: 'it will be a grand spectacle and no doubt flattering to the vanity'.[18]

Loyalism and social aspiration as show and ritual became more conspicuous than ever when the international events of 1798 and 1803 altered the context in which elite loyalism operated. Loyalist clubs and anti-Jacobin pamphleteering were replaced by volunteer reviews and patriotic sermons. The loyalist elites remained anxious about radicalism and therefore continued to assert their authority and loyalist principles, but they employed more symbolic and subtle means than they had previously. War gave the local ruling elites many more opportunities to ensure that their loyalist authority was demonstrated symbolically and physically. Volunteer regiments were reviewed in public squares, racecourses or outside commanders' mansions.[19] A sermon given by the rector of Bury on the occasion of the colours being presented to the Bury Loyal Volunteers (at that time led by Sir Robert Peel (1750–1830) and his business partner William Yates), expressed the common sentiment about the prominent role the manufacturing and commercial middle classes played in patriotism and the opportunities it offered for social advancement: 'You increase the weight and respectability of your characters, while you are adding to the general strength of the country'. This was all the more relative because Peel, the hugely successful calico printing magnate, was already an MP and lord of the manor, and

17 Cookson, *British Armed Nation*, p. 237.
18 MCL, M84/3/5/4, Philips Ms, Philips to Seward, n.d., 1803.
19 *Blackburn Mail*, 21 December 1803.

had been made a baronet in 1800 following his firm's contribution of £10,000 to the 1797 national voluntary subscription against the French.[20]

With paternalism came not simply social control but also the potential for loyalist control. As with the use of physical space, loyalist hegemony over the political public sphere remained on guard, even in the face of the apparent unanimity of patriotism during the invasion scares. Despite patriotic unanimity with the general population in the face of Napoleon, the loyalist elites remained anxious about radicalism and therefore continued to assert their authority and loyalist principles. Older histories of the volunteers linked them inextricably with Church-and-King loyalism. This view was predicated on the assumption that volunteer forces were the natural successors of the loyalist clubs and instilled in their rank and file an anti-radical political outlook. J. E. Cookson and Austin Gee have successfully challenged this direct connection, positing instead a 'national defence patriotism'.[21] As the varied political composition of many of the corps in Lancashire in 1803 demonstrated, even radicals and reformers could find an outlet for their patriotism in volunteering. This did not mean, however, that all regiments were apolitical in composition or intention and dedicated solely to national defence. This was certainly the case in 1798. Many Church-and-King magistrates and manufacturers saw the potential for using the institution both as an extension to the loyalist associations and as a means of inculcating loyalism among the rank and file. In 1797, the Bolton Volunteer Infantry participated at an Anglican celebration of the defeat of the Dissenters' campaign to repeal the Test and Corporation Acts.[22] A broadside from 1797 written by 'J. L. P.', undoubtedly Lt-Col John Leigh Philips, addressed the 'Loyal Association of Manchester on the subject of training a body of no fewer than 20,000 men in this Town alone', implying that this was taken to be a matter of political importance. The last few entries of the minutes of the Manchester Association for the Protection of Constitutional Order and Liberty in January 1797 discussed the proposal for a volunteer corps. The committee decided

[20] *Sermon Preached in the Parish Church of Bury, 18 October 1798, by Rev. Sir W. H. Clerke, Bart, Rector of Bury*. . . (Bury, 1798), p. 15; S. D. Chapman, 'Peel, Sir Robert, first baronet (1750–1830)', *Oxford Dictionary of National Biography* (Oxford, 2004).

[21] J. Western, 'The Volunteer Movement as an Anti-Revolutionary Force', *EHR* 71 (1956), 603–14; Gee, *British Volunteer Movement*, p. 59.

[22] B. D. A. Lewis, *The Middlemost and the Milltowns: Bourgeois Culture and Politics in Early Industrial England* (Stanford, 2001), p. 21.

to make a list of APCOL members willing to serve, unfortunately not extant.[23]

Certain members of the Lancashire magistrates and merchant-manufacturers were vocal in their hope that the volunteers could serve a dual role in putting down internal disorder. This was a pressing issue in 1798, with rumours that United Irish were stirring up the working classes, but it carried through to the second invasion scare of 1803. John Watson, a Preston cotton manufacturer, asked the Earl of Derby to approve his request for the Loyal Preston Volunteers to be given his blessing to act 'under the civil power when call'd out upon any riot or disturbance within the said town or five miles circumjacent', as did Furness magistrate Thomas Sunderland of the Ulverston Volunteers.[24] This was a role conventionally played by regular militia regiments, whom local authorities felt were too thin on the ground with such a level of disturbance. The prevailing worry among magistrates that Napoleon's troops would be met by a riotous, panicking, or even worse, scavenging local populace is another indication of how the image of unified Britons in patriotic propaganda papered over cracks in social relations. This policing role for the volunteers was officially sanctioned by the Commander General of the North West Military District, the Duke of Gloucester. He reported to the War Office in September 1803 that the 6,000 volunteers and five troops of the Sixth Dragoon Guards stationed in Manchester were needed for internal security and 'for keeping the disaffected in order' and would 'be able to prevent any disturbances occurring'. He insisted that the Manchester volunteers 'cannot be drawn away' to defend Liverpool in the case of trouble there, if not invasion.[25] Bolton magistrate Revd Thomas Bancroft ominously reminded Lord Derby of 'the populousness of this neighbourhood, and how needful it may be in times of apprehended commotion, to encourage a spirit of loyal Association among the numerous classes of manufacturers'.[26]

The other major feature of volunteering that marred the unanimous ideal of 'national defence patriotism' involved friction between officers over their social status. J. R. Fortescue pointed to these conflicts as evidence of the weakness of the system of defence. Though Cookson

23 MCL, f. 1797/3B, 'Copy of Two Letters'; Chetham's Library, Mun A 6.45, APCOL minutes, 1792–7, p. 41.

24 NA, HO 50/75, Internal Defence, Lancaster, January–August 1803.

25 NA, WO 30/71, Reports from officers commanding districts, Duke of Gloucester, 14 September 1803.

26 NA, HO 50/75, Bancroft to Derby, 26 August 1803.

and Gee have underlined the exaggeration in Fortescue's claims, certain incidents in Lancashire illustrate the nuances and flaws within the form of patriotism they portray.[27] The endemic conflicts about rank and status among Lancashire volunteer officers were significant and revealed that the socio-political tensions of the 1790s were channelled into the new institutions of the 1800s. Underlying currents rose to the surface, agitated by attachment to locality and civic pride. In Preston, a conflict of authority between volunteers exposed party political bias. In 1803, two rival volunteer corps were raised by two manufacturers, John Watson and Nicholas Grimshaw. Watson was commander of the Loyal Preston Volunteers and campaigner for the Derby, old Whig, interest. His cotton manufacturing business was the second largest in the town after Samuel Horrocks and Co. Grimshaw commanded the Royal Preston Volunteers and was a Tory-Anglican manufacturer, member of the Corporation, and mayor in the following year. Grimshaw's volunteers were patronized by the Horrockses together with Preston Corporation. The Tory-led tone of the corps was therefore assured, providing a contrast with the Whig leadership of Watson's volunteers. This division was reproduced in the two corps despite the new electoral 'coalition' between Horrocks and Derby cemented in 1802. Party cooperation was thus confined to the electoral sphere while the long legacy of party conflict was manifested elsewhere. Both regiments were accepted by the Home Office on the same date, but the commissions of the Loyal Preston's officers were dated a week earlier, thereby according precedence and seniority to Watson. Watson claimed that this was simply because he was first on the field; Grimshaw and his officers on the other hand believed that it had been obtained only through private solicitation, presumably the influence of Lord Derby. The dispute dragged on publicly, with Grimshaw's volunteers conceding defeat in late 1804.[28] Though the middle classes gained the most from volunteering, their patriotism thus was always shot through with the pressures affecting them in daily life: ambition, adherence to party or a political position, and the strains of local government in rapidly urbanizing and industrializing areas.

[27] Fortescue, *County Lieutenancies*, p. 66.

[28] Lancashire CRO, DDPr 137/4, Proceedings of the Royal Preston Volunteers, 1803–4; Lewis, *The Middlemost and the Milltowns*, p. 25; NA, HO 50/75, Internal Defence; N. Grimshaw, *Observations on the Reply to the Statement of the Question* (1805).

SELF-IDENTIFICATION OF THE REGION

The whole period of the French wars witnessed parallel processes of centralization and divergence of identities. As the 'national' government demanded more from its inhabitants, the provinces reacted with an assertion of their own 'independence', an idea that was much inspired by eighteenth-century Country-Whig politics. This in turn resulted in a paradoxical situation in which the provinces drew closer to the state in terms of administration, communications, and national identity, but simultaneously pulled away in terms of civic institutions, regional industries, and local identities. This process can be seen clearly in the continuing resistance to militia recruitment, which was brought into sharper focus by the different attitude manifested towards the independence of the volunteers. It could also be seen in the rituals of civic patriotism.

Lancashire inhabitants responded to nationally organized patriotic occasions in ways that revealed important aspects of their sense of regional identity. Not all civic or national events were joyful. General fasts, ordered by royal proclamation, were psychologically cathartic experiences. Government propaganda and church sermons evinced an acknowledgement that social and religious catharsis was partly the purpose of fast days. In March 1800, the 'day of national humiliation' was ritualized across the country. The volunteer regiments processed to church, while the Jewish population made a concerted effort to demonstrate their loyalty, perhaps out of fear of Anglican suspicion but also out of respect for civic ceremony. In Manchester: 'The solemnity was devoutly observed by the Jews of this town in their synagogue—in a prayer composed for the occasion—praying for the Royal Family, the Counsellors, the Nobility, the Representatives of the People and the whole nation.'[29] The public response to these occasions was perhaps influenced more by a millenarian atmosphere combined with harvest failure. Roger Wells has noted this feeling in the southern rural regions, and it also applied in the northern industrial regions, though in different ways.[30]

The atmosphere of the general fasts in Lancashire expressed recognition of the particular economic circumstances of its urban areas,

29 *MM*, 18 March 1800.

30 R. Wells, *Wretched Faces: Famine in Wartime England, 1763–1803* (Gloucester, 1988), p. 178.

especially their heavy reliance on grain imports and the direct effects of the war on the cotton trade. General fasts formed an internalized counterpart to food riots by dramatizing their recognition of the difficulties of the economic situation. In doing so, the fasts fulfilled the government's aim of using the events as a means of controlling and internalizing the passions of the population. Yet of course the introspection demanded by the fasts could also stir among individuals thoughts about the real reasons for the distress and the effects of the government's war policy. Patriotism thus might have involved different connotations for individuals according to their social roles. William Rowbottom wrote on 27 February 1799 that the general fast was observed 'throughout England and Wales' but made the sardonic comment: 'indeed in consequence of the Distressedness of the times the poor kept more fast days than the Rich although the Rich strictly adhered to His Majesty's proclamation'. His world-view, significantly, split society into the rich and poor. Local notables infused patriotism with a sense of paternal obligation, seeing it as their role to protect the common good and social order. Hence on 25 March 1799, Rowbottom wrote: 'It should be observed that in the late severe weather the Gentlemen of Oldham gave to the poor large quantities of Coals and Pea Soup which was a serviceable relief at that time.' The 'moral economy' was perhaps kept alive or rather debased by paternalistic acts of charity, but the tensions never ceased to bubble beneath the surface.[31]

Visual and vocal outpourings of emotion followed the announcement of peace in October 1801, a release of pent-up feelings that had been repressed by the closed atmosphere of Church-and-King loyalism. The peace of 1801–2 aroused extended comment in the diaries and autobiographies, and special reports in the newspapers. Most mentioned the dissemination of the news of the signing of the peace from London to the provinces, with seemingly spontaneous outbursts of rather abstract 'joy' when the reports reached the respective localities on 12 October 1801. The celebrations in the satellite towns around Manchester were described as community celebrations. In Oldham, 'the greatest demonstrations of joy took place on the occasion on the 12th at night a general Illumination took place at Oldham where all ranks of people gave convincing proofs of their joy upon the occasion'. In Bolton, John Holden wrote: 'Ratifications came—Bells sett to Ringing colours flying Roasting of

31 Rowbottom diaries; E. P. Thompson, 'The Moral Economy of the English Crowd in the Eighteenth Century', *P & P* 1 (1971), 76–136.

Sheep Drinking of Barrels of beer Drunken and at Manchester an Illumination took place which was very Grand indeed.' Such local celebrations were only precursors to the larger celebrations in Manchester on 15 October. Rowbottom and Holden described the latter as 'the grandest ever seen in this part of the country', again indicating Manchester's role in the region. The festivities there included illuminations, ringing of bells, firing of cannons, and roasting of 'several Bullocks and Sheep', accompanied by 'greatest rejoicing'.[32] The satellite towns thus looked to Manchester as the focal point of their regional identity. A geographical hierarchy was established whereby the smaller towns maintained their civic rituals, but it was now expected that Manchester would have the largest and most spectacular expression of patriotism of 'this part of the country'. In attending Manchester for the occasion, inhabitants of the surrounding towns acknowledged its role in displaying the region's identity to the rest of the nation. Elsewhere in Lancashire and across the country, celebrations followed similar patterns. In magistrate William Fleming's account of events in Furness, the first celebrations occurred in the town of Dalton, while the centre of activity was in Ulverston on 13 October. Again the focus was on visual material to demonstrate loyalty as well as patriotism: 'Ulverston was splendidly illuminated and many appropriate Emblems display'd, especially by Rev Mr Everard the Roman Catholic Clergyman and Mr Brooks an active magistrate in the Town.'[33]

The polarization of political opinion in the 1790s had thus ensured that when loyalist elites were in control, at least, patriotism had to be explicitly associated with loyalism. The patriotism of the peace celebrations could of course encompass the private radical thoughts of individuals. The peace also opened up an opportunity for the long traditions of the Grand Tour and a lingering Francophilia to resurface. Revd William Shepherd of the Liverpool 'Friends of Peace' was among the thousands of British people, loyalist and radical, who travelled over the Channel to catch a glimpse of Napoleon Bonaparte's new regime. They were absorbed with curiosity about the still unknown qualities of Napoleon's domestic rule and retained an admiration for French high culture that popular shock at the republican excesses of the 1790s had failed to exterminate. Memories of the peace of 1801–2 and the preceding war were often tarnished less by memories of the invasion scares and anti-French propaganda than by the experience of attrition

[32] Rowbottom diaries; Bolton Archives, John Holden diaries.
[33] Cumbria RO, Diaries of William Fleming of Rowe Head, vol. IV.

in the later part of the war and post-war period. It was perhaps for this reason that Benjamin Shaw, machinemaker of Dolphinholme and Preston, wrote in his reminiscences that 'Peace was of short continuence, and scarce like peace'. He attributed the resumption of war to the fact that 'there was nothing but Jalousy between the too Counterys'.[34]

The return of war in 1803 was a defining experience for most Lancashire inhabitants, but not in the ways that government intended. Participants in volunteering and civic activity enacted a distinct Lancashire patriotism. Primarily, they modified instructions from government and generic propaganda into something more suited to local sensibilities and incorporated ideas about what kind of Britishness they represented. Volunteers thought of themselves as British, but it was a Britishness which was often identified specifically with their town or neighbourhood. This was reflected in their declarations as to where volunteer corps were willing to serve. Many would serve within their military district only, though there were also pragmatic reasons for this attitude, especially employment commitments. Linda Colley attributes this to the variegated nature of a common patriotism; it was also another intimation of a form of loyalism suspicious of government impositions on provincial independence and identities.[35] John Cross's regiment of Manchester and Salford volunteers would serve only in their towns and 'vicinity', as would the Earl of Sefton's Croxteth volunteers. Liverpool port officers of customs set up the First Royal Independent Company with the proviso: 'that having regard to the importance and indispensable official duty of the individuals of this corps in collecting and guarding the revenue of Customs at this great commercial port, it is hoped that its military duty may be considered as confined to the town of Liverpool'.[36]

Volunteers who departed for service in other places within the military district stimulated an almost exaggerated reaction among those left behind. Rowbottom recounted how on 11 June 1804, the Oldham Loyal Volunteers marched to Preston to perform a fortnight's duty there; their departure was 'accompanied by a large Concourse of people', while their return was made an opportunity to display civic patriotism boldly and visually: 'they were met by the Gentlemen of Oldham and their friends accompanied by a Band of Music, Bells Ringing[,] where welcomed to

[34] *The Family Records of Benjamin Shaw, Mechanic of Dent, Dolphinholme and Preston, 1772–1841*, ed. A. Crosby, Lancashire and Cheshire Record Society, 130 (Chester, 1991), p. 44.

[35] L. Colley, *Britons: Forging the Nation, 1707–1837* (New Haven, 1992), p. 313.

[36] NA, HO 50/75, Internal Defence, Lancaster, January–August 1803.

their Homes amidst universal acclamations of Joy'.[37] This response may have resulted from the rarity of the occasion—it was usually the only experience of military service volunteers undertook—or from genuine worries on the part of relatives, as many had never travelled that distance before. Service in other towns may have enhanced awareness of the wider region, both on the part of the volunteers who marched through the countryside to their designated towns and the families with whom they lodged. There was almost an 'exchange' aspect to the volunteer service. At the beginning of May 1805, for example, the Preston and Lancaster volunteer regiments did service in each other's towns, while later in the month, regiments in south Lancashire and north Cheshire exchanged places, with Warrington going to Stockport, Chester to Warrington, and Croxteth to Chester.[38]

Britishness was disseminated through variegated and particularist means and institutions even within Lancashire. Local identities were federated to form a common awareness of the particular characteristics of the region. South Lancashire was identified and portrayed as the cotton textile manufacturing heart of Britain, and manufacturing in turn as essential to the nation's success and survival. The volunteers in south Lancashire towns ensured that their British identity was associated with industry, particularly when manufacturers enlisted their own workers in their personal corps. A significant manifestation of southern Lancashire Britishness was in September 1803, when the Prince William, Duke of Gloucester and Commander General of the North West Military District, travelled around the county inspecting troops and surveying the preparations for defence. In Manchester, the colonels of the volunteer regiments used the opportunity to demonstrate their contribution to the national economy. They gave the prince a tour of their respective factories, printing works, and warehouses, including a demonstration of 'the operation of weaving the Imperial Arms of the United Kingdom' at Greenwood and Bateman's factory.[39] The impact of this direct meeting with royalty was significant, particularly in the smaller towns which would not normally have expected such attention. The occasion produced a double-edged result, enhancing knowledge and perhaps affection for the monarchy and national ideas of patriotism, but simultaneously boosting the idiosyncrasies of civic identity. John Holden recorded the visit of the prince to Bolton and Chorley on 27 September.

[37] Rowbottom diaries. [38] *Blackburn Mail*, 1, 22 May 1805.
[39] *Blackburn Mail*, 28 September 1803.

The Bolton Regiment of Volunteer Infantry and Cavalry drilled upon Dean Moor for his inspection and the prince then proceeded to dine with Earl de Wilton at his seat at Heaton Park, Manchester.[40]

The strong confidence in the industrial Britishness of southern Lancashire differed from the way in which geographical identity was expressed in north Lancashire. Lancashire magistrates' letters to the Home Office and propaganda again expressed regional Britishness. In the south of the region, manufacturers and lower gentry had been overly enthusiastic to set up their own corps in urban centres; in north Lancashire, by contrast, there were only two volunteer regiments, in Lancaster and Ulverston. This difference was partly a product of the social and economic structure of the respective areas. The commander of the Ulverston Volunteer Corps highlighted the problem of recruitment and subscriptions from rural areas; he wrote to the Earl of Derby in August 1803 asking for funds because the local population was 'less opulent than many others'. He explained that Furness 'consists of Five Agricultural Townships, principally occupied by Tenants at Rack Rents, and thinly inhabited'. Only 380 men could be collected in a district of over thirty miles in extent, and they were 'dispersed in small bodies through twenty-nine townships'.[41]

The response from north Lancashire hinted at a divide between the conceptions of Britishness within the region. It perhaps also contributed to the growing divide between north and south Lancashire that had been painfully made clear in the 1798 dispute over the location of the quarter sessions.[42] Volunteer recruitment in Lancashire as a whole, despite the enthusiastic response in Manchester and Liverpool, was low in relation to southern counties closer to the immediate threat. Austin Gee estimates that under 14 per cent of the adult male populations of Lancashire and the West Riding of Yorkshire were enrolled in volunteer corps.[43] Perception of the possibility of invasion combined with inertia or economic concerns to dissuade northerners from signing up. Local rivalries affected service and illustrated inter-regional divisions. The Ulverston Volunteers disbanded in October 1806. Colonel Sunderland, in a private letter to the Earl of Derby, attributed this to a lack of financial support 'from the opulent on this side of the Sands'.[44] The magistrate William Fleming of Pennington went further in attributing

40 Bolton Archives, Holden diaries, 27 September 1804.

41 NA, HO 50/75, Sunderland to Derby, 13 August 1803; A. Fell, *A Furness Military Chronicle* (Ulverston, 1937), p. 124.

42 See Chapter 1.

43 Gee, 'The British Volunteer Movement', p. 86.

44 Borwick, 'An English Provincial Society', p. 139.

their failure to the divided social and economic structure of the Furness area. He noted in October 1806 that the 'Gentlemen in Furness' subscribed to the corps, 'whilst those People of property who lived in Furness Fells, secure in their native Hills, contributed very little towards their support'. When the fund failed after two years, the accounts were examined and 'it was found that they had spent near three thousand pounds and were £600 in debt'. Fleming alleged that the officers had been extravagant in their use of the money so the subscribers had refused to continue contributing.[45] The response to the state's needs for manpower was inevitably diffused through local mechanisms and could not guarantee an enthusiastic or patriotic return. Yet by contrast, funds were overflowing at the disbandment of the Manchester volunteer regiments in 1807.[46] This also suggests a class divide between north and south Lancashire. The Britishness of south Lancashire perhaps had more middle-class tones, reflecting the manufacturing composition of its officers, aspiring to social mobility, while the yeomen and failing slaving merchants in north Lancashire were conscious of their decreasing fortunes and attachment to rural life, and jealous of Liverpool's rise.

Some rank and file may not have shared their officers' 'Church-and King' definition of loyalism and the nature of patriotism, but most shared a common opposition to compulsion. This opposition evinced a lingering Country suspicion that government edicts and restrictions on the volunteers represented the first step towards the ultimate tool of despotism, co-option of all soldiers into a standing army. The issue of compulsion by the government clouded instinctive patriotism; volunteering was not akin, and indeed opposite in principle to, a 'fiscal-military state' run from London. Britishness was therefore associated with 'liberty' and freedom to the lowest levels from the intrusive edicts of the state. This belief, combined with civic pride, underlay many of the conflicts over questions of authority, state control, and pay that filled the Home Office defence papers from 1803.[47] Although their initial success and popularity must not be underestimated, nevertheless the hundreds of letters about poor pay and lack of ammunition written by respectable local notables to the Home Office indicate a patriotism that was seen through a Lancashire lens. Resignations of officers and

45 Cumbria RO, Diaries of William Fleming, vol. IV.

46 MCL, MS BR 21/BR F 356.M12, Accounts of the Treasurers to the Committee for General Defence, Manchester.

47 NA, HO 50/73, Internal defence, Lancaster, 1803.

poor attendance by rank and file from 1805 were physical testimony to their perception that the threat of invasion had lessened. By May 1805, for example, Derby was notified that the whole of the Chorley division of the Preston and Chorley Cavalry had resigned, nearly half the troop. In Lancashire, more pressing economic issues again meant more than the demands of government: many letters expressed officers' deep regret at having to resign but stressed the need to return to the quotidian business of manufacturing and trading. Lancashire patriotism was to be transmuted into contributing to the economy. Furthermore, the officers writing to the Lord Lieutenant expressed their belief that the lack of supplies from government indicated their lack of support; war-weariness became endemic well before Trafalgar. Derby was seen as the intermediary, the county representative to an increasingly distant central authority. The Earl de Wilton complained to him in January 1805: 'You will observe that Government agreed to supply me with ammunition for exercise which has since been repeatedly refused.'[48]

Radicals and loyalists alike expressed a sense of local identity entailing opposition to intrusive government orders regarding the volunteers. Once the immediate danger of invasion had faded, moves were soon afoot in the Home Office to deal with the problems caused by the heterogeneous nature of the volunteers. Orders were issued for the volunteers to be disbanded in 1807; a reduced number of officers and rank and file were then transferred into the local militia, which was both more aristocratically and centrally controlled.[49] The local response to this government move is telling. Opposition focused on loss of identity and status, and this in turn reflected the sense of independence and provincial suspicion of government that had been encapsulated in the volunteer corps. This was exemplified in the memorial to Lord Hawkesbury written by the officers of the Warrington Volunteers in 1809. They had been under the impression that transferral to militia status would not change their identity or officers, but when informed that a 'smaller neighbouring corps' would be compulsorily added to theirs, voiced indignation that: 'the command of the regiment may be committed, and two at least of our field officers as well as others of lower rank will become supernumerary'.[50] This comment emanated

[48] NA, HO 50/137, Internal defence, Lancaster, 1805.

[49] S. C. Smith, 'Loyalty and Opposition in the Napoleonic Wars: the Impact of the Local Militia, 1807–15', D.Phil thesis (Oxford, 1984), p. 57.

[50] J. A. Borron, *A Statement of Facts Relative to the Transfer of Services of the Late Warrington Volunteer Corps into the Local Militia* (Warrington, 1809), pp. 33–5.

from a strong sense of civic pride, the social status conferred by their positions, and perhaps unfamiliarity with other towns in the wider region. It was probably not just officer pretension but also reflected a genuine attachment by the rank and file to their officers, many of whom employed them. Similarly, the officers of the Hulme Volunteers retracted their original offer to transfer when they discovered that they might be consolidated with another larger corps to be placed 'under the command perhaps of a stranger, who himself not a man of Business may neglect to consult the convenience of Commercial and Mechanic persons'.[51]

Provincial suspicion of government compulsion converged on the militia ballot. The ordinary militia dated from 1757, and was first fully embodied during the American War in the late 1770s and only under wartime conditions. It was organized on a county basis under the lord lieutenant, and most able men were expected to serve, according to a ballot called at least once a year. The rich could employ a substitute, but of course this option was usually unavailable for the working man, who had to leave home and serve for an indefinite time. Though the militia regiments returning to Lancashire in 1800 after suppressing the rebellion in Ireland were greeted with adulation, it is likely that many in the crowds awaiting them were also cheered by the knowledge it had not been them. Fear of the militia ballot was probably the most common experience for all the inhabitants of the region and the country during the wars. This does not denigrate the genuine patriotism and loyalism of the population but re-emphasizes its pragmatic preference for local over nationally organized institutions. The exemption from the ballot granted to volunteers in 1799 also played a great part in the latter's popularity. Dread of the ballot was a running theme of many contemporary diaries and autobiographies, which often also dramatically recounted their authors' close shaves with press gangs as they journeyed or tramped across the country. David Whitehead of Rawtenstall expressed this in his autobiography with his sole comment on national affairs in this period: 'I had always an objection to be a soldier and for fear of being lotted for the old Militia, I volunteered for the Local Militia, as the old Militia were in constant service, but the Local Militia were only to serve a month in the year.' His choice illustrated the degree of self-interest involved, especially with regard to working time, and a suspicion of compulsion and the army. With

51 Smith, 'Loyalty and Opposition', p. 57; NA, HO 50/196, Pooley to Derby, 1 October 1808.

a typically Methodist mindset, he commented on the fact of having been dismayed by the drunken revelry of the other militiamen and how he saved the two guineas he received together with the allowance for marching to Blackburn and back for his mother.[52] The experience of compulsion also dampened some communities' response to the call for volunteer corps. Samuel Bamford 'immediately offered' himself when he heard the recruiting parties' drums in Middleton in 1803 and 1806, but his aunt reprimanded him for enlisting, saying 'it was the first time a cockade had ever been worn by one of their family, and that I was in the way to perdition'.[53] This attitude perhaps stemmed from a variety of sources, including an ethic fostered by sections of Methodism and the working class that emphasized work over the perceived foppery of the volunteer corps.

The ballot heightened awareness of the direct impact of the 'fiscal-military state' and fostered resistance to it. Loyalist patriotism during the Napoleonic War was always tempered by a strained relationship with the state and its military and financial demands. As Quakers, the Cragg family of Wyresdale expressed acute concern with any moves by the state to recruit men in their district and the nation in general.[54] The reaction to the war effort in north Lancashire recorded by the Craggs illuminated how national policy was diffused amidst local rivalries because of the politics of recruitment. The recruiting Act of December 1796 designed to raise 15,000 men for the Army and Navy resulted in three parishes fighting over the scarce resource of men who were willing to serve.[55] One of the men hired to serve for Wyresdale, named Dilworth, came from Garstang, eight miles away. One Cragg family member noted that Garstang inhabitants were 'vexed' at this and took Dilworth from Lancaster (where he was stationed) and imprisoned him in the House of Correction in Preston. The wrath of the inhabitants of Ellel was also roused when they realized 'that Wyresdale folk had hired men for less money than they could do'. Following this chain of rumour, the constable of Wyresdale went to see the High Constable at Lancaster, who made a ruling that 'Garstang folk had no business' with the fate of the substitute. The spread of this knowledge or rumour consolidated

52 *The Autobiography of David Whitehead of Rawtenstall, 1790–1865*, ed. S. Chapman (Helmshore, 2001), p. 12; Cookson, *British Armed Nation*, p. 74.

53 S. Bamford, *The Autobiography of Samuel Bamford: Early Days*, new edn, ed. W.H. Chaloner (London, 1967), p. 176.

54 Lancashire CRO, DDX 760/1, Cragg family memorandum book.

55 Lancashire CRO, QDV 1/1/13/10, Lonsdale South Army and Navy Ballot, 1796.

sub-regional identities but also created tensions between localities in times of stress. The scarcity of men in north Lancashire was so great that Lonsdale Hundred had the highest bounties for substitutes in the county and some of the highest in the country.[56] Liverpool was in any case attracting migrant rural workers away from north Lancashire with promises of higher wages. Whole communities in north Lancashire faced two pressures: having to lose some of their best men who could otherwise have been employed on the farm or were skilled and valued artisans.

Militia riots occurred across the country in 1796–7. In January 1797, a crowd broke into the lieutenant's room at Ulverston, hung a magistrate out of the window by his ankles and burned the township lists.[57] By contrast, Wyresdale and region did not resort to rioting but resolved their disputes with the system and with neighbouring townships through tense local mediatory and administrative structures. This perhaps indicates the different structure and mores of north Lancashire rural society compared with the larger, more urban population of the Ulverston region or the port of Lancaster. In all areas, the ballot was evaded through substitute clubs rather than by outright refusal, with the exception of Quakers, whose consciences required them to refuse outright. The centre of Liverpool was disrupted during major anti-impressment riots in 1809 and 1810. There had of course been many previous similar riots in the port, yet these riots were unusual for their severity and scale. The ritualized nature of the sieges of the two rendezvous houses by 'large mobs' attempting to release the men imprisoned inside prevented murder but was designed to create a high level of intimidation for the beleaguered officers guarding the men.[58] Press gangs had also always been seen as a major threat, but achieved greater notoriety during the manpower shortages of the French wars. In contrast to the joyful crowds seeing off the volunteer crowds on service, James Weatherley of Manchester portrayed the recruitment for the militia and army in the later part of the Napoleonic War as a bitter and desperate affair. Manchester recruiting parties mustered three times at the Good Samaritan pub on Oldfield Lane, and set off from Piccadilly: 'I have seen them on the going off day followed by hundreds of men women

[56] K. D. M. Snell, 'The Culture of Local Xenophobia', *SH* 28 (2003), 1–30; P. B. Park, 'The Lancashire Quota Men of 1795 and 1796', Cert. Local History dissertation (Lancaster, 2001), p. 11.

[57] Borwick, 'An English Provincial Society', pp. 264–5.

[58] NA, PL 27/8 part 2, witness statements, 24 June, 21 September 1809, 18 July, 29 August 1810.

and children lamenting and crying for they took fathers of familys as well as single men some would go east some west some north and south followed by friends and relatives for a few miles out of town heart rending to see them Parting never to meet again which was too often the case.'[59] The shortage of manpower caused by military recruitment also had detrimental effects upon local customs. William Rowbottom noted in late August 1803 that the Oldham rushbearing was 'thinly attended' 'owing to the Country being so denied of its men in consequence of the War'.[60] Tensions were thus never far under the surface of the patriotic unanimity of the invasion scares, and in many ways the increased centralization engendered by the demands of war solidified a sense of regional particularity among Lancashire inhabitants.

POPULAR PATRIOTISM

What initially held the volunteers together were a perception, an attachment, and an ideal: the perception of imminent invasion, the attachment of the volunteers to their locality, and the ideal of social unanimity within the ideal of national unity. The fear of invasion was certain, the local and regional identities complex but significant, but the hope of unanimity was transitory or unachievable. Patriotism did not involve a top-down process of indoctrination. Though both the government and local elites attempted to employ civic patriotic events to inculcate a particularly loyalist sense of patriotism among the populace, the broadly consensual nature of patriotism ensured that room for manoeuvre existed even during the height of the invasion scares. Officers had to accept that the population might be patriotic but not Church-and-King loyalist in all their views. In some cases this resulted in a compromise between the political aims of the officers and their men, with attachment to their civic identity as the bridge.

In Liverpool, one of the 'Friends of Peace', Dr James Currie, wrote about his 'valourous mood' on 30 July 1803, but contrasted the patriotism of the population with that of General Gascoigne and the other Tory-Anglican members of Liverpool Corporation: 'There is a high and generous spirit here, in the great mass—but singular coldness in

59 Chetham's Library, A.6.30–30*, autobiography of James Weatherley, transcript. Copy of typescript graciously provided by Michael Powell, chief librarian.

60 Rowbottom diaries.

some of our accustomed leaders'.[61] Currie's comment about the loyalist elites' initial detachment from popular ebullience stemmed from his radical suspicion of them. The largest towns in Lancashire contained sufficient party strife and bourgeois manpower to enact such divisions in practice: Currie was involved in the raising of a separate regiment by members of the vestry who opposed the corporation oligarchy.[62] In smaller towns, a more oblique compromise was made. Mark Philp has identified the phenomenon of 'vulgar conservatism' in the 1790s, created by loyalist writers and elites, in which their need to ensure a common loyalism through political propaganda overrode their original intent of preserving the status quo in the form of an uneducated and depoliticized populace.[63] Of course patriotism was influenced by the emotions and opinions of the ordinary populace, but as in the case of loyalism, there existed a continuing tension and negotiation over who could own and control the concept. Whereas Church-and-King elites had succeeded in enforcing their take on loyalism in the public sphere by 1803, patriotism was more ambiguous. The essence of patriotism during the French and Napoleonic wars lay in an exchange between government and governed, propaganda makers and readers, officers and privates. No single monolithic idea predominated among the organizers of civic patriotism any more than it did among its participants. Patriotism in its most basic sense was a continuing process of self-identification rather than a static collection of prejudices and xenophobia. In Lancashire, as in the rest of Britain, this self-identification involved a debate about the relationship of individuals with their locality and wider region, and of these provinces with the demands and identity of the state.

Notions of what the ideal meant differed according to class and location: for the aspirant bourgeois and gentry officers in the towns, social order could be achieved through observance of hierarchy, while the men they commanded either shared in this respect for elite dominance or acquiesced to it. In more rural and less populated areas, an ideal of community and independence, with men choosing their own officers and some notables serving as rank and file, was attempted. Though this was the most common pattern, these positions could nevertheless be reversed as well, with 'independence' stressed by civic boroughs and

61 Liverpool RO, Currie papers, 920 CUR 23.

62 Cookson, 'The English Volunteer Movement', 875.

63 M. Philp, 'Vulgar Conservatism, 1792–3', *English Historical Review* 110 (1995), 42.

the hierarchy of community enforced in villages. For example, the '4th class' was composed of men who were too old or had too many family responsibilities to belong to the regular volunteer regiments. They thus already had a distinct identity. James Weatherley's father belonged to the Manchester 4th Class volunteers and he noted that they were nicknamed the 'Old Fogeys' on account of their age. The 'Dad's Army' connotations of the volunteer corps were recognized at the time and in some cases fulfilled. Weatherley continued in his diary: 'There would perhaps be one as fat as Falstaff and another as fat as the living Skeleton that was once exhibited in Manchester, one five feet five another six feet one another bow legged and another inkneed.'[64] Many corps were based entirely around the personalities of their commanders. The rank and file appear to have been attached to the leadership of their officers, though this was probably more out of civic pride than an ideal of social communality.[65] By contrast, the regular militia and army lacked this immediacy, having aristocratic commanders and soldiers who rarely resided in the region and usually served outside it. Volunteer corps raised by the gentry firmly indicated the geographical limits of their social control: for example, John Trafford Esq of Trafford House, raised a regiment of 350 upon his estates. When they mustered in Trafford Park in August 1803, his speech proclaimed that Napoleon had pledged to deprive Englishmen of their right to England as a nation and therefore: 'The towns of Barton, Stretford and Eccles have sent Heroes to the field, and victory has crowned their zeal.'[66] This therefore, at least in the eyes of Trafford, was a localized rather than British patriotism, and a patriotism filtered through and firmly centred around the identity of the Trafford area and its resident landowner. His family had fostered recusants on their estates; it is possible that there were many Catholics in John Trafford's corps.

Volunteering also involved an attempt to restore the ideal of communality lost after the erosion of the 'moral economy' (E. P. Thompson's term for the reciprocal negotiation between 'patricians and plebs') in 1799–1801.[67] Patriotic activity in this vein allowed an element of democratic accountability that was missing from the militia and the army. The process of striving to achieve some sort of unanimity was

[64] Chetham's Library, autobiography of James Weatherley.

[65] See Warrington Library, MS 11, Warrington Volunteers Muster Roll 1807; Warrington poor rates 1802; 'A New Song in Praise of the Warrington Volunteers by J. B., One of the Corps' (1803).

[66] *Blackburn Mail*, 24 August 1803.

[67] Thompson, 'The Moral Economy of the English Crowd', 76.

important, even if it was not achieved in practice in most places in Lancashire. In many corps this sense of negotiation between elite and rank and file remained an ideal, with the middle classes using the institution to enforce social hierarchies after the tumults of the harvest failures, radical meetings and trades combinations and, as they had in promoting 'vulgar conservatism', demanding compliance more than negotiation.

The 'moral economy' had not, however, been totally destroyed. It had rather evolved to colour the ever strained relationship between local notables and the rapidly expanding industrial populations. This was demonstrated most dramatically in the case of the only major town lacking a volunteer corps in 1803: Rochdale. Volunteers had originally been enrolled in 1794, commanded by John Entwisle, landowner and magistrate. The event that made the institution legendary in local history occurred on 3 August 1795. The volunteers were called out to put down a food riot in the market place. Their chaplain, Revd Thomas Drake, vicar of Rochdale, gave the order to 'shoot o'er 'em', but it was said that the command was interpreted as 'Shoot Oram', a local manufacturer. Through inexperience and misjudgement, the volley of fire struck Robert Crompton, 'a respectable tradesman' and James Fletcher, a gentleman. The odium caused by the outrage resonated well after the event, so that when the *levée en masse* was announced in 1803, Rochdale remained strangely quiet. Compared with the fervour of the other satellite towns around Manchester and contrary to historians' assumption that 'national defence patriotism' subsumed any previous misgivings, albeit through fear or civic pride, Rochdale held out. Patriotic activity was restricted to offers to transport grain and people in the event of invasion, and sermons at the church, though it is possible that individuals signed up to neighbouring Bury, Oldham or Middleton corps.[68]

Popular celebrations of national events similarly reflected the complex layers underlying popular patriotism and loyalism. Loyalist elites and the government may have intended that national celebrations of naval victories provide a way of inculcating a deeper allegiance to the monarchy and unreformed state. The crowds at such events, although the sincerity of their patriotism and loyalism was probably mostly genuine, still maintained the capability to criticize. Popular patriotism often did not venture beyond the bounds of local defence to an unquestioning attachment to the monarchy or indeed to a wider conception of Britain.

68 P. Haythornthwaite, 'Rochdale Volunteers, 1795', *Journal of the Society for Army Historical Research*, 62 (1984), 113.

To celebrate Nelson's victory at the Nile in 1798, the boroughreeves and constables of Manchester and Salford arranged with the officers of the volunteer regiments to have a military procession with *feux de joie* through the towns. The broadside 'apprizing the public' of the event was headlined 'Admiral Nelson's Victory' in large letters.[69] This emphasis rubbed off on the diarists, as they thought it paramount to recount news of naval battles in their personal musings on the wars. Rowbottom's diary noted the 'glorious news' of the victory at St Domingo in February 1806. In most diaries and autobiographies, the conflict was described as being between England and France, not Britain, and extensive interest was shown in the leadership of the admirals. This may reflect the writers' sources of information. For example, Rowbottom appears to have relied on *Cowdroy's Manchester Gazette* for his national and international news, and editor William Cowdroy regularly took extracts from the London papers about the naval battles and was more likely to refer to 'England' than Britain. Nevertheless, this still indicates Rowbottom's judicious filtering of information, as Cowdroy and the other newspapers reported a much wider range of events and politics, particularly from French paper *Le Moniteur*. All the Lancashire diaries and autobiographies highlighted Trafalgar in the midst of their domestic detail. William Fleming recorded the illuminations at Ulverston and Dalton on 9 November 'in consequence of victory gain'd by Lord Nelson over the combined fleets of France and Spain; in this Battle the brave Lord Nelson lost his life'.[70] James Weatherley of Manchester, in his subsequently written autobiography, provided the longest description of Trafalgar and Nelson's death, though it was perhaps gilded with fifty years of Victorian sentimentality over the admiral. He claimed:

> The day of his funeral all the Mills and workshops stopt you could scarcly see that day a lad without a ribbon round his hat with a verse or something relating to the brave Nelson some of the ribbons were Paper and some Silk the one I bought was a blue Silk one I gave sixpence for it the letters on it gold Printed verse was May Nelson's Death and Britons Glory be Repeated in future Story.[71]

Navy admirals were regarded as the greatest war heroes and were commonly more popular than the monarchy, in part because of their position as renegade figures outside the corruption of politics or the court. They

[69] Broadside published by J. Harrop, Manchester, October 1798, copy graciously provided by Dr John Stevenson.

[70] Cumbria RO, Diaries of William Fleming, volume IV, 10 November 1805.

[71] Chetham's Library, Autobiography of James Weatherley.

were somewhat disassociated from both the hated press gangs and the idea of a standing army which dogged the reputation of generals in the eighteenth century. Furthermore, naval victories were regarded as separate from and even as having been achieved despite the failures of Pittite foreign policy and the lengthening war. Admiral Nelson in particular gained a personal reputation as victor and martyr. Local notables seized on the cult of Nelson to enhance their own image for civic patriotism, and the admiral featured in toasts and illuminations often at the expense of representations of the monarchy. The character of Nelson could also be construed as subversive. Individual attitudes to Nelson were more complex than xenophobic or triumphalist patriotism. Timothy Jenks has argued that Nelson's career was read in some circles as a commentary on the establishment's ingratitude for spectacular victories and on the ways in which political and social influence affected the distribution of national honours. Many perhaps preferred a somewhat maverick hero to a royal family and government that was beginning to be revealed as corrupt as soon as Nelson had been interred.[72] In January 1806, Rowbottom bemoaned the 'late disasterous events upon the Continent' and the 'unparallaled victories of Buonaparte', which had 'thrown Europe into the greatest consternation' and 'had a visable effect upon Trade and Commerce'. Yet this is followed by a contrasting statement that could almost have been lifted straight out of patriotic propaganda: 'but the glorious victory of Trafalgar, has been of great utility to the Commerce and Credit of this nation, and has placed us at present triumphant over our enemies, which may ever be the case, is the wish of every honest Englishman'.[73] Rowbottom certainly hoped for a successful end to the war, achieved quickly in order to save the burgeoning textile industry of south Lancashire, and perhaps he was more comfortable using the generic language of public patriotism to express hope than with bitter negativity over the government's economic and foreign policies. The cult of Nelson for some may have been only a passing phase or too distant to matter for quotidian life. Benjamin Shaw, machinemaker of Preston, seemed more concerned with the tactical manoeuvres of the battle and the negotiations that followed, concluding his account with the brief note: 'At the beginning of 1806, the funeral of Lord Nelson occupied the Nation awhile'.[74]

72 T. Jenks, 'Contesting the Hero: the Funeral of Admiral Lord Nelson', *JBS* 39 (2000), 423; G. Jordan and N. Rogers, 'Admirals as Heroes: Patriotism and Liberty in Hanoverian England', *JBS* 28 (1989), 222.

73 Rowbottom diaries.

74 *Family Records of Benjamin Shaw*, p. 47.

Linda Colley has highlighted the importance of George III as a rallying point for patriotism, increasingly distanced from the party faction and corruption of his ministers by his illness and by good propaganda projecting him as the father of the nation.[75] The diarists and autobiographers were relatively non-committal towards the king, especially when compared to their favourable comments about Admiral Nelson. Perhaps there was little reason for them to expound their patriotism in this way; it was either implicit or they felt that they could confine admiration for the monarch to the public sphere. Civic patriotic events focused around the king—including annual birthday commemorations and one-off celebrations, such as for his recovery from illness—were engaged in enthusiastically by the populace. Rowbottom commented on the effect of typical Lancashire weather upon the king's birthday celebrations of 4 June 1799, which were 'intended to have been ushered in with Great Pomp and festivity but it proved very unfavourable incurring by it raining which prevented a deal of public demonstrations of joy'.[76] Yet like other public occasions, their ritual and organization in effect reinforced elite loyalism. This was exemplified in the celebrations of the king's fiftieth jubilee in October 1809. Malcolm Chase has shown how the concept of jubilee in the popular political vocabulary, that is, the radical or millenarian idea of jubilee as a revolutionary event or period, was undermined by the jubilee of 1809. The 'apotheosis of George III', in which patriotism adopted the king as a kind of apolitical paternalistic saviour of the nation, culminated in the loyalist appropriation of the jubilee, leaving little room for radical interpretations of patriotism among the ritual and sermonizing. Church-and-King ideas were surreptitiously reintroduced through biblical actions such as setting debtors free from prison and an amnesty for army and navy deserters willing to rejoin their regiments. This explicitly Christian paternalism filtered down into local notables feeding the deserving poor of their parish, thereby solidifying social hierarchies and attempting to minimize popular disorder in a time of extreme hardship, poor harvests, and the increasingly ruinous economic blockade.[77] The paternalism shown by employers in manufacturing towns emphasized again the connection

[75] L. Colley, 'The Apotheosis of George III: Loyalty, Royalty and the British Nation, 1760–1820', *P & P* 102 (1984), 94–129.

[76] Rowbottom diaries.

[77] M. Chase, 'From Millennium to Anniversary: the Concept of Jubilee in Late Eighteenth-Century and Early Nineteenth-Century England', *P & P* 129 (1990), 141–2.

between Britishness and Lancashire's distinct manufacturing role in the national economy. John Holden noted in his diaries how the Bolton celebrations were stratified by trades and factories, led and patronized by their respective merchants and manufacturers:

> A great number of different Sorts of work people went in procession to the Church, Mr James Carlisle's work people to the number of 300 or upwards . . . Mr Rich'd Ainsworth of Halliwell gave meat and drink to all his men 500 and upwards and paid every man his day's wage Mr Jones gave his workpeople a meal and drinks.[78]

Using ritual and organization, the manufacturers therefore hoped that the 'mobs' of anonymous weavers and spinners which had caused havoc over the past decade could be transmuted into easily identifiable and controllable sections. Furthermore, as Chase argues, what was ostensibly an apolitical patriotic event served to entrench loyalist and establishment control over the concepts of patriotism and 'national interests'.[79] This was certainly the case in Manchester, where events were strictly organized by the loyalist elites and underlined the Church-and-King tenor of their political beliefs. After the weavers' strike and riots of the previous year the manufacturers and magistrates were acutely conscious of the need to restore loyalist control through the medium of popular patriotism. Hence the sermon at the Collegiate Church was taken from the Proverbs of Solomon, 'My son fear thou the Lord and the King and meddle not with them that are given to change.' The local newspapers focused on events featuring local notables. The customary procession through the town and firing of *feux de joie* were followed by a dinner for 250 'gentlemen' in the Exchange, where 'a transparency of His August Majesty was placed at the head of the room, bearing the following inscription at the head, "The Father of His People" '. The toasts represented the loyalist sympathies of the audience, including, 'Fixed principles and fixed bayonets opposed to French intrigues and French tactics', while 'the immortal memory of Mr Pitt' illustrated the new Pittite Toryism that J. J. Sack has argued was emerging by this time.[80]

The Jubilee celebrations of 1809 were a genuine but transient vocalization of popular patriotism. Again, they involved the creation of an ideal or collective hope for unanimity but the realities of the

78 Bolton Archives, Holden diaries, October 1809; *MM*, 31 October 1809.

79 Chase, 'From Millennium to Anniversary', 144.

80 *MM*, 31 October 1809; J. J. Sack, *From Jacobite to Conservative: Reaction and Orthodoxy in Britain, c.1760–1832* (Cambridge, 1993), p. 88.

war soon returned to create discontent. William Fleming wrote bitterly about the poor attendance at the general fast and thanksgiving for the king's recovery on 20 March 1811: 'too many were forgetful of both, and only about twenty persons attended divine service at our Church at Pennington'.[81] War-weariness and suspicion of government's conduct of the war, even among loyalists, continued through to the end of 1813 and were only assuaged after the end of the war and Waterloo. The Liverpool celebrations of Wellington's victories in December 1813 expressed an almost delirious sense of relief rather than an enduring confidence. The transparencies illuminated on the windows of the town hall illustrated the civic and commercial patriotism of the port that had fought the government's economic blockade: 'Britannia seated, leaning on her shield; in her right hand holding the Trident entwined with the symbols of Commerce, expressive of our Sovereignty of the Seas, and our extended Trade with the world.'[82] In April 1814, during the general illumination to celebrate the allied victories and the abdication of Napoleon, national symbols were amalgamated with examples of the local contribution to Britishness. Rowbottom reported that in Oldham:

> The different Manufacturers Gave Diners and ale to there Respective Work people who paraded the Streets with musick and Flags with Different Devices on a pair of looms where Drawn in a Cart where a person was weaving Callico and a person Representing Bonapart was winding Every Degradation was used to Insult the Memory of the fallen Monarch whose Tyrannical Career was at an End . . .[83]

The return of criticism of the monarchy soon after Waterloo, building up to the Queen Caroline affair, illustrated that this attachment was conditional. The monarchy was not and could not be regarded as the sole representative of true Britishness, if at all, over and above party factionalism: it was rather naval and army heroes who played that role.

Most Lancashire diarists and autobiographers of this period easily and unthinkingly elided 'England' with 'Britain'. This does not necessarily mean attachment to either, rather that the terminology was just as confused as it remains today. For example, in July 1803, William Fleming wrote about Napoleon's 'threatened Invasion of England' which 'roused the English to unparalleled exertions for the Defence of the United Kingdom. In Furness, this secluded corner of Britain, the

81 Rowbottom diaries; Cumbria RO, Diaries of William Fleming, vol. IV.

82 *CMG*, 18 December 1813.

83 Rowbottom diaries.

Inhabitants capable of bearing arms have in general enrolled themselves for the Defence of the Country'.[84] In one respect Fleming was right: the French were threatening England, as their attempts to invade Ireland and Wales had failed previously. Yet he perceived the English defending the United Kingdom, and was aware of his place in a region that he regarded geographically and politically as a remote part of Britain. Britain was thus a tangible concept but the United Kingdom less so. Scotland is rarely acknowledged in any diaries. Benjamin Shaw noted 'the political occurrences of 1801 January the first parlement of England and Ireland united met February', with no acknowledgement of Scotland or Britain. This was repeated in his terse statement about the Peace preliminaries, 'October preliminaries of Peace signed between France and England'.[85] This statement also suggests that the writers associated England with diplomatic or 'national' politics and the Westminster parliament. The generic tropes of patriotic propaganda in sermons, addresses, and ballads created a language for their consumers in the way they described patriotism, even if they did not identify with the concepts in practice; Weatherley, for example, noted 'it was in every Bodys mouth Bony is coming to take Old England'.[86]

JONE O'GRINFILT: THE LANCASHIRE JOHN BULL

Local broadside ballads were one of the most popular outlets for the amalgam of local and national. The Lancashire ballad character of 'Jone O'Grinfilt' transposed John Bull into a regional context. As the government and propagandists pushed a national or more centralized version of identity through volunteering and such characters as John Bull in pamphlets, popular response was enthusiastic but regional. Patrick Joyce has highlighted the O'Grinfilt ballads' role in nineteenth-century formations of class identity. Although elements of this were important, prior to the 1820s, its significance lay rather in what it reflected about Lancashire Britishness. Joyce has indeed argued that local knowledge reworked 'national' events and personalities in order to make them intelligible: 'Thus, local and extra-local elements co-existed, the "national" being realised through the "local", and the "local" itself being in part

84 Cumbria RO, Diaries of William Fleming, vol. IV, 27 July 1803.
85 *Family Records of Benjamin Shaw*, p. 43.
86 Chetham's Library, Autobiography of James Weatherley.

assembled by means of conventions drawn from a broad tradition.'[87] His discussion did not include a version of the ballad published between 1803 and 1805, which illustrates the popular response to the invasion scares and reveals the nature of 'Lancashire Britishness'.

Nationally-propagated broadside ballads are problematic as evidence of popular thought because of their usually anonymous provenance and the commercial motives of their sellers.[88] 'Jone O'Grinfilt', though still overlain with commercial considerations, was nevertheless composed for a specific audience at a particular time, and offers a distinct insight into local popular taste. The ballad can be regarded as 'industrial folk song', a hybrid form between traditional song and the purely commercial broadside, composed in industrializing 'neighbourhoods'.[89] It was not inherited from folklore but created in the mid-1790s by Joseph Lee (1748–1824), a schoolmaster from Glodwick, near Oldham. He may have been assisted by Joshua Coupe, a member of nearby Lees musical society.[90] The ballad was immediately a success and within a few years a dozen imitations were circulating throughout the north of England. Samuel Bamford recalled standing at the bottom of Miller Street in Manchester, viewing with surprise the enthusiasm with which a crowd purchased the verses from a ballad pedlar.[91] The various versions of 'Jone O'Grinfilt' illustrate that popular culture in urban areas did not entail an anachronistic or reactive reliance on nostalgic rural folk tradition. It was rather dynamic and responsive to new circumstances, using traditional melodies and patterns of verse as a base for innovation and social comment. The ballads also evinced a provincial suspicion of national propaganda dictated by metropolitan culture, and an irony characteristic of the North.

Jone O'Grinfilt was a version of John Bull filtered through local customs and character and had much of the ambiguity of the caricature

[87] P. Joyce, *Visions of the People: Industrial England and the Question of Class, 1848–1914* (Cambridge, 1991), pp. 233, 236–9.

[88] See D. Harker, *Fakesong: the Manufacture of British Folksong, 1700 to the Present Day* (Milton Keynes, 1985).

[89] R. Elbourne, *Music and Tradition in Early Industrial Lancashire, 1780–1840* (Woodbridge, 1980), pp. 55–6; J. Harland, *Ballads and Songs of Lancashire* (London, 1865), p. 214.

[90] B. Hollingworth, *Songs of the People, Lancashire Dialect Poetry of the Industrial Revolution* (Manchester, 1977), p. 127.

[91] M. Vicinus, *Broadsides of the Industrial North* (Newcastle, 1975), p. 18; Harland, *Ballads and Songs of Lancashire*, pp. 212–13.

image, commonly absent in the one-sided John Bull of most Church-and-King loyalist tracts. The ballad and its variations thus had a generic appeal, despite its localism, and this enabled the character to be used over and over again in different circumstances. Jone was continually portrayed as a Greenfield man, but with distribution he became a stock character representative of a general Lancashire if not a northern identity. Greenfield was a manufacturing village, separated from Oldham by the imposing Saddleworth Moor. Jone was figured comically and as simple-minded, 'Wi'my hat i'mi hont and mi' clogs full o'stumps'. In this he paralleled the figure of John Bull, which though ostensibly a national character, was portrayed (especially by James Gillray) as a Country yeoman suspicious of government demands of taxation upon the provinces.[92] Perhaps it is significant that the author came from Glodwick, which although being a small hamlet, was suspected by magistrates to contain an United Englishmen cell in 1801.[93] The verses of 'Jone O'Grinfilt' were in a dialect that was deliberately toned down in print, though the print form still retained its essence and evoked its syntax and turn of phrase. It therefore had wider commercial appeal combined with a distinct local identity.[94]

The main plot of the ballads was Jone's journey to Oldham to sign up to the volunteers in response to the French threats. The first stanza of Lees' original ballad suggested the nature of regional patriotism:

> Says Jone to his wife on a whot summers day,
> Aw'm resolv'd in Grinfilt no longer to stay,
> For aw'll go to Owdham as fast as aw con,
> . . . A soger [soldier] I'st be un brave Owdham I'st see,
> Un awll have a battle wi' th' French.[95]

The new imitation of the ballad was written in response to the French invasion scares, though it is unclear whether the original authors were involved. It related the new situation of the threat of 'Bony', and Jone's signing up to the volunteers. Jone views Oldham both as a gateway to the outside world and the epitome of military bravery. Greenfield does

92 See for example, Bodleian Library, Oxford, Curzon b.3(45), J. Gillray, 'Opening of the Budget; or: John Bull Giving his Breeches to Save his Bacon' (1796).

93 NA, HO 42/61/149–150, Hay to Portland, 7 June 1801.

94 A. Walker, conference paper, 'Identities', Annual Conference of Liverpool and Merseyside Studies, Edge Hill College, 31 March 2005.

95 Bodleian Library, Oxford, broadsides, 2806.c.16 (70).

not have these qualities; he is thus 'determined . . . no longer to stay' there, forsaking it for an Oldham identity. This Oldham identity and reputation he presumes to be known even by Britain's enemies rather than the name of England:

> Oather French, Dutch, or Spanish to me it's o one;
> . . . And aw'll tell um fro Owdham aw'm coom.[96]

This may also however have been satire by Joseph Lees of the pretensions of local pride over national identity. Jone's Aunt Margaret, by contrast, would resolutely defend her hamlet, and significantly, she equates this with remaining in England. Comically, she thus associates going to Oldham with leaving to fight abroad. Again it is the defence of England rather than Britain that is perceived to be at stake. The second ballad's development of the themes of the original demonstrated their generic appeal. In the 1790s ballad, Jone goes to fight the French because his hamlet was 'clamming and starving'. Although the militia money is mentioned, it is not the main motive, as it is in the latter half of the invasion-scares ballad, where Jone vows to fight for his King, 'Un when I return back some money I'll bring'. This emphasis perhaps had the authorial motive of either encouraging recruitment through appealing to self-interest or questioning such eagerness to serve for the material rewards. An awareness of Bonaparte's actions abroad in Egypt was either reflective of local responses to loyalist propaganda, or an authorial reminder which nevertheless assumed an awareness of events on the part of the hearer or reader.

'Jone O'Grinfilt' was particularly successful in expressing the nature of patriotic reactions to volunteering and the general circumstances of the war in a local context. Victorian antiquarian John Harland remarked that Paineite radicals issued a parody of the song. It may have circulated orally among the Taylors of Royton and other radical families, but the surviving collections indicate that the market for printed broadside ballads across Lancashire remained focused on patriotic material and the usual non-political romantic staples. The more the original Jone O'Grinfilt evolved in subsequent versions, the further away they moved from the context in which oral ballads were composed. Jone's creation and evolution nevertheless reflected aspects of how local identities were perceived and used. Jone O'Grinfilt was not the only regionalized John Bull created

[96] MCL, broadside ballads, BR f. 824.04.BA1, Vol 4, p. 155, 'Loyal Jone', printed by J. Haddock, Warrington.

during the French wars. 'Bob Cranky' was a distinctly Geordie character in dialect ballads of Newcastle-upon-Tyne from at least 1803. For example, 'Bob Cranky's Leumination Neet' of 1814 asserted: 'For oor Geordy Prince Rex;—Nyan spelt it se weel as Bob Cranky'. Admittedly, this and other 'Bob Cranky' poems were probably written by professional writers or hacks in imitation of Tyneside dialect and mannerisms rather than being a product of 'pure' dialect tradition.[97] As with many stock characters, Jone was used as a vehicle for political messages: there was a radical version concerning the Queen Caroline affair and he figured as a character during the Reform debates of the 1830s.[98]

Patriotism was a tool employed in building up the 'imagined community' of the nation, but radical and loyalist activists formed only two of many different communities competing for this identity or identified with the 'patriotic'. Popular patriotism was sincere but it was not unquestioning or acquiescent with regard to generic tropes of Boney and John Bull. Lancashire Britishness was an expression of opposition to metropolitan interference in provincial affairs, government, and identity. It was where loyalism found common ground with radicalism in what was essentially a common 'Country' opposition. It was also a means of identifying with the wider nation while maintaining a strong attachment to regional customs and allegiances, which still played an important part in the quotidian life of the population.

British identity in particular was confused because it was inherently a heterogeneous entity, a mix of different allegiances which confused contemporaries as much as it continues to confuse historians. Stuart Semmel's wider conclusions about the uncertainties of British patriotism and identity in response to Napoleon can also be applied to regional Britishness. The contemporary and historical conflation of English with British identities is obvious; the conflation of English identities with southern regions is also a factor. Contemporary observers realized that national identity was fragile and unstable, 'prone to interpretation and reinvention'.[99] Regional Britishness was just one of those reinterpretations, but in this period of industrialization and war an especially potent one.

[97] R. Colls, *The Collier's Rant, Song and Culture in the Industrial Village* (1977), pp. 25–6; See Bodleian Library, Oxford, Johnson ballads 1940, 'Bob Cranky's 'Size Sunday' (1804).

[98] Harland, *Ballads and Songs*, pp. 215–16, 227; Vicinus, *Broadsides of the Industrial North*, p. 35.

[99] S. Semmel, *Napoleon and the British* (New Haven, 2004), pp. 8–9.

Lancashire patriotism was no different from the localist, self-interested, and in some cases anti-loyalist patriotism in the rest of the country that Cookson identifies (though the lower rates of recruitment perhaps suggest that the north-west of England was worst than most).[100] Sincere as attachment to the ideal of a common Britishness no doubt often was, inhabitants of regions could only accept the reality when it was filtered through local particularities and identities. Furthermore, parallel processes of centralization and divergence of identities were occurring in the longer term. The closer Lancashire and its surrounding northern regions were linked with the Westminster parliament and the London press through 'national' edicts, orders and propaganda—and in consequence linked also to each other—the stronger the sense of provincial suspicion of government and the south. The regional nature of industrialization reinforced a situation in which attempts at national unity were often tempered by a strengthening of provincial identities.

[100] Cookson, *British Armed Nation*, p. 236.

3

Loyalism

The years of the Napoleonic invasion scares were a defining period for organizing and vocalizing patriotism in Lancashire as in the rest of the country. Their effects upon loyalism are also significant. 'Church-and-King' continued to be the toast of choice among loyalist elites, but what it meant and how it was organized under the threat of Napoleon was changing. The first invasion scare of 1798–9, moreover, coincided with another major political event that would further shape the meaning of loyalism. The events and ideologies of 1798 had as much, if not more, direct effect upon the Lancashire region as had those of 1789 or 1792. The Irish Rebellion compounded the idea among many loyalists, particularly those in positions of power, legal and religious, that loyalism entailed defence of Britain against Catholicism. The events of 1798 affected the region in a distinct way for a number of connected reasons: the region's geographical proximity to Ireland, the fact that many militia regiments were sent over to quash the uprising, the entry of United Irish exiles and emissaries, and more generally, the wave of Irish emigration, both Catholic and Protestant, into the region. These factors, together with propaganda, suspicion among magistrates about the Irish, and a basic anti-Catholicism entertained by many Lancashire inhabitants, impacted upon the nature of loyalism.

This chapter explores how loyalist elites dealt with popular loyalism after 1798. The contrast between the Church-and-King clubs and Paine effigy-burnings of the 1790s and the new forms of activity in the 1800s was noticeable. The Reevesite loyalist societies continued to meet, but lost their original roles as active propaganda producers and forces of order against sedition and became more leisurely gentlemen's dining or drinking clubs similar to the rest. The volunteer regiments raised in 1798 initially took up the mantle of the Reevesite societies, but with the more inclusive patriotism of the *levée en masse* from 1803, this loyalist hold on the military was no longer possible. Yet loyalism as a distinct organization and ideology did not disappear after 1798, nor was it subsumed totally by the activities of the volunteers. The events of 1798 in Ireland, and their effects on Lancashire society and politics, stand out in reshaping what loyalism meant and how it was organized. Lancashire was perhaps unique among its neighbouring regions and certainly in relation to national patterns of loyalism. While loyalist elites to some extent had to continue to encourage 'vulgar conservatism' under the new guise of popular patriotism, they simultaneously began to distance themselves from it. Fear of the 'mob' or at least the inconsistencies of popular fervour, aroused by United Irish activity and renewed food rioting in 1799–1801, provided one reason for this increasing exclusivity among magistrates, manufacturers, and other local notables during the Napoleonic wars.

Loyalism in Lancashire therefore developed two coexisting but in some ways antithetical strands: on the one hand, an increasingly elite or 'High' Church-and-King loyalism that was marked by a distinct puritan or conversely nonjuring inheritance; and on the other, a burgeoning Orange movement brought over directly from the counter-rebellion in Ireland. The intensity of both Church-and-King and Orange loyalisms varied across the region as across the country, but evidence of both is strongest in the most populated and industrialized districts. Manchester and Bolton were conspicuous for being centres of both. Manchester Collegiate Church, with its nonjuring links, formed the core of High Church, High Tory thinking and organization, while Bolton still had not lost its civil war reputation for being the 'Geneva of the North'.[1] Bolton magistrates were prominent in the initial transfer and creation of Orange lodges, while the English Orange Institution was inaugurated in Manchester in 1807. Both forms of loyalism again highlight the role of Protestantism in British identity. Of course tensions within the various sects of Protestantism precluded unity. The religious make-up of Lancashire was complicated and occasionally volatile. The two religio-political positions furthermore did not necessarily create a shared sense of Britishness between them, and certainly not among all Lancashire inhabitants. Nevertheless, the emergence of Church-and-King and Orange movements in the region suggests that Protestantism strengthened the nature at least of elite loyalism, as to some extent did

[1] J. C. Scholes, *History of Bolton* (Chester, 1892), p. 432.

a long-established undercurrent of anti-Catholic sentiment among the Protestant population.

CHURCH-AND-KING LOYALISM

The French Revolution was the main spur to the development of elite loyalism; but the crises of 1798–1801, principally the Irish Rebellion, the French invasion scares, and the Catholic relief bills of 1807 and 1813, also had a significant impact. Church-and-King loyalism was easy to recognize in its public manifestations but perhaps less so in terms of definitive tenets. 'Church-and-King' encompassed various political positions drawing on a wide inheritance that was refashioned in response to events. Toasts at loyalist dinners and sermons on loyalist feast days reflected some kind of common beliefs, if not entirely lucid, which shared similar principles with High Tory High Anglicanism. Lancashire Church-and-King loyalists professed loyalty to the Establishment in Church and State, though not necessarily to the current government. They swore loyalty to the king but not necessarily to the rest of the Hanoverian family, particularly the wayward and Whig-allied Prince of Wales. The positive tenets of Church-and-King centred on the king and, though drawn into sharp focus by the regicides in France, had a longer history stretching back to the Glorious Revolution, and were propagated through the calendar of celebrations and commemorations and sermons. The slogan 'Church-and-King' was also associated with the High Church Anglican party. Loyalists in Lancashire were High Church Tory in the political sense being attached to Church and State rather than through 'High' adherence to a liturgy. Peter Nockles cautions against strict labelling of political theologies. The political principles of High Churchmen were, he argues, 'invariably Tory, though by no means always in a narrowly political party sense, and were characterized by a high view of kingship and monarchical authority'.[2] This view bore the legacy of Lancashire's Jacobite and nonjuring heritage. As the eighteenth century came to a close, High Church Anglicans were distinguished by their suspicion of all forms of political and religious dissent, and maintenance of liturgical forms and practices untainted by the Evangelicalism tide rising in other regions. The strength of a

[2] P. D. Nockles, *The Oxford Movement in Context: Anglican High Churchmanship, 1760–1857* (Cambridge, 1994), pp. 26, 48.

particularly 'High' strain of Church-and-King loyalism in Lancashire influenced its popular politics and local government and distinguished it from its neighbouring regions.

Church-and-King attitudes towards the defence of the Establishment were already stoked up before the French Revolution, exacerbated by Bishop William Cleaver's tour of his diocese 'charging against Socinianism' in the summer of 1789.[3] The principles which underlay justification of mob violence against Dissenting meeting houses in the early 1790s were steeped in the prejudice that Dissenters were seditious as much as in the positive defence of the Established Church. The campaign against the bill to repeal the Test and Corporation Acts in 1788–90 was particularly vicious and became hallowed in loyalist collective memory. The diocese was not however united on the issue. In February 1790, 234 clergymen issued a conciliatory statement regarding toleration. The High Church core were nevertheless the most conspicuous protestors against relief, especially in Manchester, producing many anti-Dissenting broadsides before and after the meeting.[4] The divisions raised by the issue reverberated well into the Napoleonic wars as its tropes were re-enacted and incorporated into loyalist ritual. The central toast at the Bolton Church-and-King club's annual dinner was to '294 members of the House of Commons whose constitutional firmness secured by their decision in 1790 our civil and religious establishments'.[5] Anglican objections towards Dissenters gradually shifted from political to religious in the early nineteenth century, with the growth of Dissenting Evangelicalism, though virulent suspicion of rational Dissent as ungodly and seditious remained. The continuing use of the toast in the 1800s reflected how the religious and political prejudices of the loyalist elites were sustained long after the original causes of grievance had ceased to figure among the priorities of politicians in parliament.

The main enemies of the Church-and-King loyalists were of course secular. After moderate radicals had been silenced by the anti-seditious legislation of the mid-1790s, magistrates and other figures of local authority deliberately or unconsciously painted any individual expressing political dissent or opposition as a republican. Many loyalist authorities, in public at least, saw the politics of the people in black and white, with

[3] F. C. Mather, *High Church Prophet: Bishop Samuel Horsley and the Caroline Tradition in the Later Georgian Church* (Oxford, 1992), p. 83; W. Cleaver, *Two Sermons by William Lord Bishop of Chester Addressed to the Clergy of the Diocese* (Oxford, 1789).

[4] MCL, broadsides, f.1790/1/A; Mather, *High Church Prophet*, pp. 78–9.

[5] Chetham's Library, Hay mss, Mun A. 3.14, Scrapbook, p. 133.

no room for the grey area in between the extremes of radicalism and loyalism. They regarded 'Jacobins' in the polarized terms of propaganda, refusing to recognise the nuances of radical thought. T. Coke, magistrate in Manchester, wrote to the Home Office in April 1801: 'There are two parties in this town—one, as loyal I believe, as any in the neighbourhood and the other as Democratic.'[6] A common belief was that the ordinary populace were generally loyal but easily subverted into sedition by radical agitators, often falsely assumed to be Irish. Colonel Ralph Fletcher of Bolton wrote at the same time about the case of William Gallant, a soldier executed for attempting to seduce his colleagues from their allegiance to the crown: 'The temper of many of the lower class of the people continues in a great degree of ferment and the endeavours of the Jacobins are in part to urge them to open Rebellion.' He urged the Home Office to renew the suspension of habeas corpus and the Seditious Meetings Act, as their recent repeal had allowed radical activity to resume openly in mass meetings on the moors.[7] Although as will be seen, Fletcher had a reputation for being the most 'zealous' magistrate in the region, and his suspicions owed much to his Orange views, other magistrates, manufacturers, and notables generated a similar sense of anxiety from their Church-and-King standpoint.

Another aspect of Lancashire loyalism was the prevalence of Pittite Toryism among many of its squirearchy, manufacturers, merchants, and magistracy. Toryism as such poses problems of definition in relation to loyalism in this period. Loyalist authorities would have still regarded themselves as Whigs, and before 1819, few newspapers and periodicals called themselves 'Tory'. Yet their anti-Catholicism and anti-reform tendencies increasingly aligned them with the Tories. Lancashire was ruled by a predominantly Tory-Anglican loyalist elite in effect, but not yet in name. The Earl of Derby's influence was weak politically especially in terms of Whig influence in the boroughs: in towns where Derby had had influence, the turn of the century saw Tory manufacturers such as the Horrockses in Preston gain prominence and electoral majorities. The form of Toryism that came to predominate among Lancashire magistrates and manufacturers was less the old gentry recalcitrance inherited from the late seventeenth century and rather the dynamic Pittite Toryism that J. J. Sack has identified as emerging after the death of William Pitt the Younger in 1806. The eulogistic toasts at the dinners

6 NA, HO 42/61/432, T. Coke to Portland, 4 April 1801.
7 NA, HO 42/61/459, Fletcher to Portland, 6 April 1801.

of the newly formed Pitt clubs indicated how Toryism was refashioned around the imagined figure of an anti-Catholic, anti-reform prime minister. It crucially legitimized itself by encompassing selected Whig tropes, again including a glorification of the stability achieved in 1688. The most prominent feature of Pittite Toryism was an increasingly vocal anti-Catholicism that emerged in a manner that Pitt would never have approved.[8] Pittite Toryism was taken up enthusiastically by the local leaders in the provinces and goes some way towards explaining where Church-and-King loyalism went after the mobs and Reevesite clubs had dispersed or lost their specifically political focus.

Loyalist Elites

Church-and-King loyalism was organized within structures of local power and association that provided the bedrock of gentry and middle-class rule over the region. Again the idiosyncracies of the Lancashire situation affected loyalism. Different styles of leadership were developing to deal with the rapidly expanding boroughs. Manufacturers and merchants served on local government committees as aldermen, mayors, boroughreeves and constables. Rapid industrialization and urbanization compressed rather than amplified the distance between magistrates and the working classes, as the paternal structures in which lords of the manor overseeing their villages survived only in the more rural areas of north Lancashire and north Cheshire. For the working classes in the boroughs and large towns, and their industrializing outskirts, by contrast, their main points of contact with authority were increasingly the magistrates, their constables, and in cases of disturbance, the military. This is not to suggest a strict divide between urban and rural experiences as Carl Estabrook has portrayed for the early modern period, nor the breakdown and atomization of community that John Bohstedt suggests occurred in Manchester as a result of the Industrial Revolution.[9] Most inhabitants experienced a combination of the two forms of authority, but it is clear from the correspondence to the Home Office that magistrates and constables were most heavily involved in the enforcement of order.

[8] J. J. Sack, *From Jacobite to Conservative: Reaction and Orthodoxy in Britain, c.1760–1832* (Cambridge, 1993), pp. 66, 71.

[9] C. B. Estabrook, *Urbane and Rustic England: Cultural Ties and Social Spheres in the Provinces, 1660–1780* (Manchester, 1998); J. Bohstedt, *Riots and Community Politics in England and Wales 1790–1810* (Cambridge, Mass., 1983), p. 207.

The complicated nature of magistrates' duties was exacerbated by the pressure of the wars. Usually acting as deputy lieutenants, the magistrates became the sole source of active authority as the notionally distinct work of the county lieutenancies and the quarter sessions was combined. Pitt's anti-sedition legislation of the 1790s contributed to this process, as did the magistrates' responsibility for monitoring the registration of friendly societies from 1793. The Arbitration Act of 1800, an attachment to Combination Acts, gave them a role as arbitrators in labour relations, overseeing the processes of negotiation between master manufacturers and workers. This resulted in associating magistrates with a legal dispensation hostile to the interests of organized labour even if they strove to be objective.[10] Many had direct influence in working-class lives as employers. For example, John Singleton, JP for Wigan, wrote directly to William Pitt in 1799 against the handloom weavers' petition for a minimum wage: 'I and my brother Wm Singleton are manufacturers of Gingham, muslins etc—my brother is a half-pay Lt of Marines and we employ more than 1400 weavers and we do our duty as all true Britons do.'[11]

Many magistrates from the industrializing areas were integral members of the Church-and-King loyalist elite of the region. Certain Lancashire magistrates were prolific correspondents with the beleaguered Secretary of State in the Home Office. Frank Munger, however, did not find any correlation between the tendency of these individuals to correspond with the Home Office and relative levels of 'repression' in the region.[12] This link was indeed weak in some areas: magistrates from the northern Lancashire towns wrote infrequently, if at all. For example, magistrate William Fleming of Ulverston recorded in his diaries his suspicions and prosecutions on a scale similar to those of the southern Lancashire justices, but he rarely wrote to the Home Office about his concerns for law and order.[13] The Home Office papers nevertheless reveal that particular magistrates in south Lancashire were voluminous in their despatches. These included the infamous Bolton mine owner Colonel Ralph Fletcher (1757–1832); Revd Thomas Bancroft, vicar of Bolton (1756–1811); former spy William Chippindale; manufacturer Joseph Radcliffe (1744–1819) of Oldham and later Huddersfield;

[10] D. Eastwood, *Governing Rural England: Tradition and Transformation in Local Government, 1780–1840* (Oxford, 1994), p. 47.

[11] NA, PRO 30/8/178/2/235, J. Singleton to W. Pitt, 22 April 1799.

[12] F. Munger, 'Measuring Repression of Popular Protest by English Justices of the Peace in the Industrial Revolution', *Historical Methods*, 12 (1979), 76–83.

[13] Cumbria RO, Diaries of William Fleming.

Revd William Robert Hay (1761–1839) of the Collegiate Church, Manchester, and chair of the Salford bench, and his colleagues R. A. Farington and Thomas Butterworth Bayley; John Entwisle of Rochdale; Henry Fielden of Wigan; and John Lloyd of Stockport.[14]

These men had much in common. They presided over the most rapidly populating manufacturing districts of the region; most had manufacturing or commercial backgrounds but had risen into the gentry ranks and invested their money in coal mines, canals, and small estates; and all met regularly at petty and quarter sessions and socially in loyalist clubs and masonic lodges. Perhaps they corresponded frequently because they perceived themselves to have been in a special relationship with the government. On the other hand, their missives, some hastily scribbled late at night during agitated times, may have been a symptom of feeling more overwhelmed than most others on the Lancashire bench with the situation of disorder. These individuals may have felt more connected with the centre than their other colleagues, who were content either to involve themselves on their estates or business interests, or, perhaps like Fleming, hide from the government their sense of incompetence in relation to what was becoming an increasingly unmanageable situation in many areas. Though varied in political background, most were united in a Church-and-King desire to root out sedition and maintain social order. Loyalist civic identity was also centred upon the parish church. Clergy increasingly formed a large part of the bench, serving also as land tax commissioners and turnpike trustees, and running paternalist efforts with the gentry such as schools and charities. Certain clergy were also 'zealous' magistrates and regular correspondents to the Home Office, most notably Revd Thomas Bancroft, vicar and JP of Bolton, thus making 'the alliance of church and state more of a social reality at the end of the eighteenth century'.[15]

Prominent manufacturers and merchants comprised the other interconnected section of the loyalist elite in Lancashire. They eagerly involved themselves in civic or parish government and institutions as befitted their responsibilities as respectable members of urban society. Manchester and Salford, like Bolton, were governed by court leets of boroughreeves and constables, while Liverpool, Preston, and other large

[14] J. F. Smith (ed.), *The Admission Register of the Manchester School*, vol. 1 (Manchester, 1868).

[15] J. Walsh, C. Haydon, and S. Taylor (eds.), *The Church of England, c.1689–1833: From Toleration to Tractarianism* (Cambridge, 1993), p. 28.

towns gave the middle classes opportunities as aldermen and other members of corporations. This involvement should not be equated with either an erosion of gentry or aristocratic identity or with a 'rise' of a self-aware middle class. Most middle-class members of loyalist elites were aspirant to gentry status. The distinctiveness of the landed interest was enhanced rather than entrenched upon, albeit at considerable expense to the landed.[16] Elite loyalism allowed this alliance to operate. Loyalist notables were therefore elite not in the sense of constituting an exclusive club but rather in that there came into bring a status to which merchants and manufacturers could aspire, sharing more in terms of Church-and-King values than class identities.

Loyalism was integrated with local government and consequently with civic identity. Institutional membership made the local governing gentry and merchants active loyalists in civic society; after the suppression of the corresponding societies in 1798, the radical individuals that loyalists opposed did not have recourse to this source of identification.[17] Membership of loyalist societies was the most obvious means of demonstrating political affiliation and social status. In Manchester, the main loyalist society was the Association for the Protection of Constitutional Order and Liberty against Republicans and Levellers (APCOL). Of the eighteen boroughreeves and constables who served in Manchester between 1792 and 1797, sixteen were members of the executive committee of APCOL.[18] Membership of APCOL, and to a lesser extent, a Pitt club, were among the several social and political activities which determined the place of manufacturers and gentry in the loyalist elite. Pitt clubs spawned across the country from 1806. Most Bolton notables were members of their local Pitt Club, while its committee was composed of Colonel Ralph Fletcher, the vicar and the major manufacturers and bleachers of the area.[19] Individual loyalists were usually members of more than one club or society and thereby formed a tight network of association within a town. Dynasties of local status and authority were

[16] M. Billinge, 'Hegemony, Class and Power in Late Georgian and early Victorian England', in A. R. H. Baker and D. Gregory (eds.), *Explorations in Historical Geography: Interpretative Essays* (Cambridge, 1984), p. 29.

[17] L. Edwards, 'Popular Politics in the North West of England, 1815–21', Ph.D. thesis (Manchester, 1998), pp. 82–3.

[18] Chetham's Library, Mun A.6.45, 'Association for the Protection of Constitutional Order and Liberty Against Republicans and Levellers', minute book and constitution, 1792–9; Mun A.2.79, Manchester Pitt Club minutes.

[19] Lancashire CRO, DDHu 52/82/11, 'Minutes of the General Meeting of the Members of the Bolton Pitt Club'.

also established. Peter Drinkwater owned a factory with the highest poor-rate assessment in 1797, probably the largest single building designed for manufacture in Manchester at the time. He was constable in 1786 and a member of APCOL. His two sons also became cotton spinners and manufacturers: John was constable of Manchester in 1809, while his brother Thomas became a magistrate of Lancashire.[20]

From 1798, the nature of loyalist organization changed. APCOL, which had met every month or so in the early 1790s, tailed off in activity in 1797. By February 1798, its meeting failed to reach quorum and it did not meet again until July 1799, a meeting at which again only six members were present and which proved to be the last.[21] In part this may have been because some of its members were busy with volunteer or militia service. This was also partly a response to the decline in open radical activity following the arrests of leaders of republican societies in 1798–9. The Church-and-King clubs in most towns became less of a focus for political activism and more part of gentry associational life, while retaining a hold on civic events. This did not reflect decline, but was more a reaction to circumstances. More informal networks were maintained. Church-and-King loyalism did not necessarily need institutional structures to sustain itself. The political connections were solidified and their legacy continued. Loyalist manufacturers and magistrates were regulars at John Shaw's Punch House on Old Millgate, Manchester, where an informal club was sustained well into the nineteenth century.[22] Structures of local loyalist government were also encapsulated in the volunteers, civic ritual, and patriotic endeavours. In a time of loyalist controls on public activity, perhaps public appearances mattered the most. Having to act and speak in a loyalist way forced perhaps more hesitant members of the governing elites into an accordingly loyalist position. Whatever they may have thought privately, acting to root out sedition in public was another element of enforcement of loyalist atmosphere of repression.

Methods of Loyalist Rule

Though the loyalist elites responded warmly to popular loyalism, they also attempted to enforce compliance through both public and

20 Smith, *The Admission Register of the Manchester School*, pp. 163–4.
21 Chetham's Library, Mun A.6.45, minutes of APCOL.
22 F. S. Stancliffe, *John Shaw's, 1738–1938* (Timperley, 1938), pp. 18–32.

more subtle means. Loyalist elites almost achieved a kind of 'cultural hegemony' over politics in public and civic events by the 1800s. The political atmosphere of the 1790s ensured that it was longer acceptable for individuals openly fostering reforming views to hold positions of power and represent the views of the town. Manchester as usual proved the most extreme case, where wealthy office-holding Unitarians were subtly but firmly relegated to the prestige of their exclusive chapels in Cross Street and Mosley Street. This was most notably demonstrated by the change of position of Thomas Walker in Manchester. He had been a respected boroughreeve in 1788 and renowned for his campaign to repeal the fustian tax, but in 1794 he was put on trial for his radical activities with the Manchester Constitutional Society.[23] V. A. C. Gatrell has shown how the two prongs of Tory-Anglican attack involved an infiltration of the Literary and Philosophic Society and the creation of a Police Commission as a new source of power and civic influence. The Lit and Phil, like those in Liverpool and Birmingham, had been prominently Dissenting in membership and tone. Thirteen members of the Lit and Phil were marked out for examination by Church-and-King societies in 1794, and from the late 1790s it no longer speculated in political philosophy. By 1805, a new type of member was being admitted, who fitted the archetype of the Tory-Anglican political elite, including Hugh Hornby Birley (captain of the Manchester and Salford Yeomanry, who later cemented his infamy among radicals by leading his troops into the St Peter's Fields demonstration in 1819) and the manufacturer Sir Robert Peel and his son. Henceforth, the society allowed no opportunity for radical political involvement.[24]

The death of the prominent penal reformer Thomas Butterworth Bayley in 1802 removed the last magistrate amenable to Whig toleration and reform from the Manchester and Salford bench. Historians have pointed to his presence as an indication that loyalism in Manchester was not so extreme, but Margaret DeLacy comments on his exceptional political position as a Presbyterian 'Whig of the old school' in what had previously been a liberal city but a Tory countryside.[25] The Police

[23] *The Whole Proceedings on the Trial. . . Against Thomas Walker and others* (Manchester, 1794).

[24] V. A. C. Gatrell, 'Incorporation', in D. Fraser, ed., *Municipal Reform and the Industrial City* (Leicester, 1982), p. 33.

[25] M. DeLacy, *Prison Reform in Lancashire, 1700–1850* (Manchester, 1986), pp. 93–8.

Act of 1792 was even more effective in filtering out any opposition. It established a new body of police commissioners, who consisted of the boroughreeve and constables, the wardens and fellows of the Collegiate Church, and £30 ratepayers. The body played a lesser role than magistrates in enforcing order in the 1790s, but rose to prominence during the Napoleonic War, when ambitious members of the loyalist elite saw its potential as a tool for their rise and control of local government. Its treasurer from 1810 was the Tory dye manufacturer, Thomas Fleming, who became the effective leader of 'an allegedly corrupt but certainly Tory oligarchy which soon monopolised all significant posts in the town'.[26] Corporations, vestries, and older manorial forms of government across the region, particularly in Bolton and Preston, similarly became exclusive to loyalists. The moderate Whig loyalism represented by the earl of Derby and his interest was not eliminated by these changes, but was certainly made to play a secondary role in the suppression of radicalism in the region.

The predominance of Tory-Anglicans in Lancashire towns did not mean that loyalist authority went unchallenged by bourgeois radicals seeking a voice within local government. On the contrary, it often encouraged open conflict, especially on occasions when local 'notables' met to draw up petitions to government on such contentious topics as religious relief and parliamentary reform. Some historians have, however, suggested that civic associations overrode the political and religious differences of the middle classes and assuaged Dissenters and radicals who could not take part in local government. Alan Brooks argues that the Portico library served to unite the Manchester middle classes; its first committee included Manchester Constitutional Society members George Duckworth, George Philips, Nathaniel Heywood, and Samuel Greg, together with loyalist merchants and manufacturers Charles Frederick Brandt, John Leigh Philips, and Peter Ewart.[27] The campaign against the slave trade in 1806–7 also encouraged cross-political cooperation in many towns.[28] In Liverpool, the new Lit and Phil, Botanical Gardens, Infirmary, and Athenaeum were cross-political, cross-denominational organizations at committee level. For example, William Roscoe and Joseph Brandreth served on the committee of the

[26] Gatrell, 'Incorporation', pp. 33–5.

[27] A. Brooks and B. Haworth, *Boomtown Manchester, 1800–50: the Portico Connection* (Manchester, 1993), p. 114.

[28] House of Lords RO, HO/PO/JO/10/8/106, Manchester petition in favour of slave trade bill, 1806.

Lyceum with slave traders and ardent loyalists H. B. Hollinshead (the mayor) and Thomas Earle (magistrate and deputy-lieutenant).[29]

In the larger towns and on occasions in Liverpool, nevertheless, the experiences of 'independent' bourgeoisie outside their newspaper reading-rooms and charity committees indicate that political and religious prejudices were not wholly overcome by polite conversation indoors. Yet as long as debates about politics were conducted within the range of political discourse defined by the loyalist elites, some scope for Dissenting argument was permitted. Indeed, Anglican loyalist elites almost needed these debates to occur in order to legitimize their own hegemony. Once individuals or groups crossed acceptable political boundaries, they were either excluded or the loyalist elite enforced their dominance over them. Hence the campaign for the abolition of the slave trade was a successful movement uniting the bourgeoisie and gentry across a wide spectrum of political and religious opinion because it was conducted in terms of a single discourse aiming at an agreed end, though this did not preclude party divisions. In Liverpool, more than in most other areas, the issue of abolition was divisive in ways which reflected political divisions between the Dissenting intellectuals and the Corporation and its West Indies interests. The latter's regular motions in Council gave thanks and financial reward to members delegated to parliament to promote their case against abolition.[30] Of the fourteen presidents of the American Chamber of Commerce between 1801 and 1821, six were Unitarian and two were Quakers. In Manchester, by contrast, the Tory-Anglican manufacturers and magistrates had little truck with Unitarian radical Joseph Hanson, who directly appealed to the handloom weavers by supporting their working conditions and the question of peace in 1808. His intervention in their campaign was unacceptable behaviour for his class, because he acted outside the realms of acceptable bourgeois debate on politics, and employed working-class language about the right to a minimum wage in speeches and pamphlets.[31]

[29] A. Wilson, 'The Florence of the North? The Civic Culture of Liverpool in the Early Nineteenth Century', in A. J. Kidd and D. Nicholls (eds.), *Gender, Civic Culture, and Consumerism: Middle-Class Identity in Britain, 1800–1940* (Manchester, 1999) p. 39.

[30] Liverpool RO, 352/CLE/TRE/2/11, Liverpool Town Book, 1793–1804.

[31] See K. Navickas, 'The Defence of Manchester and Liverpool in 1803', in M. Philp (ed.), *Resisting Napoleon: the British Response to the Threat of Invasion, 1797–1815* (Aldershot, 2006), pp. 61–74.

Loyalist authorities' attempts to control the political activities of the working classes involved a more direct process of enforcing hegemony. During the wars the magistrates of the south-east maintained an atmosphere of fear and suspicion of 'sedition' within their localities, particularly by means of Home Office-funded spies. Spies have been much written about, and suffice to say most intelligence was exaggerated or at least cannot be verified.[32] Yet Colonel Fletcher and other magistrates usually believed his informants 'A', 'B', 'C', and 'D'. Home Secretaries over the years were less than credulous, and often attempted to reduce the payments given for such adventures, but felt obliged to continue from the magistrates' desperate pleading that spies were the only effective means to gather information and police a large and suspicious populace.[33] The spy system was difficult for Fletcher to manage: his informants claimed over £170, well over his allowance, in January 1805 for pursuing a United Irish suspect to Liverpool.[34] The circumstances within which the magistrates acted provide some basis for understanding if not justification for their actions or at least their beliefs and suspicions. The burden upon magistrates in rapidly populating and industrializing areas was so great that spies and special constables often offered the only resort for gathering information and maintaining order. In 1812, Joseph Radcliffe, magistrate in Oldham and later Huddersfield, referred to a militia corporal being used as a spy on the Luddites. He claimed in his letter to General Maitland, the southern commander sent to quell the disturbances, that 'desperate diseases . . . require desperate remedies'.[35] Whether or not they were true, the rumours and actions of the spies were important because they became part of the rhetorical battle between loyalist elites and radicals in Lancashire, 'a fixed point of reference in the evolving histories of conservatism and political dissent'.[36]

Freedom of speech and of physical manoeuvre were also controlled by local loyalists. Government legislation and royal proclamations against

[32] M. Elliott, *Partners in Revolution: the United Irishmen and France* (New Haven, 1982),
p. 284; see E. P. Thompson, *The Making of the English Working Class* (Harmondsworth, 1968), p. 536.

[33] NA, HO 42/65/491-2, Fletcher to King, 7 July 1802; 481, Fletcher to King, 31 July 1802.

[34] NA, HO 40/82/45, Fletcher to King, 16 January 1805.

[35] West Yorkshire RO, Leeds, WYAS 1096 (acc 3797), 4, Radcliffe to Maitland, 3 July 1812.

[36] B. Lewis, *The Middlemost and the Milltowns: Bourgeois Culture and Politics in Early Industrial England* (Stanford, 2001), p. 33.

'seditious meetings' in the 1790s defined exactly who was authorized to hold legitimate, that is, loyalist gatherings. Radical activists and bourgeois intellectuals who had formerly met openly and subsequently by the subversive tactic of 'radical dining' were forced to meet in secret. The new loyalist hegemony over the public sphere was a reaction to the specific threat of Jacobinism. E. P. Thompson focused on the 'rituals of the study of the JPs, in the Quarter Sessions, in the pomp of the assizes' to suggest how the gentry maintained social order and hierarchy in a world without a centralized military or police apparatus and with a weakened Established Church.[37] This process of domination continued to operate from the 1790s, though loyalist elites used additional means of inculcating loyalty and suppressing radicalism. As Mark Harrison has argued, the later eighteenth century witnessed a gradual but noticeable transition in towns from 'an open stage for the enactment of civic mystery and dispute' to 'a controlled set of enclosed spheres in which other than officially institutionalized mass activity was incomprehensible and alarming'.[38] Crowds could assemble legally only if the mayor or magistrates approved their purpose or they were regulated through volunteer corps, other military displays, and civic occasions. The effect was to relegate them to spectators of displays of local government authority. Loyalism at both elite and popular levels involved recognition of the governing elite's authority to name and control the symbolic meanings of place. This process was highlighted by the building sprees and civic rituals from 1789. During the 1790s, the ways in which places were distinguished reflected the loyalist reaction against radicals on all social levels.[39] Innkeepers were obliged to sign a public declaration against 'seditious' meetings on their premises. Cockhill Pump at Ashton-under-Lyne was renamed 'Jacobin's Pump' and 'during the peace of 1802, no Jacobin dared scarcely show himself in the streets without being in danger of having to undergo the dreaded pumping'. The landlord of the White Hart in the town renamed his inn the Pitt and Nelson in 1806 in honour of his two heroes.[40] Anyone unwise enough to

[37] G. Eley, 'Edward Thompson, Social History and Political Culture', in H. J. Kaye and K. McClelland (eds.), *E. P. Thompson: Critical Perspectives* (Oxford, 1990), pp. 15–16.

[38] M. Harrison, *Crowds and History: Mass Phenomena in English Towns, 1790–1835* (Cambridge, 1988), p. 141.

[39] J. Epstein, 'Understanding the Cap of Liberty: Symbolic Practice and Social Conflict in Early Nineteenth Century England', *P & P* 122 (1989), 82.

[40] W. M. Bowman, *England in Ashton-under-Lyne* (Altrincham, 1960), p. 315.

wish to honour an unauthorized hero would have been refused a licence, a fact which suggests another reason for individuals more sympathetic to reform exploiting to the full the ambiguities of heroes like Nelson.[41]

Local authorities appropriated popular rituals and ceremonies of patriotism and community in order to inspire allegiance and loyalty. Hegemony incorporated the abstract principles of loyalism into practice, thereby legitimating its assertions through widespread dissemination. In doing so, they made it appear a bottom-up process of allegiance while controlling from the top. It involved a continuation of 'vulgar conservatism' out of the page and on to the streets. The visual symbolism of the power of local notables was reiterated and reinforced through associated ritual. Traditional methods of celebration, such as paternalistic feasts and illuminations gained a new meaning in this civic context. An important part of local and national loyalist events involved a ritual and symbolic demonstration of local elite power over 'public' space. The order of processions was visually emblematic of power hierarchies within the town, with boroughreeve and constables or mayor at the forefront, leaving the general inhabitants as observers. The local elites were fully aware the masses could revolt and therefore made visually certain their domination of the new spaces. This had precedents in the practice of 'riding the boundaries', undertaken annually by members of corporations (including those of Lancaster and Liverpool) around the limits of their property and on common land to which they had rights.[42] The loyalist processions during the wars exemplified this dichotomy; private loyalist clubs displayed their social and political exclusivity in a public arena on their own terms. There was always an element of socio-political discrimination in these events. Addresses to the King or parliament were often drawn up at 'public' meetings in the new civic buildings, attended by invited 'respectable gentlemen' only. The routes of civic processions in larger towns avoided poorer areas, asserting in this way that the town was equated with places of wealth creation, consumption, and display.[43] The civic scene was deliberately incorporated into the symbolism of local politics in an enforcement of loyalist space. Focusing on the parish church also bore symbolic significance. Loyalist displays of power in urban centres were centred on processions through the main streets to

[41] Acknowledgements to Joanna Innes for this point.

[42] E. Baines, *History, Directory and Gazetteer of the County Palatine of Lancaster* (Newton Abbott, 1968 reprint), p. 546.

[43] C. P. Graves, 'Civic Ritual in Eighteenth and Nineteenth Century Newcastle', in S. Lawrence (ed.), *Archaeologies of the British* (London, 2003), p. 41.

the parish church, reaffirming the Established Church as a rallying point of loyalty. Corporation members or the boroughreeve and his officers acting as a body attended church on Sundays and public feasts and commemorations. They therefore deliberately or unconsciously confirmed at a supernatural level their secular power.[44]

In Manchester, the central area for loyalist display was St Ann's Square and the Collegiate Church, augmented by the New Exchange from 1807. Each celebration of the King's birthday followed a similar pattern. At noon, the boroughreeves and constables of Manchester and Salford and 'a number of gentlemen preceded by music and the flags of the loyal associations' processed from the Bull's Head to St Ann's Square, where the militia or dragoons on service at the time fired a *feu de joie*.[45] It is likely that the officers of the loyalist societies organized the events in consultation with the authorities, especially as most had members in common. The Bull's Head in Hanging Ditch, comprising the surviving part of the mediaeval town, was the place of choice for loyalist political meetings, thanks to its heritage as a Jacobite recruiting centre. The pub was not solely loyalist, however, probably because it had one of the only large public rooms available for hire until the new Exchange was built. St Ann's Square had already gained notoriety in loyalist politics for the Church-and-King mob riot that occurred there on 4 June 1792.[46] New political and commercial symbols were notably built on old aristocratic land. In 1804, old buildings owned by Lord Ducie in Market Place and Exchange Street were demolished and on 21 July 1806, the cornerstone of the new Exchange was laid. Medals of Lord Nelson and Pitt were enclosed in the wall with much ceremony.[47] The loyalist connotations of this were manifest. Liverpool responded almost in rivalry with their Athenaeum and fashionable residences around Great George Street from 1805. In Liverpool, expansion meant that the proportion of urban land over which the Corporation had control was declining. The new Exchange was opened in 1808.[48]

Elite loyalism was not thus just a matter of political ideology but was integral to definitions of class and social status. Local elites used civic ritual and national events to enforce their authority through the

[44] P. Borsay, 'All the Town's a Stage: Urban Ritual and Ceremony, 1660–1800', in P. Clark (ed.), *The Transformation of English Provincial Towns* (London, 1984), p. 239.

[45] *Manchester Chronicle*, 11 June 1803.

[46] Rowbottom diaries.

[47] *MM*, 22 July 1806.

[48] J. Aikin, *A Description of the Country from Thirty to Forty Miles Around Manchester*, (Manchester, 1795), p. 374.

symbolism of patriotism. Church-and-King loyalist gentry and gentry-aspirant bourgeoisie built themselves physical and visual spheres of power where they could make resolutions in private.[49] The Napoleonic wars impelled them outside their exclusive domains to lead the mass patriotism of the general population. They attempted to maintain their control over both the meaning of loyalism and the identity of the town as represented to the nation. The crowds may not have shared their social and political motivations when they participated in civic ritual, but, significantly, the organizers of events were acutely aware of this ambiguity. Ceremonies designed to display loyalist authority were always products of this tense discourse with an undercurrent of potential opposition, not only amongst the 'mob' but also amongst their own class who were left out of power.[50] They were successful in maintaining control during the period of the invasion scares, but the balance would shift later in the war.

Church-and-King and the Church

The development of loyalism in Lancashire was connected with another distinct feature of the region, its religious make-up. Two features of religion in Lancashire stand out in this period. Firstly, the Evangelical revival was relatively weak in Lancashire in comparison with Yorkshire, where the Elland society formed a network for aspirant Evangelical clergy.[51] By contrast, most Lancashire clergy were at least orthodox if not High Church in their theological outlook, and certain active members among them strenuously attempted to prevent the spread of Evangelicalism in the county. The dominance of the High Church was a legacy of Jacobitism and nonjuring that had distinguished Lancashire from other regions in the early eighteenth century. Moreover, it was mostly a result of two authorities: the Bishops of Chester and the fellows of the Collegiate Church in Manchester. The bishops in their charges and questionnaires expounded what amounted to High Church concern about religious and political subordination, which both influenced and reflected the views of their clergy. The Collegiate Church played a significant role in loyalist life, both in Manchester and Salford and in the wider region. In the early eighteenth century it was noted for its nonjuring and Jacobite sympathies, which underlined the original

49 T. Baines, *History of the Commerce and Town of Liverpool* (1852), pp. 325, 249.

50 Edwards, 'Popular Politics', p. 122.

51 Acknowledgements to Prof. John Walsh for information about this.

Divine Right meaning of 'Church-and-King' and imbued its loyalism with sacralism. The second prominent feature of Lancashire religion was that its Roman Catholic population rose faster than most other counties. Anti-Catholicism was a strong feature of Church-and-King loyalism, and was focused less on the native recusants who formed small enclaves in Lancashire society, and more on the waves of Irish immigrants who flooded its industrial areas from 1798 in search of work or refuge from the suppression of the rebellion. The region's large communities of Methodists and Evangelical Dissenters also brought to contemporary notice the weaknesses of the pre-Tractarian Church and the impact of industrialization and urbanization upon popular religion.[52] The Church-and-King element of Lancashire loyalism was infused with High Church tenets, both directly and indirectly.

Lancashire has been the subject of many studies of popular religion in the eighteenth century, most of which stress the connections between industrialization and the growth of Evangelical Dissent, particularly its cottage-based and itinerant forms that were more suited to the new environs of industrial villages. There is disagreement as to the extent to which the Established Church was willing and able to deal with these difficulties in Lancashire.[53] Yet in some ways the French Revolution eased tensions between High Church and Evangelical Anglicans through their united loyalist effort to enforce submission to the Established Church among the populace. Differences over toleration of Dissent were however quickly brought back out into the open by crises over itinerancy and the Sunday schools, battles fought particularly fiercely in Lancashire. Such events demonstrated how weak the alliance was among Anglicans and Methodists in response to radicalism and the French Revolution.

The French Revolution had a lasting impact upon all Anglican clergy and many of the Methodist hierarchy, forging Protestant unity against Jacobinism and atheism.[54] Both High Churchmen and Evangelicals

[52] J. Albers, 'Papist Traitors and Presbyterian Rogues: Religious Identities in Eighteenth Century Lancashire', in Walsh, Haydon, and Taylor, *The Church of England*, p. 318.

[53] M. A. Smith, *Religion in Industrial Society: Oldham and Saddleworth, 1740–1865* (Oxford, 1994); M. Snape, 'The Church in a Lancashire Parish: Whalley, 1689–1800', in J. Greg and J. S. Chamberlain (eds.), *The National Church in Local Perspective* (Suffolk, 2003), p. 245; P. J. Rycroft, 'Church, Chapel and Community in Craven, 1764–1851', D.Phil. thesis (Oxford, 1988).

[54] Mather, *High Church Prophet*, p. 303; R. Hole, *Pulpits, Politics and Public Order in England, 1760–1832* (Cambridge, 1989), p. 156.

were anxious to propagate passive obedience, submission to authority and a suspicion of Dissent and Methodism. Non-Evangelical clergy were much more obsessed with disobedience; hence their active participation in soup kitchens and cheap bread schemes, which they hoped would assuage the discontent of inhabitants within their parishes.[55] The message of Revd Thomas Bancroft, vicar and magistrate of Bolton, in his sermon *The Chain of Duty, or, an Exhortation to Civil and Religious Obedience* was clear: he urged adherence to the social hierarchy legitimized by paternalism and divine grace.[56] Ecumenical and cross-Anglican initiatives had been common in the 1790s, principally educational endeavours which, like the efforts of loyalist pamphleteers promoting 'vulgar conservatism', were regarded as vital to stem the flow of what the clergy called 'irreligion', an old problem that was nevertheless interpreted as a product of industrialization and Paineite radicalism.

Another significant measure of pastoral coordination underlay the deluge of Sunday schools that were set up in the later eighteenth century. Both Manchester and Stockport Sunday schools were launched in 1784 with ecumenical committees, including Roman Catholics and Dissenters, and similar arrangements were made not long after in parishes across the diocese.[57] Commitment to improving the education (and thereby obedience) of the working classes went hand-in-hand with a sense of loyalty to the social order. The atmosphere of the French wars amplified the need for cooperation over such matters, and the number of Sunday schools and their attendees shot up rapidly in the 1790s. High Churchmen and local loyalist notables cooperated willingly with Evangelicals in non-denominational bible societies, right until 1812.[58]

This ecumenicalism and apparent unity in the face of the apparent radical or atheist threat was short-lived. By the 1800s the alliance was strained and in certain parts of Lancashire crumbled. Three particular religious controversies in Lancashire during the Napoleonic wars demonstrate the role of the Church in popular loyalism and the

[55] N. Murray, 'The Influence of the French Revolution on the Church of England and its Rivals, 1789–1802', D.Phil. thesis (Oxford, 1975), p. 368.

[56] T. Bancroft, *The Chain of Duty, or, an Exhortation to Civil and Religious Obedience* (Bolton, 1797).

[57] *Reports of the British and Foreign Bible Society*, 2, 1811–13, 7th report (1813), pp. 137, 140.

[58] D. Lovegrove, *Established Church, Sectarian People: Itinerancy and Transformation* (Cambridge, 1988), p. 109; W. Ward, *Religion and Society in England, 1790–1850* (Batsford, 1972), pp. 13–14.

underlying tensions within Anglicanism which the French Revolution papered over, only for them to be torn apart again as soon as the Jacobin threat faded. It is significant for the nature of patriotism that they both occurred under the shadow of the invasion scares. The first controversy arose from the development of the Methodist New Connexion, and later Primitive Methodism, in Ashton-under-Lyne, Stalybridge, and their neighbouring industrializing villages around the border between south-east Lancashire and north-east Cheshire. Significantly, both Anglican and Wesleyan clergy associated the followers of Alexander Kilham and his New Connexion with Paineite radicalism. The Kilhamite secession in 1797 allowed the Wesleyan hierarchy to vocalize their loyalty to the state publicly and clamp down on internal dissent privately.[59] The second and third controversies were interlinked, involving Anglican reaction against Dissenters and Evangelicals over itinerancy and Sunday schools. These crises were perhaps most severe in the diocese of Chester in comparison to other dioceses. All affected the organization and principles of Church-and-King loyalism in the region. More broadly, the crises demonstrated that the alliance of the 1790s was only temporary and that sectarian and intra-denominational rivalries increasingly weakened the fibres of Church-and-King loyalism.

The struggle for control over Sunday schools was important for two reasons. Firstly, it was most disruptive and bitter in the most rapidly industrializing and urbanizing areas of the region, again reflecting its distinctive nature. As David Hempton has suggested, the conflict 'both between and within denominations was probably a more common feature of northern English life than the more publicised re-emergence of the [post-war] radical political clubs'.[60] This indicates how popular loyalism was more widespread than radicalism, though it was not the kind of loyalism than the church elites wanted. All loyalists lauded attachment to religion and to self-improvement, but the strength of support for Evangelical teaching disturbed the Church-and-King loyalist clergy. Very extensive numbers of the ordinary working population were involved, as thousands of children attended these schools. Sunday schools were part of everyday life, representing perhaps the only contact with institutionalized religion that many parents of such children

59 P. Stigant, 'Wesleyan Methodism and Working-Class Radicalism in the North, 1792–1821', *NH* 6 (1971), 103–4.

60 D. Hempton, *Methodism and Politics in British Society, 1750–1850* (1984), pp. 89–90.

experienced. Battles for control over the education of the working classes thereby translated into battles for their loyalty and demonstrated how sectarian rivalries could undermine the ideal of a united Protestantism against radicalism. Secondly, the crises affected most of the south of the Lancashire region at the exact time in 1799 and 1800 when Pitt's government was rumoured to be preparing legislation against both itinerant preaching and Sunday schools.[61] They thereby imply the connection between local denominational hostility and national policy in shaping Church-and-King loyalism.

The cosy and amenable world of the ecumenical committees began to falter in Manchester from 1795. Revd Cornelius Bayley, despite having been favourable to John Wesley, produced a Sunday school catechism enforcing a very high doctrine of the church. Anglican Sunday school preachers stopped using Dissenting chapels as venues. Bayley and C. P. Myddleton, incumbent of St Mary's, withdrew financial support from the town's committee and instigated a campaign to dissolve its ecumenical structure. Their measures led to the decision taken at a meeting of the General Committee in May 1799 that the Anglican and Dissenting Sunday schools should separate. A similar scene occurred in Stockport, where the town's committee functioned satisfactorily for nearly a decade, but then as the school associated with the Wesleyan chapel in Hillgate outstripped all others in size, a conflict arose over the proportioning of funds and the committee split.

These conflicts were partly a result of the overwhelming popularity of Methodism among the industrial working classes, as opposed to other forms of evangelical dissent. Methodism had only definitively separated from the Established Church after John Wesley's death in 1791. The Wesleyan hierarchy were highly concerned about promoting the Methodist Connexion's loyalty to the state. Though they clamped down on internal religious and political radicalism during the Plan of Pacification in 1794–5, many High Church Anglicans retained a traditional mistrust of Methodist motives, especially when new sects like the New Connexion formed in reaction to the hierarchy's loyalism. There were also political motives at work. In and about Manchester the crisis for the schools coincided or was contrived to coincide with a great push for political action from 1800. This counter-reaction by the Anglican Church against Dissenters culminated on Whit Monday, May 1801, when the Anglican

[61] This and the following paragraph draws upon Ward, *Religion and Society in England*, pp. 39–41.

Sunday school children processed to the Collegiate Church. This event established the long tradition of Whit Walks, but at the time was a political and religious show of Establishment defiance encased in symbolic ritual. It points also to the extreme of Manchester in both religion and politics. This was followed by an attempt to reunite the Church with the authority of the state when the Anglican clergy asked the boroughreeve, constables and special constables, the commander of the barracks, and Church and chapel wardens 'to enforce a more general observance of the sacred day by vigorous efforts of the police'.[62] The failure of such a policy can be witnessed in the clergy's laments in the visitation returns of 1804 and 1811. The splits were drawn out across the next decade in the manufacturing towns surrounding Manchester and in the wider region.

It is no coincidence that this tension coincided with High Church clergy acting against itinerancy. From 1798, a conspiracy theory evolved among Anglican clergy and High Church loyalists that Evangelical activity was merely a cover for radicals to disrupt the social order. Bishop Cleaver corresponded with William Pitt about the 'late increase of Dissenting Meeting Houses', and Pitt appears to have obliged in his responses. In February 1798, Cleaver claimed that preaching licenses were taken out as a means of circumventing the Seditious Meetings Act, and that 'the applications for them have frequently come from Persons better known by their Democratical Principles than Religious Zeal'.[63] His sense of alarm was much greater than that of his clergy. In November 1799, he wrote to Lord Grenville, complaining about the harm done by itinerancy. He bemoaned that without government help:

> The established religion cannot exist much longer in the country; and I think the line from Manchester through Yorkshire to Richmond, the extremity of my diocese, will convince anyone of this truth who shall pass it on horseback. I wish the Dissenters may not now be the majority in that tract.[64]

These ideas were of course circulated nationally: Grenville and Pitt were informed by representations from the diocese of Lincoln about the apparent threat. What marked Lancashire out in this respect was the extent to which the loyalist elites translated the issue as part of their political principles and into action against Evangelicalism in the Sunday schools. The legislative response was interrupted by government fear of

[62] W. E. A. Axon, *Annals of Manchester* (Manchester, 1886), pp. 127–8.

[63] NA, PRO 30/8/103, Cleaver to Pitt, 5 February 1798.

[64] *The Manuscripts of J. B. Fortescue Esq*, Historical Manuscripts Commission Society Report, 6 (1908), pp. 20–1.

social disturbance if enacted, and the renewal of the war. Lord Sidmouth did introduce an anti-itinerancy bill in 1809, and a revised form was debated in the Commons in 1811, which amounted to a more general attack on toleration. Wesleyan Methodists in Lancashire reacted in horror, desperate to prove the loyalty that they had fought for against the more suspect tendencies of the New Connexion. In fact, parliament passed a measure of toleration in 1812, making many anti-Dissenting clergy feel even more beleagured.[65] Bishop George Henry Law wrote in his 1814 charge to his diocese: 'The Parochial Minister is now more than ever called upon, to oppose and check that spirit of itinerancy, which appears to be gaining ground.'[66]

The anti-Jacobin atmosphere of the 1790s had already fostered prejudices against evangelical zeal among not only Methodists but also Anglican Evangelicals. The strength of the High Church within Lancashire thereby snuffed out any open opportunities there may have been in many parishes for Evangelical endeavour, despite the apparent unanimity of elite adherences of the two camps against radicalism. The village of Littleborough was not too far from the Oldham parish that Mark Smith has lauded for its Evangelical response to the difficulties of serving an industrial congregation. The minister of Littleborough was less favourable to this fervour, seeing danger to tenets of the Established Church. He recounted to the Bishop in his return to the visitation questionnaire:

> I have often been urgently solicited to baptise children without sponsors in private houses—at funerals and upon days when there is no congregation which I have never acceded to. I have consequently incurred much ill-will because there are clergymen not far distant who make no scruple about these matters. Dr Cleaver and Dr Majendie strenuously discountenanced such practices yet I am told they are still persisted in.[67]

The orthodox influence of the bishops is thus clear; the situation in Oldham was unusual and regarded as suspect by even nearby clergy. Pressure against Evangelicals increased during the rest of the war. In 1812, the SPCK established one of its new diocesan committees in

[65] Hole, *Pulpits, Politics and Public Order*, p. 195; Lovegrove, *Established Church, Sectarian People*, p. 140.

[66] *Resolutions of the Methodist Ministers of the Manchester District assembled at Liverpool, 23 May 1811* (Liverpool, 1811); *A Charge Delivered to the Clergy of the Diocese of Chester . . . by George Henry Law* (1814), p. 21.

[67] Cheshire RO, EDV 7/3, Bishop of Chester visitation returns, 1804.

Cheshire and Bishop Law recommended in his charge that his clergy support the society rather than what was now perceived as its rival, the non-denominational British and Foreign Bible Society, which was, he thought 'unfavourable to our Church Establishment'.[68] The implication from what is said in the visitation returns is that the bishops and many of the clergy saw education as the salvation of the Established Church. The vicar of Heywood, near Rochdale, praised the achievements of Sir Robert Peel's act of 1802 to improve the condition of children apprenticed to factories, which he claimed, had 'been attended with great service to the Establishment here. By his decree, I take care that they are properly instructed and throughout the Parish, 500 children belonging to his factories who formerly went to no place of worship now regularly attend the Church or chapels of the Establishment.'[69] Again, loyalism in these respects was less about Protestant unanimity than about the establishment of a Church-and-King hegemony and the beginning of a slow process of Anglican renewal that would continue well into the nineteenth century.

The Clergy and Popular Religion

The returns to the bishop's questionnaire of 1804 suggest that clergy regarded the political impact of the French Revolution as fading and therefore turned to look inwards at threats to popular loyalty to Church-and-King hegemony that lay closer to home. Despite the preponderance of anti-Jacobin sentiment in the sermons and pamphlets which continued to be circulated during the Napoleonic wars (and are used as evidence of clerical attitudes by historians), the shift during these years towards more positive patriotic messages appears to have affected clerical thought about the politics of their parishioners. Few clergy regarded the influence of Paineite radicalism upon the religious tendencies of inhabitants in the North West as lasting or significant. Some clergy did comment on the issue, but they stand out as unusual. The ministers at Bacup and Colne, two rapidly expanding Pennine industrial villages, used the term 'poison' to describe the influence of Paine's writings among the working classes of their parishes, both 'politically and religiously'. J. Hartley of Colne used the language of

68 B. E. Harris (ed.), *A History of the County of Chester*, iii (Oxford, reprint, 1980), p. 59.

69 Cheshire RO, EDV 7/3, Bishop of Chester visitation returns, 1804.

anti-Jacobin propaganda, either out of genuine belief in its veracity or in order to impress the bishop. He railed against:

> the infamous Paine, and his diabolical associates in the same horrid cause, during the progress of the French Revolution [,] that phenomenon in History which has given a new character to man and shewn him when perverted by irreligion and false philosophy, to be capable of greater wickedness than any records of his former corruptions, could give any reason even to imagine him equal to.[70]

Most clergy by contrast hoped that Paineite radicalism was a passing phase rather than a long-term development or did not mention it at all. The cleric at Colne attempted to assure the Bishop that 'the number of Revolutionary Spirits' were 'much upon the decline' as a result of the 'termination' of the Revolution and its effects. The relatively few mentions of Paineite radicalism in the returns do not negate the fact that the *Rights of Man* continued to be sold and disseminated among the textile workers of the North. Nor does it suggest that all inhabitants and indeed all clergy were loyal in the anti-radical Church-and-King sense. It perhaps suggests that, as Stuart Semmel has argued, the ambiguous status of Napoleon Bonaparte was confusing matters about defining the enemy as Jacobins, or, more likely, that there was a general acceptance that patriotism had diminished radicalism at home.[71] It might also suggest that the clergy were beginning to understand that their fears of Jacobinism had been based on the exaggerations of loyalist propaganda rather than real knowledge of its (rather more limited) influence on the ordinary populace. The minister of Hollinwood in 1811 believed the number of absentees would 'still diminish as the infamous doctrines of Tom Paine sink into oblivion'. A more telling reason why mentions of Paineite radicalism were few in the returns was that the clergy were careful to distinguish absenteeism from what they called 'irreligion' or atheism. Only a low percentage of parishes claimed that there were many 'irreligious': 20 per cent of the returns did so in 1804, falling to 14 per cent in 1811. Furthermore, they recognized that most absentees 'did not openly profess irreligion'.[72] Wilful disobedience was attributed to

[70] Cheshire RO, EDV 7/3, Bishop of Chester visitation returns, 1804.

[71] S. Semmel, *Napoleon and the British* (New Haven, 2004), p. 16.

[72] Cheshire RO, EDV 7/3–4, Bishop of Chester visitation returns, 1804, 1811. Calculations are taken from analysis of 163 chapelries in the 1804 visitation returns and 121 chapelries in the returns of 1811. Not all parishes responded to all questions, and some are vague or implied. The returns for 1804 only run from parishes beginning with the letters A to P. Some returns from 1811 are missing. The percentages should therefore

longer term causes of the effects of industrialization and rapid population growth rather than the short-term disruption of Paine.

The changes that the clergy witnessed between the visitations of 1787, 1804, and 1811 were less to do with politics and more to do with longer-term social patterns. Certain clerics gave the impression in 1804 that they were desperately struggling to cope against industrialization and urbanization. This anxiety was no doubt sparked also by high-profile debates in parliament about clerical non-residence, which resulted in several bills attempting to restrict multiple livings in 1802.[73] The problem that both clergy and the bishops recognized was that church building had halted because of the war and economic scarcity, yet this was precisely the time when the population was increasing at a faster rate than at any time in the eighteenth century. Furthermore, the booming population was concentrated in areas where churches and chapels were not traditionally built, primarily the industrial colonies of the Pennines. Many clergy reported that they were unaware of what occurred in the 'extremes' of their parishes, and it was in these areas where itinerant preachers and evangelical cottage and camp meetings flourished. The incumbent of Gorton highlighted the problem of the thickening outlying villages 'where there is not any place of worship of the Established Church—as Reddish and Aston Smith, where there is a Methodist meeting house; Audenshaw, a Calvinist Chapel; Fairfield, a Moravian Congregation; Openshaw, Methodist'.[74] By 1811, only a few specifically blamed the growth of Dissent for poaching potential attendees from the Established Church, perhaps because most took it to be inevitable or unstoppable.

The effects of industrialization on the work and leisure of the working classes undoubtedly affected church attendance and practice, although this was mentioned by fewer clergy than there were industrial parishes. Reasons for non-attendance were often simply described as 'indolence' or 'indifference' or 'worldly matters', all terms which could encompass the wider social effects of industrialization but which also were complained about whatever the century or circumstance. A few clergy were more explicit. The minister of Flookborough in Cartmel was unable to keep track of the number of Catholics in the area because of 'a large

be understood as rough estimates and not a definite indication of the opinions of all the clergy in the diocese.

[73] See for example, 'Bill to amend Act abridging Spiritual Persons from having Pluralities of Livings', *19th Century House of Commons Sessional Papers*, vol. 1 (1801–2), p. 153.

[74] Cheshire RO, EDV 7/4, Bishop of Chester visitation returns, 1811.

cotton mill in it, employing nearly 700 people, the workers at which being continually changing, I cannot say whether there may be papists amongst them or not'.[75] The vicar of Ashton-under-Lyne wrote about families in Audenshaw and Charlestown, settlements that had newly grown up around factories:

> The Heads of many Families among the lower ranks of the community even persist and encourage their children to wander up and down during the time of divine service. The Parents themselves allege that, as their children are confined in the Factories during the Week, therefore they think it necessary that they should have some relaxation on the Sunday . . . The cotton manufacturers make a constant and common practice of employing engineers and wheelwrights to repair their engines and machines of the Lord's Day.[76]

This was symptomatic of the Lancashire clergy fearing rapid economic, more than ideological, disruption. It also implies that many clergy did not see themselves to be fighting a battle against impiety: it was rather a matter of form and practice.

Popular loyalism was not seen to require a strict adherence to the Established Church as a political entity in the same way that 'Church-and-King' elites hoped that it should be. Personal piety involved a sense of diffuse Christianity that did not necessarily entail attendance at formal structures of Sunday service or positive allegiance to the doctrines and practices of the Established Church. Religious identity was cultural, encompassing a broader range of adherences which could include family and community networks, in which the rites of passage of baptisms, marriages and funerals were focused more on social rather than on theological values. Nor was loyalty to the Church when it was present a result of its imposing hegemony from above; rather a long-term process of communities and individuals taking what they wanted from religion. As Jan Albers has deftly stated, 'A cultural understanding of religious identity does not preclude theological awareness or active piety, but does not base itself upon them.'[77] Popular identities were constructed not from absolute principles but from a combination of pragmatic factors. The conviviality of cottage and camp meetings that characterized early Methodism and its later off-shoots often fitted better with the busy but humble lives of many members of the working and middle classes.

Many individuals cannot be pigeonholed as adhering to any one denomination or set of doctrines; especially at a time when there were

[75] EDV 7/3, 1804. [76] EDV 7/4, 1811.
[77] Albers, 'Papist Traitors and Presbyterian rogues', pp. 333, 319.

various Protestant sects, it was common to drift in and out of different churches in response to life events, personal contacts, and migration. Lancashire diarists provide examples of this freedom of religious choice. Benjamin Shaw (1772–1841), a machinemaker of Dolphinholme and Preston, wrote that his father joined the Methodists once he 'began to feel and see his need of inward religion', but afterwards joined the Independents. Shaw himself came into contact with a Baptist spinning master at his work in 1800. Shaw was invited to the Baptist chapel after he 'pretended to defend the Church of England; I prated much though I seldom went to Church, but was much attatched [sic] to it for all that'. He oscillated between chapel and church, 'for I was still prejudiced in favour of the Church, but found nothing that I wanted there'.[78] Shaw's last comment supports the view of some historians that popular loyalty to the Church of England was based much less on theological conviction and much more on an inherent or cultural awareness that it was the right thing to do.[79] The idea of a national church was appealing in principle, even if it was not achieved in practice.

Church-and-King loyalism among the populace was therefore inspired and confirmed in many cases by experience of the church's communal role. Some clergy were aware of the nuances of popular piety but felt unable to deal with it; the most common complaint was about non-attendance on Sundays. The clergy were so caught up in this aspect of what they regarded as the major fault of their parishioners that they often forgot to acknowledge that loyalty to the church was expressed in a different way. Inhabitants willingly observed rites of passage, marriages and funerals being the most obvious, and customs associated with their parish church including the celebrations of the king's birthday and volunteer services. Historians (and indeed the clergy writing to the bishop) have found it easy to stereotype the Established Church as an agency of social control neglected or despised by the working classes, but on the parish level at least, the church played a positive role and was respected.[80] Popular loyalism was not Church-and-King in the same

[78] *The Family Records of Benjamin Shaw: Mechanic of Dent, Dolphinholme and Preston, 1772–1841*, ed. A. G. Crosby, Record Society of Lancashire and Cheshire, 130 (Chester, 1991), p. 38.

[79] T. Claydon and I. McBride (eds.), *Protestantism and National Identity: Britain and Ireland, c.1650–c.1850* (Cambridge, 1998), pp. 3–32.

[80] Snape, 'The Church in a Lancashire Parish', p. 249; Walsh, Hay, and Taylor, *The Church of England*, p. 27.

way as the Anglican elites wanted it to be; this does not make it less genuine, only less institutionalized.

The 'Church' in Church-and-King was therefore disunited theologically and institutionally. Throughout the eighteenth century, it failed to cope with long-term pastoral and organizational challenges that the new forces of urbanization and industrialization created. This did not mean, however, that it had lost its entire role, and as P. J. Rycroft has argued about the parish of Craven, 'where the Church had a base, it could continue to function as a social focus'.[81] It was to this embodiment of a continuing tradition that communities directed their loyalty, and which provided the basis for resilience among Church-and-King loyalists, both lay and clerical, High Church and Evangelical. Nevertheless, the Church's role as a beacon of loyalty towards the Established state was fading in areas of rapid economic change and Dissent, or where wealthier clergy (often magistrates) demonstrated hypocrisy or indifference that was only later alleviated by Evangelical zeal in the nineteenth century. The bishops' visitation returns reveal on the one hand exaggeration on the part of some clerics, particularly the fellows of the Collegiate Church, and on the other some underplaying of the problems by other clerics. There was nonetheless a sense of defiance in adversity; the 1811 return of Manchester Collegiate Church proclaimed: 'Yet amidst these papists and Calvinists and Methodists common foes I hope it may be said, "Fear not o little flock" to our Established Church!'[82]

Popular support for state and Church was thus not a product of an unthinking consumption of Church-and-King propaganda. Its relationship with the government, the state, and the Church was nuanced and conditional. It became increasingly separated from the aims of local loyalist authorities. This relationship was developed through a process of negotiation played out in the civic ritual of processions and addresses to the king. When local elites came to feel that 'vulgar conservatism' was becoming too popular to control, they sought to find other methods of asserting their loyalist authority and exclusivity, principally in the Orange movement.

THE ORANGE MOVEMENT

The English Orange movement fed upon two connected elements during the Napoleonic wars: Protestant anxiety about apparent attacks on

[81] Rycroft, 'Church, Chapel and Community in Craven', p. 146.
[82] Cheshire RO, EDV 7/4, visitation returns, 1811.

the Established Church and sectarian tension among immigrant Irish workers. The movement has not received the attention it warrants by historians of loyalism because of its association with immigrant sectarianism. This image of the early movement is misleading. The Orange Institution was not merely a working-class social phenomenon. On the contrary, its first lodges were formed by the gentry, magistrates, and clergy. It facilitated and shaped their enforcement of law and order during industrial disturbances. It was no coincidence that some of the very men who repressed the 'Peterloo' radical meeting in Manchester in 1819 had been officers of militia regiments that had quelled the Irish Rebellion with their fellow Irish Orangemen. Orangeism provided the opening for the subsequent transformation of loyalism into 'ultra' Toryism among politicians and a large section of the northern working classes.

Anti-Catholicism

Anti-Catholicism was an underlying current in Lancashire society. This was not of course entirely a result of the propagation of such tenets in Anglican sermons. Jan Albers has described how overt sectarian violence in Lancashire prior to 1790 always occurred at times of 'heightened sense of social, political or religious threat' and centred on the most extreme stereotypes of Presbyterians and Roman Catholics. Yet even in periods of widespread pressure, violence was localized and depended upon other pre-existing tensions within communities.[83] As in the case of the Church-and-King mobs, this also applied after 1790. By 1795, once attacks on Dissenting places of worship had ceased, religious prejudice expressed itself in the public eye instead in the rhetoric of pamphlets and petitions, and more covertly through discrimination and organization.

Anti-Catholicism in Lancashire in the 1800s fed from, as well as contributed to, religious initiatives in parliament. The Union with Ireland and the consequent question of Catholic emancipation which resulted in the resignation of William Pitt from the prime ministership in 1801 coincided with the state of alert over the United Irish emissaries attempting to incite revolution in the region. The Catholic petition for relief in 1805 renewed Protestant anxiety, further exacerbated by the pledge of the new Ministry of All the Talents in 1806–7 to relieve Irish Catholics, and Lord Howick's motion in April 1807 for a

83 Albers, 'Papist Traitors and Presbyterian Rogues', pp. 321, 324–6.

Roman Catholic Army and Navy Service Bill which would have allowed Catholics to become military officers.

These parliamentary initiatives and debates inspired expressions of anti-Catholic loyalism. The year 1807 marked an especially significant flashpoint in Lancashire. Loyal addresses were sent from across the country to the king congratulating him on the defeat of Howick's bill. The Manchester address against the bill was composed at a meeting at the Bull's Head Inn by a committee consisting of fellows of the Collegiate Church and some major manufacturers.[84] The response by radicals and other opponents of the High Anglicans was to accuse them of religious bigotry. On 9 May, the radical editor of the *Manchester Gazette*, William Cowdroy, claimed that anti-popery was being infused into electoral politics: 'The moderation of the Catholics presents a striking contrast to the conduct of certain *Protestants* who are setting every engine at work to excite the popular fury against them.'[85] In Preston, the Mayor, Aldermen, and burgesses of the borough drew up an address to the king similar to the Manchester address in tone and in its use of Protestant tropes. The Catholic priest in Preston, Father Joseph Tate, felt compelled to publish his sermon on the topic in response. He defended his congregation's loyalty, highlighted Catholic participation in British military victories to support his case and, in stating that Pitt had been in favour of Catholic relief, pointed to the hypocrisy of Pittite ministers and their supporters' anti-Popery.[86]

The ferment aroused by the bill was evident across the region and broke out into actual violence through the medium of election riots. In Liverpool, the Whig-radical Unitarian William Roscoe stood down from seeking re-election for the seat in the next month, blaming the prejudices of crowds shouting 'No Popery' in riots upon his return. Vivid anti-Catholic election squibs stirred up the disturbances. They latched onto Roscoe's support in parliament for Catholic relief as the main point of satire and criticism, rather than what should have been more contentious in Liverpool, his key role in the abolition of the slave trade. Further evidence illustrates that 1807 was a high-point of religious tension. The *Liverpool Courier* was established by Thomas Kaye at the end of the year. Victorian historian Thomas Baines claimed that it was

[84] *CMG*, 25 April 1807. [85] *CMG*, 9 May 1807.

[86] *MM*, 25 April 1807; *A Discourse Delivered in the Catholic Chapel Preston before the Catholic Association for the Relief of the Sick on Monday May 25, 1807, by Rev Joseph Tate* (Preston, 1807).

the first openly political provincial newspaper to flourish because of its overt High Church-and-King principles.[87]

Another round of anti-Catholicism was stirred up in 1813 by a similar provincial reaction to Henry Grattan's Catholic relief bill. Local clergy and 'principal inhabitants' across the country sent petitions against the Catholic relief bill in February 1813. The magistrates, clergy, and 'other inhabitants of different denominations of Protestant Christians' of Bolton were adamant in their petition that Catholic participation in the political process would endanger the 'spirit' and 'stability' of the 'constitution purely Protestant'. Collegiate Church fellow Revd C. W. Ethelston wrote the Manchester petition, which included the usual tropes: 'the Roman Catholics could give no security against the abuse of [power]'.[88] These attitudes had been common since the Glorious Revolution and indeed before. They were important in the context of the 1800s because suspicion was aroused by the frequency of Catholic relief bills in parliament, compounded by the unique circumstances of the Irish Rebellion and Union. These events seem to have made a deeper impact upon Lancashire loyalism than by the Anglican reaction to the atheism promoted by the French Revolution.

The Bishops of Chester naturally encouraged such Church-and-King attitudes among their clergy by their visitation questionnaires, with their standard questions about whether members of their congregations had been converted by marriage or by the proselytism by 'popish priests'. Clergy in predominantly Catholic-dominated areas expressed anti-Catholic sentiments in their replies, even though they associated and cooperated freely with priests in civic occasions. The vicar of Preston, Revd William Starkie, wrote in 1804, 'This Quarter of Great Britain is supposed to constitute the Head Quarters of Popery', and complained, 'A new and most commodious place of worship for the adoration of dead men and women as well as Angelic beings was erected about eleven years ago capable of containing at least 2000 devotees.' Using typical anti-Catholic tropes, he denigrated the ostentation of the Abbess with her 'gold crozier' and expressed a sense of being swamped by the nunnery and the Catholic church off Winckley Square: 'These two buildings are within a few yards of each other and both are very close to the back of my house which stands between the popish parsonage

[87] Baines, *History of the Commerce and Town of Liverpool*, p. 527.

[88] *Hansard*, XXIV, 8 February 1813, 411–4; F. R. Raines, *Lives of the Fellows and Chaplains of the Collegiate Church of Manchester*, Part II (Manchester, 1891), p. 308.

inhabited by two Jesuits.'[89] This response was what the Bishop wanted to hear rather than quotidian reality. Revd Starkie had partaken in cross-denominational activity with Father Joseph Dunn. The committee for a subscription to help the wounded and orphans after Admiral Duncan's victory of 1797 began at a non-sectarian dinner including Starkie, Dunn, and the Independent Minister Revd J. McQuhae.[90] Other clergy in the diocese did not endorse the anti-papist assumptions in the Bishop's questionnaire. The vicar of Altham-with-Accrington described the Catholic priest at Dunkenhaulgh (near Church, owned by the Catholic peer Robert Lord Petre) that he was 'a respectable, candid man and by no means gives offence to any of the neighbouring clergy'.[91] Significantly, the majority of the replies to the visitation questionnaires claimed that Roman Catholics were either not numerous or not increasing (around 70 per cent in both the 1804 and 1811 returns). This may have been an underestimate because the clergy wished to give the bishops the impression that they were coping satisfactorily with Catholicism. On the other hand, it may have reflected both reality and the separation in the clergy's minds between native and immigrant Catholics. The native Catholic population of the diocese, mainly recusant gentry and their tenants, was stable or in decline; the Irish immigrant population was notably on the rise.

On a general level, the region can be divided into two, in terms of its religious make-up, by a line from north to south roughly passing over Wigan and Preston. Catholic recusant families survived to the west of this line, while virulent Protestantism and Dissenting sects were the major feature in the east.[92] This pattern was vital in shaping the nature of Church-and-King loyalism in the different areas of the region. The influx of Irish reapers and weavers to the industrializing areas in Lancashire was seen there as the main problem. Revd Thomas Bancroft, vicar and magistrate of the Orange heartland of Bolton, wrote in his 1804 return: 'Papists are numerous but have rather increased from the influx of Irish on account of Manufacturers [sic].'[93] The Pennine areas of Lancashire and the West Riding of Yorkshire had been

[89] Cheshire RO, EDV 7/3, visitation returns, 1804.

[90] Lewis, *The Middlemost and the Milltowns*, p. 20.

[91] EDV 7/3, visitation returns, 1804.

[92] J. Langton, 'The Continuity of Regional Culture: Lancashire Catholicism from the Late Sixteenth to the Early Nineteenth Century', in E. Royle (ed.), *Issues of Regional Identity in Honour of John Marshall* (Manchester, 1998), pp. 82–101.

[93] EDV 7/3, visitation returns, 1804.

strongly Protestant across all denominations since the Reformation. What initially fostered anti-Catholicism there was the relative weakness of Catholic presence and the consequent myths built up from ignorance. These places then became the heartland of the industrializing North to which the Irish emigrated. Large-scale Irish immigration into England and Scotland began from 1798, on a different scale and intensity from traditional patterns of seasonal labour migration that characterized the Irish Sea throughout the eighteenth century.[94] The Manchester Collegiate Church complained of a rapid increase in Catholics because of 'the great influx of Irish' and 'proselytising' priests.[95]

Parliament had investigated the effects of the Irish influx upon the poor laws and vagrancy in the 1810s, but the first major comprehensive survey was conducted by a Commons select committee in 1836. Some manufacturers testifying to the committee indicated that the first wave into Lancashire occurred when they had invited Irish weavers over to replace native workers turned out during the strikes of 1799. The witnesses focused on the leading question of whether the immigrant Irish maintained a separate identity through self-imposed or enforced residential segregation and Roman Catholicism. An overlooker in a Dukinfield cotton factory reported that the latter had been the case in Stalybridge: 'The masters began to build cottage-houses, because the natives would not take in the Irish. A great many Irish have come over since to Staley Bridge at different turnouts.'[96] The vicar of nearby Disley in Cheshire wrote in his visitation return of 1811 that a 'continued variety' of journeymen calico printers from Ireland and north Lancashire came to work at printing works along the river Goyt. This contrasted with his previous experience of only two native Catholics in the area. He perceived that the Irish were distinguishable from English Catholics because they did not practise their religion, either out of atheism or a lack of priests.[97] Most witnesses to the select committee had strong anti-Irish prejudices, stereotyping the immigrants as drunken, unwilling to work, and prone to crime, disease, and violence. These stereotypes were directly compared with what they claimed was the apparent sobriety of the English working classes and occasionally

[94] D. MacRaild, *Irish Migrants in Modern Britain, 1750–1922* (Basingstoke, 1999), p. 111.

[95] EDV 7/3, visitation returns, 1804.

[96] PP 1836, XXXIV (427), *Report of the Select Committee into the Condition of the Irish Poor in Great Britain*, pp. 558–9.

[97] EDV 7/4, visitation returns, 1811.

more favourable views of Welsh and Scottish immigrants (though this contradicted manufacturers' accusations about English workers' idleness in select committees on petitions for minimum wage legislation).[98]

The number of Irish residents in Manchester and Salford was estimated in 1793 at 5,000 or about 8 per cent of the population. The 1836 select committee report surmised that the Irish in Manchester and its environs had risen to two-thirds of a Catholic population totalling from 30 to 40,000.[99] Some residential segregation was in evidence. The Irish-dominated streets in Manchester were in the north, parts of 'New Town or Irish Town' by the river Irk and the streets south of Angel Meadow. Rapid urban expansion of Irish Town occurred between 1795 and 1831, encompassing all the area between the Rochdale Road and the river Irk.[100] According to the 1798 poor rate assessment, 'Newtown Irish Row' was composed of 28 terraced cottages; the inhabitants mostly had Irish surnames and were listed as poor and unable to pay. There was some brief residential stability, in that 16 of the names were listed in the previous year's assessment. By 1811, 'Irish Row' contained almost completely new inhabitants, but all were Irish.[101] In 1798, Hannah Greg, wife of Samuel the Unitarian manufacturer, wrote that a magistrate had told her that Mancunians associated all Irish with Jacobinism. Hence 'he thinks it very well the Irish all inhabit the Q[uarter] (about Newtown Lane) or else they would all be murdered'.[102] The Manchester overseers anxiously responded to the influx of Irish. Their reports showed that by 1808, a separate account was kept for casual relief given to 'Irish resident poor'. The amount expended in 1808–9 was £2,456.[103] The situation in Liverpool required extraparochial assistance. Liverpool's Hibernian School was founded in 1807 by the Benevolent Society of St Patrick to educate 'Poor Children descended from Poor Irish Parents'.[104] Irish societies were another example of distinct identities, though membership of course did not preclude integration into general

[98] PP 1803, III, part IV, *Minutes of Evidence on . . . Petitions Relating to the Act For Settling Disputes between Masters and Servants* (1803), p. 47.

[99] PP 1836, XXXIV, p. 430.

[100] M. Busteed and R. Hodgson, 'Coping with Industrialization: the Irish in Early Manchester', in S. J. Neary *et al.* (eds.), *The Urban Experience, A People-Environment Perspective* (London, 1994), p. 478.

[101] MCL, Mancnester Poor Rates, 1797, 1798, 1811.

[102] Liverpool University Special Collections, RP.II.1.60-9, Greg to Mrs Rathbone, April 1798.

[103] MCL, BR f. 942.72.L15, local broadsides, 20–1.

[104] *Liverpool Chronicle*, March 1807.

friendly societies. In 1812, St Patrick's Day was celebrated by 'about eighty' at the Fox Tavern in Manchester, where 'a number of patriotic toasts were given'.[105]

The situation on the ground may not however have been as dire as magistrates and others suspicious of the Irish feared. In living close to friends and relatives, the Irish were no different from other migrants in most large towns. The slums by the Medlock known as 'Little Ireland' did not develop until the late 1820s, and in Liverpool, although the Irish lived in cellars and courtyards, so did many other migrant labourers.[106] Residential concentration cannot be automatically assumed to mean segregation or isolation, although witnesses to the 1836 select committee certainly saw it that way. Some witnesses by contrast claimed that the Irish quickly adapted to speaking English and that the children used English as their sole language. Nor were the Irish a coherent body in unionized activity. Although the Manchester manufacturer John Potter was certain that 'the Irish are more given to combinations', by contrast the owner of Newton Heath silk mill boasted of using the Irish as strike breakers.[107] Furthermore, the experiences of Irish migrants were far more varied than nineteenth-century stereotyping of them suggested. They differed with the rate and timing of the migrant inflow, the size and economic structure of the place of destination and the religious composition of its population, its local history and civic leadership. The Leinster Irish, who included Protestants among their number, sailed from Dublin to Liverpool. Most Irish migrants to the Manchester region appear to have come from the predominantly Catholic north-western counties of Roscommon, Sligo, and Leitrim.[108] Lack of evidence prohibits a full assessment of the effects of Irish regional variations on the region's migrants, but it is likely that distinct patterns were maintained into the nineteenth century. The increasing frequency of riots each 12 July indicated that intra-Irish sectarian tension was carried over the Irish Sea. The Protestant Irish are likely to have assimilated more readily to English society than their Catholic counterparts, especially when serving under manufacturers favourable to Orangeism.

105 *CMG*, 21 March 1812.

106 P. Laxton, 'Liverpool in 1801: a Manuscript Return for the First National Census of Population', *THSLC* 130 (1981), 88.

107 MacRaild, *Irish Migrants*, p. 53.

108 M. Busteed and R. Hodgson, 'Irish Migrant Responses to Urban Life in Early Nineteenth Century Manchester', *Geographical Journal*, 162 (1996), 141; D. MacRaild, *Culture, Conflict and Migration; the Irish in Victorian Cumbria* (Liverpool, 1998), p. 40.

The Irish Rebellion of 1798 was as defining a moment as the French Revolution in those parts of the region which received both Catholic and Protestant Irish exiles. During the United English and Irishmen agitation at the turn of the century, most correspondence to the Home Office came from magistrates who were obsessed about the Irish threat. Colonel Ralph Fletcher of Bolton believed weavers campaigning for the minimum wage were seditious and linked to the United Irish, despite their protestations of loyalty.[109] He spent much of his allowance from the government on spies who followed suspicious Irishmen across the country. He sincerely believed that former United Irishmen were looking for an opportunity to seduce the 'deluded' lower classes and incite revolution. Even as late as 1805, Fletcher expressed his continued suspicions on the basis of information from his spies, who (he told the Home Office) had 'connections both with the Irish who are resident and those who have lately passed through Manchester'. They had intimated that 'an Insurrection will be soon attempted in that part of the United Kingdom'.[110] A commonplace book compiled by Manchester magistrate Revd William Robert Hay contains much material on the Irish Rebellion and Catholic emancipation petitions, and ballads such as 'Dying Rebel air' and 'The Popish Address to a Great Lady'.[111]

Whether a United Irish or English insurrection could have taken place in Lancashire or was just a figment of the spies' commission-hungry imagination is still debatable.[112] What is important is that Fletcher and his colleagues believed it. The connection which loyalists made between the Emmet and Despard conspiracies and the French had sunk deep into their political consciousness and influenced their dealings with the working classes well after 1801. This continued to be the case throughout the war. During the handloom weavers' strikes of 1808, for example, the magistrates demonstrated some understanding of the demands of the weavers, yet often assumed the agitators were Irish and associated with 'sedition'. Manchester magistrate R. A. Farington commented on the 'great number of Irish weavers' whom he regarded

[109] NA, HO 42/80/93-4, Fletcher to Home Office, 16 February 1805; HO 42/82/45, Fletcher to Home Office, 16 January 1805; HO 42/95/5, Fletcher to Home Office, n.d, 1808.

[110] HO 42/65/442, Fletcher to Pelham, 3 April 1802.

[111] Chetham's Library, Mun A.3.13., Hay MS, Scrapbook 4.

[112] R. Wells, *Insurrection: the British Experience, 1795–1803*, (Gloucester, 1983), p. 198.

as 'the foremost and most turbulent in all the proceedings'.[113] Publicly, therefore, anti-Catholicism was intertwined with civic patriotism and local government, and this was manifest in the making and organizing of the petitions and addresses. Privately, by contrast, it flourished in certain areas through more surreptitious methods of action, particularly the Orange movement.

The Orange Movement

By 1830, 230 Orange lodges existed in Great Britain, but Lancashire had by far the greatest number: 77, compared with 36 in Yorkshire, and 39 in southern Scotland.[114] Orangeism has been neglected in studies of both loyalism and the suppression of disorder in this period because it was not a national phenomenon and because historians have regarded the lodges as simple vehicles of sectarianism and working-class sociability not worth investigating.[115] J. J. Sack has commented on the difficulty of knowing 'how seriously to take' the early nineteenth century Orange movement. He generally dismisses its significance by concentrating on parliament's rejection of the institution, but suggests that it 'might repay the type of close local study often given to radical associations and unions'.[116] Although Orangeism was 'deserted' by the upper classes after the war, most notably by its Grand Master, Lord Kenyon, this is no reason to deny it a role in loyalism. It expressed the values of the section of Lancashire society who enforced law and order against 'sedition' and working-class combinations. It was because of its provincialism that the Orange Order was able to survive official liquidation in 1835 and become a feature of Tory working-class community life. The strength of Orangeism in the region, particularly among magistrates and gentrified bourgeoisie, again points to the central role of anti-Catholicism in

113 Farington to Hawkesbury, 4 June 1808, in A. Aspinall, *Early English Trade Unions: Documents from the Home Office Papers in the Public Record Office* (London, 1949), p. 99.

114 MacRaild, *Culture, Conflict and Migration*, p. 165.

115 The most comprehensive study remains H. Senior, *Orangeism in Ireland and Britain, 1795–1836* (London, 1966). See F. Neal, 'Manchester's Origins of the English Orange Order', *MRHR* 4 (1990), 12–24.

116 Sack, *From Jacobite to Conservative*, p. 107. The later nineteenth century is well covered in D. MacRaild, *Faith, Fraternity and Fighting: The Orange Order and Irish Migrants in Northern England, c.1850–1920* (Liverpool, 2005).

creating or sustaining loyalist and British identities among certain sections of society in the region.

Orangeism comprised three forms of structure and identity. Firstly, the Orange Institution was an organizational structure for gentry and the middle classes. Secondly, Orange societies provided welfare for immigrant Irish working classes. Finally, the ideology of Orangeism was originally a collection of mystical Protestant tropes which developed over the century into a more nebulous conservative value system. All interacted to produce a movement that was diffuse, yet able to unite in response to attacks from either radicals or parliamentary politicians on its general ideology and membership.

Evidence of the early Orange movement is patchy. Records from individual Lancashire lodges are non-existent before 1817. A House of Commons select committee report was set up in 1835 to investigate the spread of the Orange movement. Although the witness statements to the committee were littered with inaccuracies and prejudices, other evidence abounds that enable the historian to peel back some of the myths and conspiracies surrounding the movement.[117] One revealing source is a pamphlet entitled *Orange Miscellany*, compiled by antiquarian and Orangeman William Nuttall of Rochdale in 1815. Another key document is a comprehensive list of rules of the Orange Institution from 1810, sent to the Home Office by Joseph Radcliffe, JP of Huddersfield. He requested the Home Secretary's assent to these rules under the corresponding society legislation, but the latter refused. The document listed Colonel Samuel Taylor of Manchester as Grand Master, and James Lever, Esq. of Bolton as Grand Treasurer of the Grand Lodge.[118] Radcliffe shared many of the attributes of magistrates like Colonel Fletcher. Born in Ashton-under-Lyne, he acquired interests in all the major canal companies, and served as magistrate at Royton and Oldham before moving to Huddersfield. He travelled regularly over the Pennines to see Fletcher and used spies to counteract disorder. He became one of the most active magistrates against Luddism.[119]

[117] PP 1835 (605), XVII, *Select Committee Report into the Origins, Nature, Extent and Tendency of Orange Institutions in Great Britain and the Colonies*; see B. Turner, 'A Loyal Englishman?: John Lloyd and Aspects of Oath-Taking in 1812', in M. T. Davis, *Radicalism and Revolution in Britain, 1775–1848* (Basingstoke, 2000), pp. 133–42.

[118] NA, HO 42/101/162-5, Radcliffe to Ryder, 29 June 1810.

[119] R. Reid, *Land of Lost Content: the Luddite Revolt, 1812* (London, 1986), pp. 19–22; West Yorkshire RO, RAD, Papers and correspondence of Sir Joseph Radcliffe of Rudding Park, 1796–1818.

The Orange movement in Lancashire had its roots in the regiments of volunteers and militia sent over to Ireland to suppress the Irish Rebellion, who returned to their home towns with new ideas and possibly new Irish recruits. The Lancashire militia officers mixed in Irish Protestant gentry circles and indeed some of them already held land in Ireland. In June 1799, Lieutenant James Radford, Paymaster in the Royal Lancashire Militia wrote from New Ross, county Wexford, that he, Colonel Stanley, and Major Orlando Bridgeman of Wigan breakfasted with a 'Col. Totting-ham MP', presumably John or Charles Tottenham, barons Loftus.[120] His correspondence revealed the close bonds formed through frequent balls and dinners held by the gentry for the officers. The return of Earl de Wilton's regiment in May 1802 was greeted with much ceremony by the Manchester loyal associations, whom Wilton praised for keeping order in the locality during his absence.[121] Toasts at a 12 July commemoration in Bury in 1803 congratulated the British regiments sent to Ireland. Several were from the Manchester area, principally Colonel Stanley's First Regiment of Lancashire Militia, the Second Battalion of the Manchester and Salford Volunteer Rifles, and Lord Wilton's Corps of Lancashire Volunteers. The Grand Orange Lodge in Ireland granted warrants to individual soldiers, who then enrolled others in their private lodges.[122] It is therefore almost certain that ex-officers were important in the process of establishing Orangeism in Lancashire. There was a lodge in the Manchester and Salford Rifle Volunteers, commanded by Colonel John Silvester, which held Irish warrant 1128. Silvester was a magistrate and owned mills in Atherton and Chorley. Five hundred members of his regiment of Manchester militia were called out by the magistrates against Luddism in the area in May 1812.[123] His regiment had been raised and financed by the Grand Master, Colonel Samuel Taylor. Taylor was one of Fletcher's compatriots on the Bench and commander of a battalion of the Manchester and Salford Volunteers. Colonel Stanley's regiment held warrant 320, which was converted to English warrant 43.[124]

Nuttall listed over seventy lodges in existence in 1811. All early lodges originated in already fertile ground provided by the military regiments

120 Lancashire CRO, LM1/1, Lancashire Lieutenancy correspondence; D. Hayton, 'Charles Tottenham (1685–1758)', *Oxford Dictionary of National Biography*.

121 *MM*, 18 May, 8 June 1802.

122 Neal, 'Manchester Origins', 13; R. J. T. Williamson and J. Lawson Whalley, *History of the Old County Regiment of Lancashire Militia* (1888), p. 156.

123 F. O. Darvall, *Popular Disturbances and Public Order* (Oxford, 1969), p. 256.

124 W. Nuttall, *Orange Miscellany* (Huddersfield, 1815) p. 200.

and displayed analogous patterns of transmission of ideology, organization, and personnel. Each 'Orange' town had a combination of large numbers of textile workers, rapid Irish immigration, and 'zealous' magistrates.[125] The first seventeen English warrants were assigned to lodges in Manchester and its satellite towns. The first Orange lodge meeting recorded in the local newspapers occurred on 12 July 1802 in Stockport. It was clearly respectable, beginning with a service in the parish church, 'where an excellent sermon was preached by the Rev William Harrison, MA, from the first epistle of St. Peter—"love the Brotherhood; fear God, honour the King"'. Their dinner was held at the Britannia Inn, with President Joseph Hearnet in the chair. The toasts included the Grand Master, Sir George Ogle (governor of county Wexford where the regiments had been sent), and 'Major Watson of the late Stockport Volunteers'.[126] Most Orange societies met in pubs as friendly societies, although warrant 14 was held at Grand Master Col. Samuel Taylor's house in Ashton-under-Lyne and warrant 15 at Shaw Chapel near Oldham. By July 1804, an 'Orange Loyal Beneficial Association' had been established in Oldham. An 'Orange Society or Orange Boys' was held at the Reed Inn in Rochdale, with the innkeeper in charge of the box.[127]

Magistrates in Manchester and its satellite towns were integral to the organization of the Orange movement. Revd William Robert Hay, chairman of the Salford Quarter Sessions, was a prominent suppressor of the 'seditious' from 1798 to Peterloo. One of his scrapbooks contains an account of the 12 July dinner in Bury in 1803. This suggests very strongly that he and several of his colleagues were Orangemen. The toasts reiterated the common hope that the Duke of York would become Grand Master and congratulated the Bishop of Chester: 'may he still continue to support the Protestant interest'. Finally, they thanked Revd Hay himself and his colleagues on the bench: 'R A Farington Esq. of Manchester, Matthew Fletcher Esq. of Bolton, the magistrates of Stockport, Mr Winter of Oldham'.[128] William Rowbottom's diary recorded that the first Orange meeting in Oldham occurred on 12 July 1803, and that they heard a sermon by Revd William Winter, 'one of the members'. It is therefore reasonable to suggest that all the magistrates and clergy mentioned in the Bury toasts had Orange sympathies at

[125] MacRaild, *Irish Migrants*, p. 111. [126] *MM*, 20 July 1802.

[127] Nuttall, *Orange Miscellany*, appendix; NA, FS 2/4, no. 1361, 16 July 1804; *Preston Journal*, 9 September 1809.

[128] Chetham's Library, Mun A. 3.10, Hay mss, Scrapbook vol. 2.

least.[129] High Church clergy were prominent in their own right and as magistrates. The various 12 July celebrations in Oldham, Mottram, and Bolton were centred around the parish churches in which the vicars gave 'appropriate sermons'. Revd C. W. Ethelston and Revd Hay were the Orange exceptions among the clergy of the Manchester Collegiate Church.[130] Significantly, Ethelston was chaplain of Lieutenant-Colonel John Silvester's volunteer regiment.

Canvassing of potential magnates was pursued in earnest. In 1808, Lord Grey Egerton (1756–1829), eighth earl of Bridgewater, wrote to John Lloyd Broughton on his receiving a request to take up the position of County District Grand Master: 'Induced I think the aspect of the times such that it is of the utmost importance to know friends from foes, and at the same time to belong to a Loyal Protestant organized association.' He hoped to see him for a 'little Orange Conversation'.[131] The first peer actively to encourage the movement was George Kenyon (1776–1855), second Baron Kenyon of Peel Hall, south of Bolton, who joined the Grand Lodge in the same year. At the select committee of 1835, Lord Kenyon stated that Colonel Taylor of Bolton inspired him to join the Orange Institution 'from the statement he made to me of the benefit he conceived from the cause of good order received in his neighbourhood from the Institution'.[132] Kenyon published the inflammatory pamphlet *Observations on the Roman Catholic Question* in 1810 and was active in the late 1820s among ultra Tories against Catholic Emancipation.[133] Together with Francis Seymour-Conway (1777–1842), Lord Yarmouth, later third marquess of Hertford, he was instrumental in coaching Frederick, Duke of York, to become a member. The Duke of York assumed the office of Grand Master in 1821, although he later resigned his position in the wake of parliamentary suspicion of its illegality.[134]

At the very time that petitions were being raised against the bill to allow Catholics to become army officers, in 1807, the English Grand Orange Institution was instituted at the Star Inn in Manchester, following a riot in Newton Lane. Orange parades on 12 July re-emerged during the

129 Rowbottom diaries, 17 July 1803.

130 Nuttall, *Orange Miscellany*, p. 132.

131 Lancashire CRO, DDX 24/24, Egerton to Broughton, n.d., 1808.

132 PP 1835, XVII, *Select Committee Report*, q.2604.

133 Lord Kenyon, *Observations on the Roman Catholic Question* (J. J. Stockdale, 1810); J. Wolffe, 'George Kenyon (1776–1855)', *Oxford Dictionary of National Biography*.

134 W. S. Marshall, *The Billy Boys: A Concise History of Orangeism in Scotland* (Edinburgh, 1996); *The Times*, 14 June 1821.

sectarian tension fostered by that year's 'No Popery' election, though such parading had been forbidden by the boroughreeve after trouble in 1803. A letter in the *Liverpool Chronicle* referred to the atmosphere surrounding an Orange parade in Manchester: 'in consistence with the spirit of the times, it was conducted with extraordinary pomp'. It stated that the Orangemen were 'guarded by the civil officers of the town'. Irish Catholics met the Orange parade en route and violence ensued.[135] The magistrates, usually zealous in any matter of popular disturbance, did not report the incident to the Home Office. Secretary Ralph Nixon wrote to the Manchester loyalist newspaper, the *British Volunteer*, to defend the riot as an attack by Irish Catholics on what he saw as a peaceful Orange parade. Conversely, radical newspaper editor William Cowdroy claimed that 'No Popery' slogans had been chalked on walls, and when the local regiments sent recruiting parties into Manchester, their bands paraded the streets playing Orange tunes, particularly 'Croppies Lie Down'. It is significant that Lieutenant-Colonel Silvester's regiment, experienced in Ireland and later involved at Peterloo, put down the disturbance.[136] From then on 12 July parades caused more riots; the disturbances following the parade in 1811 'originated in a party spirit amongst the Orangemen and others'. Cowdroy commented: "Tis a pity but the Societies would altogether abandon the ostentatious parade of our populous streets.'[137]

Orangeism bound together the loyalties of many magistrates and clergy in south-east Lancashire. A tradition of virulent Protestantism and insignificant Catholic recusancy was integral to an active response. By contrast, the two major ports, Liverpool and Lancaster, despite having their fair share of Irish immigration, seem to have been devoid of Orangeism, at least until after the war. Orangeist anti-Irish tropes were not used amidst the virulent anti-Catholic rhetoric of election propaganda during the Liverpool contest of 1807, nor is there any surviving description of Orangemen being involved in the riots about the Catholic relief bills there. The wealthy corporation families and merchants on Liverpool Corporation, though staunch Church-and-King Tories, played no part in initiating Orange lodges, which only appeared there after 1815. The first recorded riot between Orangemen and Catholics in Liverpool occurred in 1819, and in 1830 there were

[135] *Liverpool Chronicle*, 12 August 1807; *MM*, 21 July 1807.

[136] *MM*, 21 July 1807; Senior, *Orangeism in Ireland and Britain*, pp. 152–3; Neal, 'Manchester Origins', 15.

[137] *CMG*, 20 July 1811.

only three lodges, the first having appeared in 1815. Rural areas also lack evidence of Orange activity. North Lancashire gentry had little need of the movement, having neither factories to defend nor major labour combinations to contend with.[138]

The social aspirations of middle-class and gentry Orangemen in Lancashire were clear, and Orangeism became integrated into the established patterns of civic government. The Bolton Orange Society celebrated the birthday of King William III on 4 November 1808. Associational rituals were followed, including attending a special service in the Old Church and a dinner with toasts. The toasts included notables favourable to the Orange cause, national and local: Earl de Wilton of Heaton Hall, Manchester, Sir Richard Musgrave, Col. Samuel Taylor, Col. Ralph Fletcher and the Bolton Volunteer Infantry, John Pilkington, and Revd Thomas Bancroft 'with thanks for his excellent sermon'.[139] Pilkington was a dimity manufacturer, commander of the Bolton Light Horse Volunteers and Deputy Lieutenant for Lancashire.[140] Donald MacRaild has shown that the movement in west Cumbria was similarly neither purely proletarian nor completely Irish.[141] Orange clubs also became a visible part of the associational world of loyalism and the provincial elites' representation of loyalism to the nation. Orangemen were visible in industrializing towns from the time of the Napoleonic wars. This was exemplified in national celebrations of George III's fiftieth Jubilee in October 1809. In Manchester, among the rifle regiments, musicians and freemasons who formed the procession to the Collegiate church were 'the Orangemen . . . in their orange scarves'. William Rowbottom recorded that in Oldham: 'Public service was performed at both Church and chapel and the Orange Societies walked in grand procession and made a fine show.' In Bolton, John Holden noted that factory workers marched together to church, 'with the Orange Men from John Baron's, Church Bank and the Freemasons from two Lodges'. The Orange lodges of Oldham played a prominent part in the celebrations for the overthrow of Bonaparte on 25 April 1814, joining the gentlemen and the freemasons in the procession through the town to the parish church.[142]

138 F. Neal, *Sectarian Violence: the Liverpool Experience, 1819–1914* (Manchester, 1988), pp. 15, 39.

139 *MM*, 15 November 1808.

140 J. Brereton, *Chain Mail: the History of the Duke of Lancaster's Own Yeomanry* (Chippenham, 1994), p. 4.

141 MacRaild, *Culture, Conflict and Migration*, pp. 150–1.

142 Rowbottom diaries; Bolton Archives, Holden diaries.

The ideology of Orangeism invoked the established repertoire of Whig ideals, so it may seem paradoxical that magistrates and clergy of a mainly Tory persuasion were the earliest participants in the movement. Whig tropes were integral to the songs and oaths that formed the textual element of the lodges' ritual, especially William III, the 'balanced constitution' of King, Lords and Commons as founded in 1688, the battle of the Boyne, and a political defence of the Established Church. The birthday of King William III on 4 November was publicly commemorated by Orange societies, as in Bolton parish church and Assembly Rooms in 1808.[143] This reinforces the argument of J. J. Sack and Kathleen Wilson that Pittite Toryism appropriated the symbols of the Glorious Revolution in order to legitimize itself and drag its reputation away from its disgraced Jacobite past.[144] Though the party boundaries should not be drawn too sharply, other elements of Orangeism were less provincial or mundane and distinguished themselves from mainstream Whiggism. They indicate the reason why the movement was taken up by the new generation of Tory rather than Whig gentry on the whole. These common reference points were embellished by an amalgam of masonic imagery and mysticism familiar from the associational world of gentry societies. The *Orange Miscellany* contained, for example, 'An Address delivered in the Theatre, Rochdale, January 1814', which attempted to emulate the male bonds and exclusivity that lay at the heart of freemasonry:

> True Orangemen, whom mystic rites engage;
> While Orient lore illumes the sacred page.
> . . . while furious malice howls around,
> Shall Orangery lie prostrate on the ground?[145]

The Orange oath to defend the King and his heirs was initially conditional; it only applied 'so long as he or they shall support the Protestant ascendancy'. A right of resistance was implied. 'Church-and-King' loyalism had meant loyalty to the king and his government; loyalty for Orangemen involved defending Protestantism, a priority which came before both monarch and state. Implicit was the idea, derived from Huguenot and Calvinist beliefs, that there was a right of

143 *MM*, 15 November 1808.

144 J. J. Sack, 'The Memory of Burke and the Memory of Pitt: English Conservatism Confronts its Past, 1806–1829', *HJ* 30 (1987), 624; K. Wilson, 'Inventing Revolution: 1688 and Eighteenth Century Popular Politics', *JBS* 28 (1989), 353.

145 Nuttall, *Orange Miscellany*, p. 33.

lawful resistance to monarchical tyranny.[146] These ideas complicated loyalism. They took root in an atmosphere of suspicion about the activities of parliament in religious affairs. Orange magistrates feared that the Established Church was giving away its right to enforce its tenets and status too easily, because of the government's successive Catholic relief bills in parliament, together with the seemingly inexorable tide of nonconformity. A common Orange demand was the maintenance of true Protestant principles and order. This definition of loyalism was formed in the context of magistrates' and gentry's belief that government and even the Crown were abandoning the 'Protestant Constitution' as established in 1688. Nuttall's *Orange Miscellany* declared: 'the confidential advisers of the sovereign have thought fit to abandon, as a cabinet, the protection of the Protestant Ascendancy, and of the Whig principles, which seated the House of Brunswick on the throne . . . the Protestant Ascendancy has now no support'.[147] Some of the towns that organized petitions against Howick's Bill fostered Orange lodges that federated to the new Institution. One immediate role of the Orange Institution was therefore to defend the Church against these attacks by those in government who 'misunderstood' the lodges and their aims.

The first controversy over Orangeism was raised in relation to the existence of lodges in the regular army in 1810. This was regarded as compromising soldiers' loyalty. Joseph Radcliffe then attempted to diffuse these suspicions by sending the rules of the Orange Institution to the Home Office. This merely led to a second controversy concerning the contractual nature of the Orange oath to the King. During a debate in the House of Commons on 29 June 1813, objections were expressed about the Orange Institution's secretive organization and particularly about the illegality of its oath. Charles Watkins William Wynn, Grenvillite MP for Montgomeryshire, proclaimed: 'What could be thought of such an oath? Conditional allegiance!—Loyalty depending upon the maintenance of the Protestant ascendancy! Terms hitherto unknown in this country.' His complaints were supported by Samuel Whitbread, amongst others in opposition. *The Times* raised analogies to the Protestant associations that had provoked the Gordon Riots in 1780, and secret societies on the Continent.[148] The Secretary of the Orange Institution attempted to forestall

[146] E. W. McFarland, *Protestants First: Orangeism in Nineteenth Century Scotland* (Edinburgh, 1990), p. 5.

[147] J. J. Stockdale, *The Orange Institution: a Slight Sketch* (1813), pp. 3–4.

[148] *Hansard*, XXVI, 29 June 1813, pp. 974–86; *The Times*, 23, 30 June 1813; Senior, *Orangeism in Ireland and Britain*, pp. 163, 167, 170.

legal action against the lodges by revising the oath to remove the contractual clause, but both versions caused outrage in the Commons debate. The issue was temporarily settled in 1814 with another set of rules which omitted the oath altogether.[149] The significance of these episodes was that it showed how the ideological debates over the French Revolution and English radicalism had not yet settled what 'loyalism' meant.

The hollow mysticism and Protestant ideology of Orangeism were important constituencies of its identity, but they were less of a binding force than its activities of the institution in practice. The Orange Institution could not be repressed by its opponents in the same way as seditious societies had been in the 1790s because it was integral to the gentry associational world in some areas. The movement flourished in parts of Britain because it underpinned a practical network of activism against the 'seditious' working classes during the wartime crises of public order. The 'mobs' who had burned effigies of Thomas Paine and the pamphleteering loyalist clubs of the 1790s had seemingly ceased to be an active part of the fight against radicals, and the lodges perhaps provided a more coordinated substitute. The Orange oath was explicit in stating: 'I solemnly swear that I will aid and assist all magistrates, and all high and petty constables in the lawful execution of their office, when called upon.'[150] This was a major element of their association. The oath, swearing that the member is not a Roman Catholic, a United Irishman or, significantly in the local context, a United Englishman, indicated how this aspect of loyalism was shaped less by the French than by the troubles of 1798–1801. It is conceivable that northern magistrates, obsessed with tracking down seditious combinations, composed this oath and oversaw working-class members taking it in their own factory or mine. The emphasis throughout Joseph Radcliffe's 1810 document was on the enforcement of order against sedition.[151]

Orangeism was thus not just about gentry show and sociability. Underneath the civic patriotism, Orange-influenced institutions of local government contained more sinister and private aspects. Though the castigations of Bolton radical Dr Robert Taylor were exaggerated, the most energetic employers of spies were indeed Orangemen and it is very likely that the spies themselves belonged to Orange clubs or lodges. Magistrates' military connections and their obsession with tracking down 'sedition' enabled Orangeism to provide a crucial network

[149] Nuttall, *Orange Miscellany*, p. 144. [150] Stockdale, *Orange Institution*, p. 22.
[151] NA, HO 42/101/165, Radcliffe to Ryder, 29 June 1810.

during the crisis years of the war. Orangeism was thus integral to the organization of elite Church-and-King loyalism in Lancashire during the Napoleonic wars. One of the witnesses to the 1835 select committee, Deputy Grand Secretary, Eustace Chetwoode, admitted: 'being in communication with the late Colonel Fletcher and others in that quarter, I understood that the society was considered useful by the magistrates', and that 'the great manufacturers felt that their men being embodied in the Orange Society, they were ready at all times to come forward in the suppression of disturbances'.[152] Nuttall's *Orange Miscellany* reported that at a dinner at the *Spread Eagle* in Manchester on 4 November 1814, Colonel Fletcher gave a speech in which he proclaimed: 'He had witnessed the utility of the Orange Institution, in the cheerful co-operation of its members with the civil and military powers, at an alarming period, in maintaining the peace of the country, and he knew nothing better calculated for public good than a great diffusion of its principles.' The pamphlet then claimed: 'The Orange Institution has wrestled successfully against the Institutions of King Lud'.[153] A pamphlet of 1813 printed by J. J. Stockdale again exposed the links between religion, Ireland, and maintaining order in the minds of Orangemen: 'The rebellious associations of the followers of King Lud, closely resembling, in many material features, the principles and practices of the United Irishmen, caused the aid of the Orange institution to be invoked in Lancashire, where it has much extension.'[154] The Irish Grand Lodge issued a declaration to its English counterpart on 12 July 1813 which proclaimed: 'Following your loyal example, the British Orangemen have saved their country by suppressing the treasonable bands calling themselves Luddites.'[155] It was therefore no coincidence that the Orangemen Fletcher, Radcliffe, and Hay, and their friends and colleagues Charles Prescott, John Lloyd, and William Chippendale, were the most active magistrates against Luddism and later played a key role in suppressing the Peterloo radical meeting in 1819, including among their number Revd C. W. Ethelston and William Hulton, owner of mines and land around Wigan.[156]

152 PP 1835, XVII, *Select Committee Report*, p. 33.

153 Nuttall, *Orange Miscellany*, pp. 131–2, 138.

154 Stockdale, *Orange Institution*, p. 2.

155 Senior, *Orangeism in Ireland and Britain*, p. 157; PP 1825 (181), IX, *House of Lords Select Committee Report to Inquire into the State of Ireland*, p. 352.

156 Darvall, *Popular Disturbances*, p. 244.

It is more difficult to discern the motivations of Orange rank-and-file. Socially less-elite Orange societies were much less Masonic in organization and symbolism than were the lodges, and functioned much more as friendly societies for Irish Protestant immigrants. Their spread in areas of Protestant Irish immigration reflected a migration of culture over the Irish Sea as well as a means of pooling resources and sustaining a shared identity.[157] Members may have been influenced by the manufacturers' Orange lodges and the apparent existence of United Irish agitation and personalities in the Manchester area and therefore formed their own clubs. Continued military comradeship was certainly a factor. At the trial of the Westhoughton Luddites, prosecution witness Robert Martin claimed a suspect attempted to twist him into the Luddites, to which his alleged response was that he was in the local militia and an Orangeman and as such would never desert his colours. Colonel Silvester testified that Martin was indeed in his regiment of Manchester local militia and he had given him two pounds for his passage to Ireland for convalescence. Samuel Fleming, the main prosecution witness, was a member of Colonel Silvester's regiment and an Irishman, having previously served in Lord Rosmore's regiment.[158] The use of Orange privates as the sole prosecution witnesses at the trial led to the accusations of prejudice from the radical Dr Taylor to Henry Brougham. Brougham voiced these concerns in the Commons at the debate on the preservation of the Peace Bill in July 1812.[159]

Among the Irish working classes, Manchester rather than Liverpool again formed the centre for sectarian rivalry in the 1800s. In February 1802, a riot among Irishmen occurred at the Goat on Stafford Street. Cowdroy reported that 'the quarrel arose from a dispute on the subject of the Union'.[160] During the Luddite disturbances, John Moore, a sergeant of Colonel Silvester's regiment, was attacked outside an Ancoats inn and thrown into the canal, seemingly by Catholic Irish. *Aston's Exchange Herald* stated that Moore was 'a Protestant Irishman, and was or had been a member of the Orange Society'. His widow received a day's pay from all the members of his regiment. Revd Hay knew about the incident and reported it to the Home Office although he did not

[157] Acknowledgements to Donald MacRaild for this suggestion.

[158] NA, Treasury Solicitor papers, TS 11/1059, Trial of Lancashire Luddites, 1812.

[159] Taylor, *Letters on the Subject of the Lancashire Riots* (Bolton, 1812); *Hansard*, XXIII, 13 July 1812, 1021; see *Hansard*, XXVI, 29 June 1813, 974–86; Turner, 'John Lloyd', p. 138.

[160] *CMG*, 20 February 1802.

mention the sectarianism involved.[161] Manchester Orangemen may have been involved in Colonel Silvester's cavalry regiment or as special constables during the Peterloo disturbances, although many other factors were involved in the suppression of the crowds. The clash of Liverpool Orangemen with their mayor in 1812 attracted more attention in the newspapers and crucially in parliament. The Mayor stopped a 12 July parade, which was reported to have carried a mock pope and cardinal to be burned at the church door. The Orange Grand Lodge took the matter to court and lost. The legal expenses of £200 were relieved in part by Lord Kenyon, but the incident provoked another attack on the Orange institution in parliament.[162] It was from this point that Liverpudlian Orangeism grew in strength compared with Manchester.

The formal Orange lodges did not serve the social and welfare roles of the Orange clubs, and the two together did not exhaust Orangeism as a diffuse conservative value system. In England, Orangeism internalized what was to become a defence of the principles of the Established Church and the Tory party. This was much more acceptable to a broad swathe of Victorian working and middle classes than was the Masonic symbolism of the Orange Institution. This gave the impression of a much broader support for Orangeism than mere lodge membership would account for. Orangeism could be seen as forming part of the root or at least as having helped to shape the emergence of a Tory working class in nineteenth-century Lancashire.

Loyalism in Lancashire during the Napoleonic wars took a variety of forms and fulfilled various roles. It spanned the political spectrum from Church-and-King High Anglican High Toryism, through moderate Whig attachment to the legacy of the Glorious Revolution, to a bitter Orange struggle against radicalism and Irish Catholicism. It could be popular when it was integrated with the principles and public institutions of patriotism; but during the 1800s, it fragmented into more closed and private societies in order to distinguish itself from the very 'vulgar conservatism' that it had sought to encourage in the reaction to the French Revolution. Class had much to do with this, as the local governing elites feared the Church-and-King 'mob' almost as much as the radicals did. The 1798 Irish Rebellion also played a large part in causing loyalism to evolve, especially in the directions of Orangeism

[161] *Aston's Exchange Herald*, 12 May 1812; NA, HO 40/1/1/117, Hay to Ryder, 20 May 1812.

[162] Senior, *Orangeism in Ireland and Britain*, p. 171.

and 'Ultra' Toryism. The Established Church exercised some influence through its sermons and by encouraging rallying at the time of crisis, but its internal divisions and weaknesses against the power of Dissent in Lancashire lessened its role within Church-and-King. Loyalism survived into the nineteenth century because it maintained its cultural and political hegemony among a naturally reactive social elite and conservative populace. Yet while its control was not complete, it needed the stimulus of radical challenges to renew its legitimacy and inspire it to quell opposition. These challenges are explored in the following chapters.

4

Radicalism, 1798–1805

> Who blushes at the name of democrat or shrinks from the term Jacobin, when it is applied to those who rejoice in the improvement of society and the subversion of every thing that is inimical to the happiness of mankind?

William Clegg employed this provocative rhetoric in his pamphlet *Freedom Defended, or the Practice of Despots Exposed* in 1798.[1] Clegg was a radical Stockport schoolmaster, and proud to be a 'Jacobin', and in particular, an English Jacobin. He was however in the minority: by this time, most individuals holding radical political views would have indeed 'shrunk from the term Jacobin'. Radicalism in the 1800s was not the outspoken, association-based, openly popular movement of the early 1790s. There were few opportunities to be a respectable and vocal radical without fear of arrest.

A combination of national and local factors contributed to this silencing of British radicals. Many radicals had shunned republicanism altogether from 1793, when the Terror in France dashed their hopes of a non-violent constitutional revolution.[2] The legislation against seditious writings and meetings of October 1795 induced an atmosphere of fear. Combined with local suppression, this atmosphere had made actively organized radicalism inchoate and secret by 1798. The loyalist reaction decisively fixed the boundaries of political activity for the rest of the wars, and an atmosphere of suspicion and repression was later maintained by the magistrates' network of spies. Clegg's declaration was therefore also a

[1] W. Clegg, *Freedom Defended, or the Practice of Despots Exposed* (Manchester, 1798), pp. 11–12.

[2] M. Philp, *The French Revolution and British Popular Politics* (Cambridge, 1991), p. 84.

reaction against the polarization of political opinion which was enforced by loyalist elites after the French Revolution. He was speaking out during a closely monitored time when any individual who expressed sympathy for political or social reform would be tarred with the brush of 'Jacobin', even if they were not republican. Only a few individuals like Clegg were prepared to break the silence. This chapter charts their progress until the political atmosphere lightened in the later part of the decade and a larger section of the discontented could express their opinions more freely.

Clegg was involved with the United Englishmen, the republican movement that attempted to foster small cells within the south-eastern towns and villages of Lancashire. Apart from a few studies dedicated to the movement, the United Englishmen and United Irishmen usually mark the coda to the story of radicalism after the French Revolution, conceived as representing an ephemeral and desperate burst of extreme and violent republicanism that imploded within its enforced secrecy. E. P. Thompson argued that radicalism persisted through concrete but hidden personal and ideological connections which bridged the Jacobinism of the 1790s and the 'mass platform' of the 1810s.[3] These speculations result in part from lack of evidence. It is understandably difficult to track down artisans who left little or no personal documents, and who were likely to be mobile or migratory. The most extreme radicals seem to dominate in the 1800s, but this may be because that they left most evidence. It is likely however that more moderate radicalism continued in subtle ways that were harder to detect. Magistrates spent more energy tracking and writing about the United movements and republicans precisely because their radicalism was easier to identify and was rightly regarded as a greater threat. They frequently and often deliberately confused more moderate or constitutionalist radical activity and trade unionism with what they termed 'Jacobinism'.

From 1798 until at least 1807, the silence of radicalism was only occasionally interrupted by a few outbursts and demonstrations, chiefly during the economic distress and millenarian atmosphere of the turn of the century. Clegg's pamphlet is one indication that radical principles were kept alive by individuals within local communities during the Napoleonic wars, until the opportunity arose to be more vocal, organized, and regional. Clegg was one of the few who kept the legacy of Paine alive and vocal around Stockport and Ashton-under-Lyne during the Napoleonic wars. There were many more, however, who were less

[3] E. P. Thompson, 'Hunting the Jacobin Fox', *P & P* 142 (1994), 94–140.

radical and content to follow quietly. A distinction must be made between committed, active leaders or promoters of radicalism and the ordinary population whom they led. This chapter discusses expressions of radical discontent during the war, and the different responses they evoked from activists and local populations.

RADICAL ACTIVISTS

During the Napoleonic wars, certain groups of activists remained committed to maintaining the vestiges of radical principles and identity. The first group were 'English Jacobins' like Clegg, who had been inspired by Thomas Paine's *Rights of Man* but had not had a high enough profile in public life to suffer arrest or exile in the 1790s. They fostered a continued opposition to the war with France and braved showing their heads above the loyalist parapet, at least locally, to publish radical pamphlets and organize meetings at opportune moments. Among these were local families who maintained a radical reputation in particular villages in the region. Another group were bourgeois Dissenting intellectuals prominent in Liverpool, Manchester, and Bolton, the 'Friends of Peace'. The events of the 1800s perpetuated turbulence in their political outlooks. All had learnt lessons from the conflicts with Church-and-King loyalists in the 1790s and experienced mixed emotions about the military successes of Napoleon Bonaparte. The Friends of Peace differed from others in their moderate or 'romantic' radicalism. Intent on maintaining middle-class respectability, like their counterparts in Westminster, they became increasingly fearful of involvement with the war-weary working classes. They were willing to support financially, albeit silently, a final group of activists, the new generation of radicals who emerged towards the end of the war to lead the organization and oratorical display of the 'mass platform' until 1819.

'English Jacobins' flirted with the 'United' movements but were never fully committed to their republicanism. They had their own motives for activism, resulting from a commitment to the ideal of parliamentary reform and to Paineite social equality and from aversion to the repressive actions of local loyalists. William Clegg published his pamphlet, *Freedom Defended*, in retort to *Democratic Principles Illustrated by Example*, the pamphlet by the then-loyalist William Cobbett, or more particularly, to its distribution around Stockport by the Orange magistrate John Philips in 1798. Cobbett reiterated well-propagated arguments about the horrors of French Jacobinism.[4] Clegg responded with a fierce defence of the French Revolution which indicated his ideological involvement with the United Englishmen. The pamphlet reiterated the usual radical complaints and tropes, including denouncing the futility of the loyalists' apparent aim of restoring the Bourbons to the French throne. 'The Hoary Apostate' Edmund Burke and his 'specious rhetoric' were other obvious target of attack on grounds of hypocrisy. Though most of Clegg's argument was old hat, the pamphlet illustrates that radicalism was not totally silent after 1795. Clegg struck one note of caution among his vitriol. He implied that democracy only applied to rational individuals; he assured the reader that rule 'by the people' did not mean by 'mobs or clubs'.[5] Clegg may not have believed that democracy would be achieved through the United Englishmen or indeed conversely by the rhetoric of pamphlets like his. He perhaps knew that activism on a regional scale, without the secrecy that cloaked the UE, would be most effective, and he displayed this preference in his own activities. Bolton magistrate Colonel Ralph Fletcher sent the pamphlet as evidence to the Home Office in April 1802, accompanied by a note informing them that Clegg was 'indefatigable in organising the Neighbourhood'.[6]

Clegg continued to regard rhetoric as a valuable tool of opposition during a time when open activity was difficult. *Cowdroy's Manchester Gazette* published his 'Ode to France' at the height of the invasion scares in 1803. It bemoaned the 'scepter'd despotism' of Bonaparte which was destroying 'thy dear-bought conquer'd Liberty' and wasting 'all the blood for freedom spill'd' during the French Revolution:

> By Heav'n! great land, thy glory shall not rest
> Beneath a vain Usurper's haughty crest![7]

This execration of Napoleon was common amongst radicals, including, as will be seen later, the 'Friends of Peace'. They bitterly regretted Napoleon's imperialist and dictatorial government as it had destroyed their hopes of the egalitarianism of the Revolution coming to fruition. Radicalism therefore utilized the language of loyalism against Napoleon in an attempt to legitimize radical patriotism. By denouncing his clampdown upon the freedom of representation and speech in France,

[4] Acknowledgements to Robert Glen for extra information about this; 'Peter Porcupine' [W. Cobbett], *Democratic Principles Illustrated by Example* (1798).

[5] Clegg, *Freedom Defended*, 4–5, 22.

[6] NA, HO 42/65/442, Fletcher to Pelham, 3 April 1802.

[7] *CMG*, 10 December 1803.

radicals could skilfully subvert the expression of similar sentiments as loyalists, to uncover what they saw as parallels with repressions under Pitt's government.[8] The manipulation of loyalist language to support radical arguments remained one way in which radicals could express their views on the war, albeit only entirely safely when anonymously. Another correspondent to *Cowdroy's Manchester Gazette* during 1803 went under the pseudonym 'ALFRED'. His radicalism was of a more traditional constitutionalist stamp. He expressed radical patriotism in his call to defend the nation from corruption, as government could 'never be restored to its ancient purity by foreign interposition'. He also echoed the common radical complaint that British anti-Gallican rhetoric had inflamed the French and brought about the disintegration of the Treaty of Amiens: 'Will not calm reasoning infuse more real and lasting courage into British bosoms, than an inhuman exhortation "to inflict a terrible vengeance" on the "savage hordes" of France; for that is one of the appellations with which that civilized people have lately been branded.'[9]

Gradually during the 1800s, even the republicans moved from employing rhetoric that openly supported French democracy to more traditional attacks on the 'Old Corruption' of the British government that could only be purified by parliamentary reform. This formed part of the radical patriotic reaction against Napoleon's absolutism, but it perhaps also indicated a wish to be accepted as reasonable in the public eye. In November 1807, Clegg achieved most prominence when he served as secretary at a meeting in Ashton-under-Lyne to draw up a petition to parliament for peace.[10] Cowdroy printed another of Clegg's poems, 'Petitionary Lines for Peace', as accompaniment to the renewed peace campaign of 1807–8. The poem addressed the King, invoking ideas of the need to withstand corruption:

> Rather banish ev'ry knave,
> Purge thy councils, gracious Sire!
> Quick the British State to save,
> Bid the friends of war retire.[11]

[8] J. E. Cookson, *The Friends of Peace: Anti-War Liberalism in England, 1793–1815* (Cambridge, 1982), p. 180; See S. Semmel, 'Radicals and Legitimacy: Napoleon in the Mirror of History', *P & P* 167 (2000), 140–75.

[9] MCL, Broadside dated 29 August 1803, 'To the Inhabitants of the Town and Neighbourhood of Manchester', by ALFRED, printed by William Cowdroy.

[10] R. Glen, *Urban Workers in the Early Industrial Revolution* (New York, 1984), p. 154.

[11] *CMG*, 2 January 1808.

Clegg must have aimed his poem at ordinary inhabitants in the hope of encouraging them to petition the king, keeping his personal Paineite tenets private for the sake of the immediate cause.

The patriotism of radical activists was thus a complex mix of romantic Francophilia tarnished by dislike of Napoleon, and a love of country compared with a bitter hatred of governments pursuing what they regarded as the 'Pitt system' that pursued corruption and war-mongering, against the interests of British inhabitants in parliamentary representation and foreign policy. These sentiments were expressed even more forcefully by a contemporary of Clegg's, someone he may never have met: Robert Walker, the self-styled 'Tim Bobbin the Second'. Walker was born in Audenshaw in 1728 and was a handloom weaver in Rochdale. He composed the comic dialogue *Plebeian Politics* in response to the signing of the peace preliminaries of November 1801. It was printed in instalments in *Cowdroy's Manchester Gazette* and was 'so well received' that William Cowdroy republished it as a pamphlet. It was reprinted again in 1812.[12] *Plebeian Politics* is highly important as a dialect text, as one of its many rhetorical levels was directed at south-east Lancashire communities who knew that there were isolated radical cores within their midst. It is furthermore a solid example of the survival of radicalism in the early 1800s and reveals much about reactions to the peace. Walker obviously felt that the situation in November 1801 was safe enough for him to publish before retreating back into a less contentious career as a dialect writer; he may have died in 1803. Like Clegg, Walker was self-conscious about the role of radical rhetoric and tropes. He used the theme of pigs in conscious reference to Edmund Burke's invective and to Thomas Spence's republican riposte *Pig's Meat* of 1795. He thereby simultaneously aimed to appeal to radical audiences and to satirize critics of Spence. Walker explained that his characters had gained their political education through reading *An Impartial History of the War* (printed by Sowler and Russell of Manchester in 1799) and Thomas Erskine's *A View of the Causes and Consequence of the Present War with France*, first published in 1797. Walker recommended these books as a wider background to his own propagandic purposes of the dialogue. He furthermore advertised that the works were available for borrowing from 'Jim Street, in Sugar Lane' (in Dobcross, nestled within

[12] W. E. A. Axon, *Annals of Manchester* (Manchester, 1886), p. 131; *CMG*, 27 March 1802; R. Walker, *Plebeian Politics: Or the Principles and Practices of Certain Mole-Eyed Maniacs Vulgarly Called Warrites* (Manchester, 1802).

Saddleworth Moor).[13] This indicates two features of the dissemination of printed information: that the texts were available to the ordinary population other than through one-off sale; and the local and personal nature of this informal distribution. National distribution of print was thus dependent upon sometimes fragile local means of transmission.

The comic dialogue between the characters of 'Tum' and 'Whistlepig' employed a common device of both radical and loyalist propagandists. It aimed to expose the hypocrisy of Church-and-King loyalist elites, celebrating the preliminaries after having refused demands for peace from 1795. In the concluding part, Tum declares that a local 'nabob' who illuminated his house on the event of the peace is: 'Just like th'rest o'th' foos ot han no oppinnions o'the'r own: bod grunt'n afthr eawer nashonal pig-leaders, one dey for war, an another for peeoss'. ['Just like the rest of the fools that have no opinions of their own: but grunt after our national pig-leaders, one day for war, and another for peace'.] The purpose of the tract was less to explain radical principles than to attempt to convince or remind readers about the ways in which both local and national government were 'wetherkok, fawnink, krinjink, hypokritical, sykofantine skeawndrils'. A particular target was the use of religion by Church-and-King loyalists to support their case for war. Tum expressed disgust at his local clergy leading militia regiments into their parish church, sanctioned by the magistrates and government: 'when the'n drunm't an ekorsis't foke o the' Sundy o'er, heaw fort' kill the'r fello kreturs; ods flesh mon! th' kristian religion teaches no sitch wark'.[14] ['when they drilled and exercised folk all the Sunday over how to kill their fellow creatures; God's flesh man! The Christian religion teaches no such work'.] Walker thereby used comic rhetoric to subvert Church-and-King religious arguments and exhibit Christian pacifism.

Of course it is unclear how widely these pamphlets were distributed or how far their rhetoric was effectual in changing minds about the war, but they must have confirmed and sustained the views of some committed radicals among the regional population. It was still a risky business producing material expounding such overtly radical tenets, particularly in an environment where loyalist patriotism was being propagated more widely than ever as the government attempted to unify the population in defence of the nation against the French. In *Plebeian Politics*, Walker indicated the isolation of radicals after the Two Acts by lamenting a litany of radical martyrs. These included the national figures Thomas

[13] *Ibid.*, 14–15. [14] *Ibid.*, 52–3.

Hardy, John Horne Tooke, Joseph Priestley, and John Thelwall as well as local heroes William and John Knight of Saddleworth and the printers Matthew Faulkner and William Birch (who published the *Manchester Herald* and radical pamphlets). He continued:

> Le meh naw forget Measter Tummus Wawker, o'Manchester, a mon persekutet an prosekutet to his utter ruin, uppo th'evidense ov a for-sworn skeawndril, for no other krime, thin beink a knone frend to liberty.[15]
> [Let me not forget Mr Thomas Walker of Manchester, a man persecuted and prosecuted to his utter ruin, upon the evidence of a forsworn scoundrel, for no other crime than being a known friend to liberty.]

This was one of the few published recognitions of the heritage contemporary radicals had inherited from the 1790s. These hagiographic sketches were written from a position of radical isolation when activists were no longer public or well known, but rather silent and community-based.

Most of Thomas Walker's political contemporaries did not 'interfere much in public life' from their arrest or the moment when suspicion was aroused against them.[16] Many of the original members of the MCS had either died or gone into exile. The destinations of members of less prominent radical circles in smaller towns are even harder to trace. Very few names reappear on petitions; for example, there is little correlation between the signatories of the peace petitions of 1795 and 1808 or the popular addresses concerning the Duke of York corruption scandal in 1809. Former MCS members John, Jeremiah, Abraham, and Arthur Clegg continued as timber merchants in Manchester. George Duckworth, former member of the MCS and Lit and Phil and anti-slavery campaigns, continued his career as an attorney, remaining in the relatively high-profile role of notary public of Manchester, which involved dealings with many local notables.[17] Duckworth was one of the four buyers of the Chorlton Hall estate which was leased for redevelopment in 1796. He continued as a respectable figure, acting as Master extra in Chancery and hearing the oaths of prominent manufacturers for legal agreements.[18] The only political petition he signed during the Napoleonic War, however, was the Manchester petition in support of the slave

[15] Walker, *Plebeian Politics*, 27–9. [16] *CMG*, 8 February 1817.

[17] MCL, BR f. 942.7389 Sc 13, Scrapbook 1808–24; M156/53/4/39, bond of John Clegg, 1807.

[18] MCL, L4/1/5,6, John Bury papers, arbitration bonds, May and July 1802; NA, HO 42/82/94, Peter Marsland oath, 25 May 1805.

trade abolition bill in May 1806. The abolition campaign brought other radicals briefly back into public action, including Ashworth Clegg, merchant trustee of Stand Unitarian Chapel and member of the Manchester Literary and Philosophic Society; Bolton radicals, the manufacturer Robert Heywood (1786–1868) and physician Dr Robert Everleigh Taylor (1773–1827); William Clegg of Stockport; and 'James, Joshua, John, Sam, Charles and William Taylor', probably from Royton.[19] As many members of loyalist elites also supported the abolition campaign, its depoliticized character enabled former radical activists to express their opinion within a legitimate and respectable setting.

Certain individuals sustained a pattern of radical activity throughout the wars, though they were unusual in this respect. Manchester radical Thomas Walker took part in later agitation, associating with the United Englishmen, abolitionists, and the Luddites. He was regarded by each new movement as something of a veteran.[20] John Knight of Saddleworth was probably the most involved among the disparate few. He was arrested as a radical leader in 1794, joined the United Englishmen's county executive in 1801 and was again arrested in Manchester in 1812 for what the magistrates regarded as his leading part in the renewed reform activity. He became editor of the *Manchester Register* in 1817 and was arrested a fourth time in 1819. He was still politically active in the 1830s. His activities are unrecorded between 1803 and 1811, on the other hand, which suggests that like many others, he laid low or focused his efforts on patriotic endeavour.[21] The radical pamphleteer George Philips also remained in Manchester. In January 1807, he was elected a member of the 'King of Clubs' dining club of London, joining the company of leading Whig-radicals such as Lord Holland, the Marquess of Lansdowne, and Henry Brougham.[22] He continued to vent his political frustrations in frequent but private correspondence with William Roscoe and the Liverpool 'Friends of Peace'. Like Clegg, he developed a sense of radical patriotic disgust about the government's conduct of the war in its later

[19] House of Lords RO, HO/PO/JO/10/8/106, Manchester petition in favour of slave trade abolition bill, 14 May 1806.

[20] *CMG*, 8 February 1817.

[21] J. Foster, *Class Struggle in the Industrial Revolution: Early Industrial Capitalism in Three Towns* (London, 1974), p. 43; NA, HO 42/117/524, Fletcher to Home Office, 21 November 1811; *The Trial at Full Length of the Thirty Eight Men from Manchester, 27 August 1812* (Manchester, 1812); Oldham Local Studies, E/BUT/F, Butterworth diaries, 1830–9.

[22] MCL, M/C 2688, lease for building in Mosley St., June 1802; British Library, Additional MS 37337, Register of the King of Clubs dining club, 1798–1823.

stages which aroused him to communicate. On 20 February 1808, he sycophantically thanked Roscoe for sending him a copy of his new peace pamphlet, commenting: 'It is impossible to avoid shuddering at the retrospect of those follies which have led to the subjugation of Europe; or to read without alarm your able description of the probable consequences of the continuance of that infatuation in our councils from which the evils of our present situation are observed.'[23] Although his radical mind thus remained active, his public face was quiet. The fortunes of 1790s radical activists in Lancashire were therefore mixed, and how vocal they were depended largely upon local circumstances and individual personalities.

THE UNITED ENGLISHMEN AND THEIR SUPPORTERS

Though loyalist local elites saw these individuals as a nuisance, their potential to disrupt the social order operated only at the level of text and rhetoric in the early part of the war. What magistrates feared the most from 1798 were the United Irishmen and United Englishmen. The united movements in England and Scotland have been studied in detail by Marianne Elliott and Roger Wells, amongst others, and their conclusions need only be recited in brief in relation to Lancashire. Elliott and Wells argue that secret-cell organization, republican aims, and French backing could have combined to result in something approaching a revolution. The United Englishmen could not, however, effect their aims as a result of various factors, principally their small numbers, personal feuds within the leadership, and government repression of the movement.[24] The Lancashire evidence demonstrates that the planned revolution dissipated into malcoordinated conspiracies because of unresolved differences between the United Irishmen and United Englishmen, and between the United movements and the remnants of what could potentially have been a welcoming group of Paineite radicals in the region.

Three elements of the United Englishmen conspiracies in Lancashire stand out in relation to popular radicalism. Firstly, local bourgeois radicals were sympathetic towards the home-grown artisanal UE, but they

[23] Liverpool RO, 920 ROS 2977, Philips to Roscoe, 20 February 1808.

[24] M. Elliott, *Partners in Revolution: the United Irishmen and France* (New Haven, 1982); R. Wells, *Insurrection: the British Experience, 1795–1803* (Gloucester, 1983), p. 235.

were simultaneously distant and occasionally distrustful of their ultimate aims and of the UI emissaries sent over from Ireland to foment unrest. Their patchy involvement in the movement reveals a calculated appraisal of risks on the part of many radicals in Lancashire. Secondly, conflicting attitudes about religion separated the Lancashire UE from the UI emissaries, and from the London-based United Britons.[25] Thirdly, the UE in Lancashire acted and drew support from a distinctly regional basis.

Evidence for the United movements is, because of their very nature, either sparse or based on the suspicions and speculations of magistrates and their spies. It seems that the Lancashire UE were not created by the itinerant Irish delegates whom the magistrates' spies followed around the country, but 'grew naturally out of the MCS'. Alan Booth has found continuities between the membership of the MCS and those arrested as United Englishmen, naming James Dixon, Richard Stansfield, and four others as possibly being involved in both.[26] This paralleled the movement's growth in London, where, as Francis Place later admitted in his autobiography, the negotiations between his London Corresponding Society and UI emissary John O'Coigley resulted in a UE branch being formed. The LCS, UI, and UE were legislatively prohibited by name by an act of July 1799.[27] There is on the other hand little evidence that this 'radical underground' continued into the reform campaigns later in the 1800s, as individuals from the MCS or UE cannot be identified as active in this later period. Dissensions were endemic within the Lancashire movement from the start. In early 1797, disputes arose between former MCS members after 'a quarrel between the Gentlemen who had given great support to the MCS' and 'the mechanics of the Society'.[28] Only the most dedicated henceforth continued, spending most of their efforts travelling around the North looking for new recruits to the UE. Arrests of the most well-known emissaries, John O'Coigley and John O'Connor, en route to France, left the radicals around Manchester in constant fear of arrest and thereby brought any concrete planning to a standstill. Some UI delegates remaining in the area proved elusive, but escaped to Ireland via Liverpool. The confining of UE suspects in Cold Bath Fields Prison in London, though it aroused

25 *Ibid*., p. 151.

26 A. Booth, 'The United Englishmen and Radical Politics in the Industrial North-West of England, 1795–1803', *International Review of Social History*, 31 (1986), 276.

27 *The Autobiography of Francis Place*, ed. M. Thrale (Cambridge, 1972), p. 177.

28 Wells, *Insurrection*, p. 74.

sympathy for them, and the failed attempt of Colonel Despard to spark a revolution, effectually put an end to the movement.[29]

The residual anti-Catholicism, or perhaps more accurately, anti-Irish sentiment, of the UE played a large part in fragmenting them and their plans. The UE were decidedly *English* Jacobins who kept their distance from the UI and were less concerned about the French invasion of the mainland and about freeing Ireland from British rule than they were about championing Paineite values of universal suffrage and equal representation. The UE, having grown out of the remnants of constitutional societies, thus had sympathies with Enlightenment atheism and were suspicious of established churches, while the identity of the UI by contrast had centred around Catholicism since their alliance with the Catholic Committee and the Irish Rebellion. Hatred of the Church-and-King alliance underlay much of William Cowdroy's rhetoric and his opinions mirrored those of the UE. In January 1798, Cowdroy criticized William Pitt, the 'haughty Monarch of Downing Street', for his attempts 'to root out Jacobinism, to starve Republicans and to disseminate the principles of Christianity by the sword and the bayonet'.[30] Such tropes surfaced regularly in radical rhetoric: Robert Walker used the character Whistlepig to allege that the 'war-lovink tinkor' Pitt used his budgets (and the new income tax) to maintain 'a parel o'French runagates, ot wurn'n komn to this kuntry, ot te kode'n t'klergy and Laety'.[31] ['A group of French refugees that had come to this country, that they called the clergy and laity'.] In his examination during the trial of the Lancashire UE, the spy Robert Gray had alleged that Cowdroy had told him that England had no defence against the French 'as long as Priestcraft was suffered in the country'.[32] This was reflective of the anti-hierarchical elements in his radicalism and pointed towards a significant theme underlying much of Lancashire radicalism. William Clegg criticized Burke's rhetoric, which was 'in support of a war for the continuation of popish superstition and regal despotism'.[33] Such anti-Catholic tenets continued even into the new forms of radicalism that would emerge from the later part of the war. Hence two peace petitions from Chowbent and Chorley to the House of Commons in 1812 both pointed to the fund for exiled Catholic clergy and laity as proof of the

[29] Booth, 'The United Englishmen', 282; NA, HO 42/65/481, Fletcher to King, 31 July 1802; Wells, *Insurrection*, pp. 231–2.

[30] *CMG*, 20 January 1798.

[31] Clegg, *Freedom Defended*, p. 20.

[32] NA, Privy Council, PC 1/42/A140, examination of Robert Gray, 15 April 1798.

[33] Clegg, *Freedom Defended*, pp. 4–5.

government's hypocritical disengagement from the economic plight of the working classes.[34]

The UE were also distinguished by their regional concentration. E. P. Thompson emphasized the distinctive sense of identity and propensity to radicalism that characterized artisans in the Pennines. Informer Robert Gray claimed there were UE divisions in most of the satellite towns and villages around Manchester.[35] Two large meetings occurred on 3 May 1801, at Buckton Castle, a Pennine moor overlooking Mossley, and at Greenacres Moor on the outskirts of Oldham. Over two hundred people reputedly attended another meeting upon Rivington Pike (a moor overlooking Horwich to the north-west of Bolton) on a Sunday morning later in the month. The purposes and intentions of the meetings were unclear, but the magistrates saw them as a major threat.[36] Twenty-one people were arrested, mainly artisans from the wider Wigan to Bolton area, though it cannot be verified whether these men were really interested in the UE or merely convenient scapegoats.

The UE can be regarded as a product of political desperation as much as a genuine commitment to republicanism, though their attempts to co-opt the resident radicals in Manchester and its satellite towns raised their importance beyond that of mere provocation to the zealous magistrates. The physical-force radicalism of the UE arose, as Booth and Thompson noted, out of depressed artisanal districts of mixed ethnic origin.[37] Three-quarters of the secretaries of the society named by the spy Robert Gray in 1798 lived in the mixed Irish–English artisanal area around Ancoats and Newton Lane. None marked were identified as 'poor' in the poor rate lists and one member, Moses Fry, was listed as the ratepayer of a high-value house on Church Street, a main street.[38] Gray himself was a cotton manufacturer and an important figure for both UE and magistrates in 1798–1801. He became secretary of the UE in Manchester and was employed as an informer by the magistrate Thomas Butterworth Bayley. William Cheetham, the acknowledged leader of Manchester UE, derided him because of his hostility to republicanism,

34 See Chapter 6.

35 Booth, 'The United Englishmen', 277; NA, HO 42/62/149–50, Hay to Portland, June 1801.

36 Rowbottom diaries; Bolton Archives, Holden diaries, 3 May 1801; NA, HO 42/62/110, Hay to Portland, 27 May 1801.

37 Booth, 'The United Englishmen', 276–7.

38 NA, PC 1/3118, Papers relating to United Irishmen and United Englishmen, 1798; MCL, Manchester poor rate, 1798, district 4; Fry was marked 'in jail'. Note Lancashire CRO, WCW 1802 and 1808, wills of David Dougherty and James Dixon.

his religiosity, and ignorance of Paine.[39] Hannah Greg, wife of Samuel the Unitarian manufacturer of Manchester and later Quarry Bank, identified him as 'the Informer' as early as April 1798 in a letter to William Rathbone of Liverpool. She argued that United activity and the tendency to violence in Manchester was the result of Gray 'spiriting them up'. Greg's comment indicates a common knowledge of the UE among radical sympathisers; she indeed mentioned 'our united friend' having given her the information.[40] Middle-class radicals who had stepped down from active involvement in radicalism continued in the background by keeping up these connections and knowledge.

The UE were far from anonymous in their immediate local communities. William Rowbottom provided personal evidence about the fate of Lancashire individuals arrested for seditious activities at this time. It is testimony to the strength of local community in and around Oldham that he remembered who they were and furthermore what had happened to them. He wrote in 1808:

> 19th August–last night John Jackson of near Chaderton arrived at his house after serving seven years transportation.
> 20th–Stansfield and Buckly the two unfortunate companions of the above Jackson have died some time since on the coast of Guinea the vollonteers for soldiers in preference to serving as transports.[41]

As Rowbottom had already noted in 1801, John Jackson, John Buckley, John Stansfield, and John Bradley, all labourers late of Chadderton, were indeed indicted at the Lancaster Assizes for seditious activity after the Buckton Castle meeting and were transported.[42] The men appear to have been known locals, and thus Rowbottom's comment suggests some sense of community identity or awareness. It is unlikely that returnees from transportation fell back publicly into radical activism. Colonel Fletcher stridently reported after a peace meeting on Oldham Edge on Christmas Day 1807: 'I need only observe that the leaders in this meeting were intimately connected with several of those persons who were at the Autumn Assizes for this County in the year 1801, transported for having administered unlawful oaths.'[43] Rowbottom's observation on the return of radicals in 1808 contradicts Fletcher's claim. John Foster

[39] NA, PC 1/41/A139; Wells, *Insurrection,* p. 125.

[40] Liverpool University Special Collections, Rathbone papers, RP.II.1.65, Greg to Rathbone, April 1798.

[41] Rowbottom diaries.

[42] NA, PL 28/4, Crown Office minute book.

[43] NA, HO 42/91/963, Fletcher to Hawkesbury, 27 December 1807.

also exaggerated continuities of action in his study of Oldham radicals; he stated that amongst others, John Jackson of Chadderton was active from 1797 to 1808. It is clear from Rowbottom's account that Jackson was serving his sentence of transportation between 1801 and 1808.[44]

The possibility remains that former United Englishmen supported renewed and broader campaigns for peace and reform after their return or when the local political atmosphere lightened. Hence it is difficult to confirm or deny Colonel Fletcher's claim in February 1808 about the Bolton peace petition: 'Three of those who went round the Country with the Petition are known by myself to have been of the Affiliated Jacobin Societies . . . their names were transmitted to Government as such as nine or eight years ago.'[45] Most United Englishmen remain untraceable. William Cheetham, the main delegate from Manchester, was imprisoned in Coldbath Fields 1798–1801. On his release, he acted as a delegate to London radical committees and was still arousing Colonel Fletcher's suspicion in May 1803, but there is no surviving evidence of his activities after this.[46] It is likely that some UI and UE joined the navy as a means of avoiding incarceration or deportation. Yet others, notably William Cowdroy, were able to find more fruitful careers and continued to influence the political views of the population in new ways.

WILLIAM COWDROY, RADICAL FATHER AND SON

Cowdroy's Manchester Gazette provides sustained evidence of radicalism throughout this period. William Cowdroy (1752–1814) and his son William (1775–1822) were two key individuals in Lancashire, linking silent bourgeois radicals and active working-class 'Jacobins'. William Cowdroy Senior was born in Chester and moved to Salford in 1794, where he went into partnership with Thomas Boden, bookseller and stationer of Deansgate, who was already known for printing the trial of Thomas Walker. In November 1795, they bought the *Manchester Gazette* and radicalized its editorial content. This was a remarkably brave move in the circumstances, as memories of the suppression of the *Manchester Herald*

44 Foster, *Class Struggle in the Industrial Revolution*, p. 151.

45 NA, HO 42/95/5, Fletcher to Home Office, February 1808.

46 A. Hone, *For the Cause of Truth: Radicalism in London, 1796–1821* (Oxford, 1982), p. 136; NA, PC 1/42/148; HO 42/65/442, Fletcher to Home Office, 3 April 1802; HO 42/65/491–2, Fletcher to Home Office, 7 July 1802.

were fresh amongst both radicals and loyalists in the town. His eldest son, William, began business as a printer and publisher in Salford in 1803 and took over the *Gazette* on his death.[47] Cowdroy's radical credentials were certified not least by the Liverpudlian republican poet Edward Rushton, who wrote an elegy for him. William Senior named one of his other sons 'Citizen', born in 1799 or 1800, which again boldly indicated his Francophile sympathies and his brazenness about expressing them.[48]

Cowdroy's Manchester Gazette was the main channel through which radical writers were able to get their opinion voiced in the region during this period. The location of the paper again demonstrated how Manchester remained central for radicalism; or at least suggests that radicals from across the region had no choice but to look to the city for a voice. The only comparable paper was the *Chester Chronicle*, as John Singleton JP of Wigan commented in 1801: 'Two Country papers are doing and have done a deal of mischief by corrupting the minds of the lower orders. One of these papers is published in Chester and the other in Manchester.'[49] Clegg and Walker among other radicals offered their writings to the newspaper, but Cowdroy also contributed more actively to sustaining the radical message. His editorials were crucial in maintaining the vestiges of radicalism in Lancashire and beyond during the period following 1798 until 1812, when the upsurge in popular radicalism gave openings for new radical newspapers. The tone of the political rhetoric in his editorials was clear and it remains a mystery why the authorities did not force him into silence. Sales of the *Gazette* reached a wartime high of 1,700 a week in the summer of 1796 and apparently never fell below a thousand.[50] One copy could go a long way. In 1797, when the stamp tax was increased, Cowdroy wrote about 'the little circle of friends who subscribe their pence for a single paper' who would have to 'either extend these circles by taking more into the firm, or advance (if four of them) their halfpenny each week, rather than shut up their weekly channels of information'. He estimated that each copy of his paper was read on average by 'ten different persons . . . although the most of them are individually read by considerably

[47] C. Horner, 'William Cowdroy (1752-1814)', *Oxford Dictionary of National Biography*; MCL, Biographical cuttings.

[48] Lancashire CRO, WCW/1815, will of William Cowdroy of Manchester; MCL, MFPR 43, Manchester Cathedral marriage register, p. 384, no. 1150.

[49] NA, HO 42/62/112, J. Singleton to Portland, 27 May 1801.

[50] M. Turner, 'The Making of a Middle-Class Liberalism in Manchester, c. 1815–32: A study of politics and the press', D.Phil. thesis (Oxford, 1991), p. 57.

more'.[51] Cowdroy also took up the role of the Faulkner printers, whom Church-and-King rioters had forced to shut down in the 1790s, in publishing pamphlets, peace and reform petitions and addresses, and providing a venue for those petitions to be signed.

In March 1798, William Cowdroy junior was arrested for printing the 'Declarations of the United Englishmen' for the spy Robert Gray. Other 'United men taken at meetings at Manchester' included William Cheetham, James Dixon, Moses Fry, and four other men.[52] Cowdroy junior was tried at Middlesex, but bailed in June. On being shown Thomas Paine's pamphlet, 'Letter to Thomas Erskine' during his examination, he claimed that 'he had a dozen of them from America and that he sold them'. Cowdroy Senior was almost prosecuted after donating two shillings to assist UI John O'Coigley's passage to France, but the spy Gray's evidence was insufficient to convict him.[53] The paper ceased publication for a few months, but was up and running again after William junior's release. Their most important and remarkable achievement was the paper's survival long after the Cowdroys were suspected of UE involvement. It remained the main non-Tory newspaper in the region until the new generation of radicals felt secure enough to begin publishing once the reform campaign renewed from 1811.[54] He remained under surveillance: information transmitted by Colonel Fletcher to the Duke of Portland in July 1801 indicated the local and national radical circles he was mixing with or at least was perceived to be so:

> Thelwall was at Manchester on the 2nd inst. at the House of Cowdroy the Printer of the Manchester Gazette of whose character I presume your Grace is not wholly ignorant . . . Thelwall has been with several Jacobins of the higher order in Manchester particularly with Thomas Walker, William Hanson and Preston the younger.[55]

Thomas Walker here reappeared together with William Hanson, silk manufacturer of Cannon Street and father of Joseph, who would organize Manchester radicalism in the 1800s. William had signed the Manchester peace petition of 1795 (he also signed petitions against the

51 *CMG*, 24 June 1797, 25 June 1796.

52 NA, PC 1/44/158, 'United men taken at meetings at Manchester, March 1798'.

53 NA, PC 1/42/140, Middlesex Quarter Sessions, Trial of William Cheetham, April 1798.

54 See Chapter 6 for the establishment of the *Liverpool Mercury*.

55 NA, HO 42/62/238, Fletcher to Portland, 8 July 1801.

abolition of the slave trade in 1788 and 1794).[56] In their examinations at the Middlesex Quarter Sessions in 1798, Cowdroy junior and his brother Thomas admitted that they borrowed money from Joseph Hanson 'for the use of the office'.[57]

The Hanson family were amongst the section of the middle class who, though not openly involved in radical activism in the 1790s, became crucial to its maintenance in the 1800s. A letter from the magistrate Mr Floud to the Home Secretary of 12 April 1798 described how wealthy patrons supported suspected UE members. The informant Gray implicated Hanson, 'a young man in partnership with his Father, a Merchant and who is supposed to be worth £100,000', together with Jackson, 'also a considerable merchant and the man who was tried with Walker of Manchester five years ago', the bookseller Hopper and the manufacturer Robert Norris.[58] On both occasions that O'Coigley passed through Manchester, the resident UE felt able to turn to these 'gentlemen radicals' for financial assistance: Joseph Hanson, the veteran Thomas Walker, and three others, Thomas Collier, Thomas Norris, and Samuel Jackson. The remnants of the 1790s radicals were connected with these 'gentlemen radicals'. A legal document of October 1803, concerning sales related to the bankruptcy of Thomas Walker and his brother Richard, listed their assignees as Joseph Hanson and his fellow Dissenting and abolitionist merchants James Darbishire and William Marsden.[59] Tacit financial support from middle-class sympathizers was experienced in other towns marked by radical agitation. In May 1801, nine out of the twenty-one men arrested at the radical meeting on Rivington Pike were bailed by Bolton 'cotton manufacturers' presumably favourable to their cause.[60] Fear of repression and arrest, however, made the welcome accorded to United emissaries decidedly frosty. When they called upon Joseph Hanson in connection with the subscription for O'Coigley, Hanson allegedly replied: 'You never come but [when] you want something.'[61] This fear, together with lukewarmness on the part of those who potentially had the organization and funds to help the UE succeed, contributed to its eventual demise.

[56] House of Lords RO, HL/PO/JO/10/3/286/3, Manchester petition against the slave trade bill, 25 March 1794.

[57] NA, PC 1/42/140. [58] *Ibid.*

[59] House of Lords RO, HO/PO/JO/10/8/106, Manchester petition in favour of slave trade bill, 14 May 1806; MCL, deeds, m/c 129, 8 October 1803; m/c 132, 3 March 1804; *Manchester Herald*, 9 March 1793.

[60] Wells, *Insurrection*, p. 217; HO 42/62/111, Bancroft to Portland, 27 May 1801.

[61] Booth, 'The United Englishmen', 280.

William Cowdroy, father and son, nevertheless continued to risk their freedom to aid the UE in this period. William Senior collected subscriptions on behalf of the London-based committee to relieve the families of those imprisoned in 1798. The remnants of the UE used his newspaper for communication with the wider public. Cowdroy published their addresses appealing for money and defending their innocence. In May and June 1800, the five members of the Manchester UE imprisoned in Cold Bath Fields wrote to the London committee for relief, stating that they wished to 'confine any correspondence to Mr Cowdroy, Printer of the Manchester Gazette, whose amiable deposition and zeal in the cause of Freedom', they believed contrasted significantly with that of other 'Manchester Patriots', who 'have been very cold in the cause of Freedom, since the bug-bear—the pretended Plott, were discovered'. This suspicion again illustrated that the silence of Mancunian bourgeois radicals owed much to fear of arrest as well as their desire to distance themselves from the UE's extremism. The monetary support that the UE received was however far from substantial, as in July they thanked the relief committee for a total of £3, 17s, 6d.[62] Cowdroy maintained his support for their cause in 1801. In April, his editorial commented on William Cheetham, 'the last of the Manchester TRAITORS', being discharged from Coldbath Fields after three years without trial, thereby, in his view, confirming both Cheetham's innocence and the corruption of the state. This episode also marked Sir Francis Burdett and Horne Tooke's first new foray into the public light. Cowdroy believed that Burdett intended 'to move the house to indemnify these long afflicted men and their families, for the ruinous losses they have sustained in consequence of their captivity'.[63] Local interests were therefore paramount; Cowdroy focused on this aspect rather than on their campaign against the governor of the prison, which was what made Burdett's name in metropolitan radical circles.

The centrality of *Cowdroy's Manchester Gazette* to radical life in the region was clear. William Cowdroy often proclaimed that he intended to influence public opinion directly through the *Gazette*. His hopes were apparently fulfilled. Readers indeed gleaned from the paper information and radical viewpoints about the government and the effect of the war. William Rowbottom, for example, noted the 'National Debt as it appears

[62] BL, Additional MS 27816, Place papers, fo. 571, W. Cheetham, J. Dods, A. Donoughy to M. Hewitt, 14 June 1800; fo. 573, 7 July 1800.

[63] *CMG*, 11 April 1801; see also 30 May 1801, 12 June 1802.

in Manchester Gazette of June 26th 1802'.[64] On 31 October 1801, Cowdroy's response to the preliminaries of peace included a restatement of his intention to follow the 'undeviating and immutable' path of 'proclaiming to the world that the war was neither just nor necessary'. He recognized the significance of the paper in the preceding and current political atmosphere: 'Our paper has been often burnt, after *solemn* and *salient* debate, in public bars, by the hands of pitiable ignorance and inveteracy:—And for what?—"For *disaffection and Jacobinism*!" .' He argued against the loyalist view that opposing the war was Jacobinical. Hence in a manner recalling *Plebeian Politics*, Cowdroy ironically commented on the hypocrisy of loyalists celebrating the Peace: '*John Bull* himself is a Jacobin and frantic joy that pervaded the kingdom from one end to the other is an incontestable sentiment—that *Jacobinism* is now "the order of the day" .'[65]

The ideal of unanimity through patriotism that was propagated during the invasion scares failed to silence Cowdroy's radical editorials. The peace had given him both a breathing space and a psychological break allowing him to vent his fury. Once war resumed, though initially quiet, he sensed that the atmosphere was still more amenable to calls for change than it had been during the more repressive loyalist atmosphere of the previous invasion scare. He therefore criticized the government's conduct of the war as early as 10 September 1803, again using the radical trick of employing the rhetoric of patriotism to insulate his comments from loyalist taunts of sedition: 'There is a littleness in their conjectures, a narrowness in their systems, an instability in their judgement, a timidity in their prudence, and a rashness in their courage, which disqualify them from their posts at the present important crisis.' Much of this opinion was shaped by his dissatisfaction with the Treaty of Amiens and the short-lived peace, and his Country suspicion of centralized demands from the government. By 31 December 1803, Cowdroy felt confident enough to speak out again: 'A parliamentary reform among the rotten boroughs has long been called for and the danger of making a beginning is the principal reason, probably, that has so long withheld it . . . Ten pounds for a single vote, twenty for a plumper—a system apparently as current as common exchange and barter'.[66]

Cowdroy's editorials did not progressively become either more or less radical during the war. Rather, he dexterously employed elements from

64 Rowbottom diaries.

65 *CMG*, 31 October 1801.

66 *CMG*, 31 December 1803.

the whole range of radical repertoire according to the circumstances. He called for parliamentary reform at opportune moments when it was less likely to provoke arrest; for example, during the peace on 20 February 1802, he combined an appeal for reform with one for abolition of the slave trade. His New Year editorial each year exhibited aspects of his political opinions most clearly: radical patriotism and opposition to Pittite repression and corruption. From 1805, he again expressed repeated demands for peace. By 4 January 1812, he renewed complaints recalling the war-weary distress of 1800, castigating 'the errors of our Rulers' who by 'procrastinating the evils of War . . . thereby palsied our trade and manufactures'. He asserted the radical patriotic belief in the unity of Britain against France: 'the printer has only to add that he shall still pursue the part of, and invariably be the advocate for, PEACE and REFORM'.[67] The paper continued its role as a focus for reformist sentiment into the post-war era of mass-platform radicalism. Though it is possible that his rhetoric was exaggerated for the sake of selling more papers or sparking debate, the newspaper nevertheless stood out as being as the sole constant propagator of such radical views at a time of prohibition of 'seditious writings'.

The impact of the UE agitation of 1799–1801 may have been limited in the longer term, but during its brief appearance it perhaps provided the only means of radical expression during the unusual circumstances of economic distress and popular uncertainty about both the direction of the war and uncertainty about the fallout from the government's restrictions on political meetings and writings. A millenarian atmosphere was also evident at the turn of the century, with propaganda abounding about Bonaparte as the incarnation of Satan. This may have influenced the extremities of radicalism propagated in this period; hence the rumours that the UE oath was similar 'to the form taken out of the Prophet Ezekiel'.[68] More moderate radical individuals like the Cowdroys and Joseph Hanson took calculated risks and rightly treated the UE with caution, but men such as these weathered the storm until opportunities arose later in the decade for more open radical action.

LOCAL RADICAL CIRCLES

Radicalism in Lancashire was variegated in terms of its principles and its membership; its geographical spread similarly displayed a patchwork

[67] *CMG*, 7 January 1804, 4 January 1812.
[68] NA, HO 42/61/432, Coke to Portland, 4 April 1801.

of differing strength. Certain areas were more 'Jacobin' than others. In part this was a result of circumstance, particularly the existence or not of close-knit families and circles of activists who were prepared to foster the right environment for such views to be held. John Foster termed these 'more permanent cells of opposition, isolated groupings of families which provided at least some of the long-term continuity of language and direction'.[69] Once radical activists retreated into their communities after 1795, their thinking was shaped less by textual or ideological abstraction than by local circumstances.

One of the hotspots of radicalism throughout this period was the village of Royton, near Oldham, despite having a population of only about 3,500. Royton's radical reputation was most likely a direct consequence of the influence and organization of the Taylors, the most commonly mentioned family in the Lancashire magistrates' reports to the Home Office. In his memoirs, Samuel Bamford commented that Royton was 'looked upon as the chief resort of Jacobins on that side of Manchester'.[70] The reputation of the village continued and spread across the region. When Lieutenant-Colonel Joseph Hanson stood as an independent candidate for Preston in 1807, an election squib, 'Hanson and Bony, A New Song', hinted at Royton's radical history, cemented by the 'Royton Races', the infamous Church-and-King mob attack of 1794. Of Hanson it was said:

> To Royton he once went to make revolutions,
> For like his friend Bony he hates constitutions;
> But the King's Dragoons, in all that saw no fun,
> And a charge sword in hand, made the jacobins run.
> . . . We'll soon make him run and we'll soon make him sweat,
> In spite of his green men and *Cowdroy's Gazette*.[71]

UE gatherings and peace and reform meetings were often held on Tandle Hill on the outskirts of the township. The politics expressed at such events were also distinguished by the unique and markedly Paineite character of Royton radicalism. The resolutions passed at a peace meeting there on 5 April 1801, for example, expressed considerably greater awareness of the economic relationships than was apparent in the usual constitutionalist rhetoric of other addresses and petitions from

[69] Foster, *Class Struggle in the Industrial Revolution*, p. 31.

[70] S. Bamford, *The Autobiography of Samuel Bamford: Early Days*, new edn, ed. W. H. Chaloner (London, 1967), p. 44.

[71] *Account of the Election at Preston. . . 1807*, p. 16.

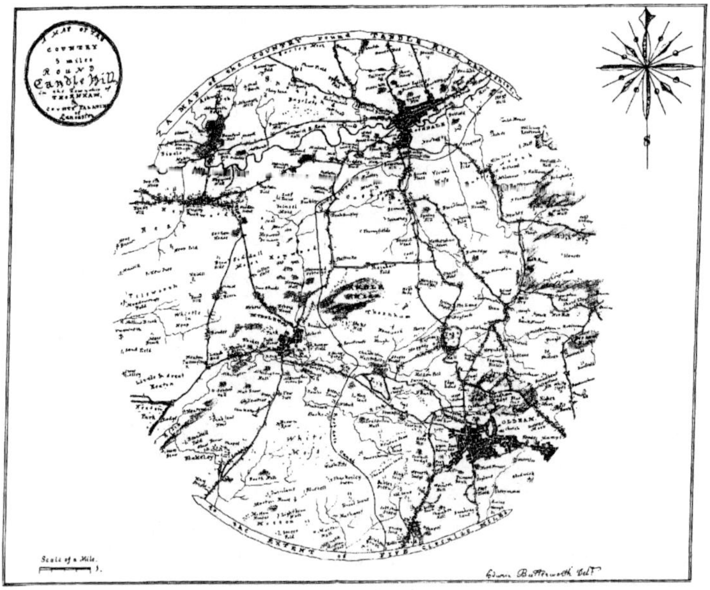

Map 2. 'A map of the country five miles round Tandle Hill', by Edwin Butterworth, *c.*1824. Source: Oldham Local Studies and Archives.

elsewhere. They included the assertion, in terminology reminiscent of Paine's *Agrarian Justice* and the political economy of John Thelwall: 'that nothing is produced without labour, however taxes are laid in the first instance, they ultimately fall upon the labouring poor'. They demanded 'nothing less than an immediate peace, a thorough reform in the representative system and a reduction of the national debt'. The Taylors were probably the originators of this rhetoric. The petition suggested the lasting effect of the economic depression of 1795 and 1799–1801 in sustaining thoughts of social welfare among the local populace. Paineite radicals took this connection one step further by linking it with reform. Handbills fixed to the trees attempted to conceptualize and politicize the distress by demanding 'An equal Representation of all the People of England by universal suffrage', 'a Reduction of the National Debt', and 'a lowering of [the prices of] Provisions of All Sorts'.[72] Despite the republicanism of the Taylors, the idea of 'thorough' reform at this point did not explicitly include an extension of the franchise and perhaps the

[72] NA, HO 42/61/459, Fletcher to Portland, 6 April 1801.

petition was written in a general way to appear constitutionalist enough to the magistrates as well as to parliament whom they were petitioning.

The resurgence of the peace reform movement in the later 1800s seems also to have been promoted by the Taylors in the Royton-Oldham area. Former spy turned magistrate William Chippindale gave an account of the peace meeting on Oldham Edge on Christmas Day 1807, in which the Taylors were identified as the leading radicals. According to his report, the speaker was 'attended by several of the family of the Taylors, whom I have mentioned to you under the name of O'Calebs, viz Jo' O'Calebs, Caleb O'Calebs and many more'.[73] Caleb Taylor had been an United Englishman suspect in 1801, and in 1802, Colonel Fletcher reported that William Cheetham had been sent as a delegate to London to procure instructions 'of which they have been in want since Taylor of Royton died'.[74] The report by Chippindale was perhaps unreliable, as it came from an 'informant' who was convinced that the meeting was called to create discontent, 'which they think favourable to the ultimate attainment of their revolutionary designs'.[75] There are sufficient references in magistrates' letters to the Taylors of Royton, on the other hand, to imply that they continued to play a significant role in maintaining radicalism in the village and its neighbourhood. J. E. Cookson points out that the inhabitants of Royton were the first to declare in favour of petitioning the House of Commons in 1807 and their petition was the most offensive to the government, alleging that the ministry was committed to 'perpetual war'. Their legacy continued to be felt through the post-war radical movement: the first Hampden club in Lancashire was formed in Royton in August 1816.[76]

The Wilsons of Manchester were another family who kept the radical tradition alive within a community context. They originated from Edinburgh, settling in Manchester in the late eighteenth century. Charles Wilson became a handloom weaver in Newton Lane. His son Michael (a furniture broker from 1806) and grandsons Thomas and Alexander became locally infamous for expressing their radical principles in some of the many oral ballads they composed. Michael Wilson commissioned a portrait of himself, which 'he said would leave no mistake as to either

[73] HO 42/91/967, Chippindale to Hawkesbury, 25 December 1807.

[74] HO 42/65/442, Fletcher to Home Office, 3 April 1802; Hone, *For the Cause of Truth*, p. 103.

[75] HO 42/91/967, Chippindale to Hawkesbury, 25 December 1807.

[76] Cookson, *Friends of Peace*, p. 211; J. Dinwiddy, 'Luddism and Politics in the Northern Counties', *SH* 4 (1979), 40.

his religious or political views and opinions'. He was represented with his hand resting on two volumes, one a work labelled 'Democracy' and the other a 'Life of John Wesley', which no doubt would have irked the now staunchly loyalist Methodist hierarchy. The Victorian antiquarian John Harland noted this anecdote about his regular confrontations with Revd Joshua Brookes of the Collegiate Church:

> The Rev Joshua Brookes had a speaking acquaintance with him and sneered much at his politics. Passing the shop door one day, the parson saw Michael sitting at the door reading; and called out—'Well Michael, reading Tom Paine I suppose'. The ready reply was 'Well I might read a worse book, Mr Brookes'.[77]

One example of their radical material was the 'best song in Mr Wilson's estimation that he ever wrote', entitled 'An Ode to Freedom'. No record remains except the first line: 'Great goddess of Freedom, appear to thy sons'. Harland also noted an incident recounted by Michael's son Alexander about his brother Samuel. Samuel composed a ballad shortly after the mass meeting of striking handloom weavers at St George's Fields in Manchester in April 1808:

> It was in the year one thousand eight hundred and eight,
> A lot of bold weavers stood in a line straight
> Then coom th'barrack sogers [soldiers] o in a splutter,
> And knock'd the poor weavers right into the gutter.[78]

Radical tenets and knowledge were thus transmitted through oral ballads, but Wilson's song, like many others, was not printed. Printers were obviously reluctant to publish radical ballads and there were almost certainly fewer radical writers than loyalist and patriotic propagandists. Radical ballads sold less well and perhaps were therefore better suited to oral transmission. Some intriguing printed examples survive and hint at a larger circulation for such material than historians can quantify. *A Political Garland*, printed in Preston in the late 1790s, included pro-French anti-war ballads and a 'Song for the Thinking Club' of Manchester. This castigated ministers as 'ye detestable foes to mankind' whose legislation had forced radicals to meet in silence.[79] The radical verses of Samuel Bamford's father were recorded only in his son's *Early Days*; for example, his 'God help the Poor' of 1792. Some of the songs of the Wilsons seemingly only survived because of the antiquarian efforts of Harland. He claimed that he was publishing much of their work for the

[77] J. Harland (ed.), *The Songs of the Wilsons* (Manchester, 1865), pp. 3–4, 25.
[78] *Ibid.*, pp. 6, 14–15. [79] *A Political Garland* (Preston, n.d.).

first time. There may have been many other radical poets in Lancashire like the Wilsons whose work has been lost or never recorded. The ballads may just have been treated as curiosities by the ordinary populace but, on the other hand, though people were publicly unreactive to the sentiments expressed, the ballads may have struck a chord privately. Though in the minority, such ballads indicate how radicalism just as much as conservatism could be part of popular culture, and that there was an oral tradition which enabled radicalism to sustain itself in local communities. They also suggest the richness of radical culture which did not just express itself in conflicts with loyalist authorities.

The 'Friends of Peace' and 'Romantic' Radicalism

Such radical circles as the Taylors' and Wilsons', though influential within their own communities, did not stretch out across the region. One group which had the potential to form a wider network were the radical-thinking among Dissenters, particularly the proscribed Unitarians. The Church-and-King attacks on Presbyterians and other groups in the 1790s however had dealt a major blow. Thomas Walker, in his account of his trial in 1794, reflected bitterly on the failures of the English reform movement and pointed to the timidity of the Dissenters:

> They have, as a body, constantly fallen short of their own principles; they have excited opposition which they have never compleatly supported; and through fear, or some other motive, they have been so strongly the advocates of an overstrained moderation, that they have been rather the enemies than the friends of those who have ventured the most for the rights of the people.[80]

Expressing the spleen of a dedicated activist, Walker was sorely disappointed at the Rational Dissenters' failure to live up to the example of Priestley. Walker's criticism had force for Rational Dissenters as a whole after 1800 and their conduct is understandable in a Mancunian context, as repression and fear had driven the Unitarians behind the safety of the elite Cross Street Chapel doors. Vocal radicalism did not surface in towns such as Preston and Blackburn, at least not after the 1790s. In both towns, there were few prominent bourgeois intellectuals amongst local Unitarians, who were largely made up of artisans, tradesmen, and shopkeepers. The radical intellectuals who had been involved in the

[80] Cited in J. Seed, 'A Set of Men Powerful in Many Things', in K. Haakonssen, (ed.), *Enlightenment and Religion: Rational Dissent in Eighteenth Century Britain* (Cambridge, 1996), p. 167.

Warrington Academy mainly dissipated to Manchester and Liverpool after its closure in 1786 or remained quiet. Other old Warringtonians died before radicalism revived: for example, the physician Thomas Percival died in 1804 and George Walker, president of the Lit and Phil, died in London in 1807.[81]

The level of radical activity in large manufacturing towns in the 1800s correlated better with the presence of wealthy bourgeois than with that of lower middle-class Rational Dissenters. Yet Walker neglected to look across Chat Moss to Rational Dissenters in Liverpool. Dr James Currie (1756–1805) was part of the 'small circle of literary friends', whom he believed were 'remarkable for a prompt discussion and open declaration of their opinions on public questions'.[82] The Liverpool 'Friends of Peace' were important but unusual because of their acute self-awareness of their own identity and principles. The other prominent members included: the American merchant William Rathbone (1757–1809); the banker and intellectual William Roscoe (1753–1831); Unitarian ministers James Yates (1755–1826) and William Shepherd; printer and poet Edward Rushton; and the Spanish poet Joseph Blanco White (1775–1841). Families associated with this intellectual circle gathered at the Presbyterian and Unitarian chapels of the port, especially Benn's Garden and Gateacre, where Revd William Shepherd preached from 1791 to 1847.[83] They appear to have been much more cohesive than other groups of radicals, regularly discussing their ideals in correspondence though rarely disagreeing with each other. They had much wider connections across the region and country than other radicals, while retaining a distinctive Liverpool identity within the larger intellectual and Unitarian community.[84]

The Rational Dissenters of Bolton also appear to have been more active than their co-religionists in neighbouring towns. Despite the close watch kept on Bolton inhabitants by Orange magistrates and loyalist manufacturers, a small circle of opposition was sustained by

[81] A. Nicholson and J. Pickstone, 'Thomas Percival (1740–1804)', *Oxford Dictionary of National Bibliography*.

[82] W. W. Currie, *Memoir of the Life, Writings, and Correspondence of James Currie of Liverpool* (1831), vol. 1, p. 500.

[83] A. M. Wilson, 'Culture and Commerce, Liverpool's Merchant Elite, c.1790–1850', Ph.D. thesis (Liverpool, 1996), p. 51; S. Checkland, 'Economic Attitudes in Liverpool, 1793–1807', *Economic History Review*, 2nd ser., 5 (1952), 63.

[84] J. Seed, 'Theologies of Power, Unitarians and the Social Relations of Religious Discourse, 1800–50', in R. J. Morris, ed., *Class, Power and Social Structure in British Nineteenth Century Towns* (Leicester, 1986), pp. 107–56.

the Heywood family and Dr Robert Everleigh Taylor. This circle can be considered part of the Friends of Peace on account of their cross-regional links and their expressions of 'romantic' patriotism. Again, this does not mean that all Rational Dissenters were radical, but it does suggest that Unitarians felt enough of a sense of personal community to support each other and transmit political information through their discussion networks concerned with philosophy and religion. Colonel Ralph Fletcher wrote about their cross-regional links during the peace agitation in February 1808. He identified the Unitarian John Brandreth, 'the ostensible leader of those clamouring for peace', as the brother of Dr Brandreth of Liverpool, 'who is much connected with Roscoe one of the representatives of that borough in the late parliament'.[85] In 1800, Revd William Shepherd visited his friends across the region. He wrote to his wife from Lancaster that he had met Benjamin Heywood, Dr Robert Everleigh Taylor, and John Pilkington's wife at Bolton. After Bolton, Shepherd went to Chorley to see the inventor of the spinning mule, Samuel Crompton, who was receiving treatment from Dr Taylor. He then travelled to Preston, where he 'saw Lloyd for whom Mr. Duckworth had collected 15 guineas in Manchester'.[86] This also indicates that George Duckworth was still radically active in a private capacity in support of George Lloyd, the former MCS member, who had moved to Bath.[87] Shepherd also corresponded with Gilbert Wakefield and cared for his young son during Gilbert's imprisonment.[88] Dr John Aikin of Warrington, writer of *Twenty to Thirty Miles Around Manchester*, was a correspondent of the Liverpool circle throughout 1790s and 1800s, as was George Philips of Manchester.[89] The women of the circle also maintained their own pan-regional links. Mary Rathbone of Liverpool and Hannah Greg of Styal Mill and Manchester wrote regularly to each other, though only occasionally on political matters.[90] Their correspondence appears however to mark the limit of these forthright

85 NA, HO 42/95/5, Fletcher to Home Office, February 1808; see Liverpool RO, Roscoe papers, 920 ROS 423, Brandreth to Roscoe, 5 June 1808; 920 ROS 430, Roscoe to Brandreth, 1810; Lancashire CRO, WCW/1815, will of Joseph Brandreth, testified by John Pilkington of Bolton.

86 Harris Manchester College, Oxford, William Shepherd papers, vol. iv, p. 20, Shepherd to Wakefield, March 1799.

87 *The Admission Register of the Manchester School*, VI, ed. J. F. Smith (Manchester, 1868), pp. 99–100.

88 Harris Manchester College, Oxford, William Shepherd papers, iv, p. 29.

89 Liverpool RO, 920 ROS 15, Aikin to Roscoe, 30 April 1808.

90 Liverpool University Special Collections, RP.II.1.64, H. Greg to M. Rathbone, 31 July 1798.

women's active involvement in radical politics at this time, though no doubt they contributed to promoting 'independent' candidates at election time, as when Roscoe stood for Liverpool in 1806.

The circle kept radical principles alive during the Napoleonic wars, but their radicalism was of the moderate, constitutional if not 'reactionary' kind that shared many elements of patriotism with loyalism. J. E. Cookson and Peter Spence have discussed their position in relation to what Spence has termed the 'romantic radicalism' shared by the Westminster circles around Sir Francis Burdett, Major Cartwright, and William Cobbett in the 1800s. This chapter highlights by contrast their separation, both from other Lancashire radicals, and from Westminster circles and the post-war 'mass platform'. They were inspired by Burdett but remained consciously aloof from him and the 'mob' that followed him. Their conscious defence of their bourgeois intellectualism suggests that like the loyalties of their own class, they had fostered if not inspired 'vulgar reformism' in their writings, but increasingly wished to distance themselves from its consequences.

Despite their sympathies for revolutionary France in the 1790s, the Friends of Peace were not English Jacobins in the 1800s. Cookson applied the epithet 'liberal' to their political views while Spence has termed them reactionary or 'romantic radicals'. The Friends of Peace exhibited three phases of romantic patriotism: a Francophilic pacifism in 1789–98, a state of confusion over Bonaparte combined with hostility to Pitt in 1798–1805, and finally a move to anti-corruption patriotism from 1806. Reactionary or romantic radicalism did not involve new Paineite ideas; it had its roots in a Burkeite or Country Whig emphasis on an organic constitution and state. A central theme was defence of the constitution against corruption. From the 1790s, this coalesced into a vocal opposition to a Pittite 'boroughmongering faction' who had encroached upon the liberties of the press and judiciary and extended the libel and treason laws.[91] Another element of the platform of the Friends of Peace that set them apart from the other radicals was their concern for the plight of Ireland and their active campaign for Catholic Relief. Reform was in essence Whiggish in tone and aim. Roscoe's recommendations on reform in his 1810 pamphlet addressed to Henry Brougham were moderate: a limit on numbers of inferior placemen in the House of Commons, a correction of the corrupt representation

[91] P. Spence, *The Birth of Romantic Radicalism: War, Popular Politics and English Radical Reformism, 1800–1815* (Aldershot, 1996), p. 20.

of Scotland, the elective franchise to English copyholders, and the foundations of borough reform.[92] They had no truck with the universal suffrage and annual parliaments demanded by Paineite radicals.

The Friends of Peace illustrated Stuart Semmel's conjecture that the contradictory nature of Napoleon's position and rule confused both radical and loyalist attitudes towards revolutionary France, and thereby complicated their patriotism.[93] Their Francophile radical optimism continued into the first few years of Napoleonic rule, partly out of a misguided hope that Napoleon would fulfil the original aims of the revolution. Dr James Currie wrote to his lifelong friend Thomas Creevey MP (later member of the radical 'Mountain' faction of the Whig party) on 25 January 1801: 'What an astonishing being is this Corsican! Since the days of Julius Caesar, there has not been such a combination of great gracious talents with great power.'[94] This attitude paralleled William Cowdroy's curious editorial of April 1802, in which he ensured the reader 'we are far indeed from being the panegyrists of Bonaparte', but highlighted the paradoxical contrast he perhaps naively believed was occurring under his rule when he secured the Peace of Amiens: 'The more dishonest we admit the Chief Consul to be in his professions, the more we behold him, in order to secure his situation, compelled to consult the will of the people . . . the more we behold the Triumph of Public Opinion.'[95] The Friends of Peace were also bitterly dissatisfied with the British government and press's attitudes towards France during the negotiations for peace in 1801. Currie for his part believed that 'Buonaparte was not disposed to war' but 'the irritations of the press have had more share in producing war than any other cause'.[96] With the renewal of the war in 1803, their hopes gave way to disillusionment with Napoleon and his autocratic imperialism.

Though ostensibly similar patterns of radical activity occurred in the other towns in Lancashire as in the country as a whole, Liverpool was unusual, as it was in many other aspects of socio-political life. The continuity of personalities among radical activists throughout the period and the more bourgeois (and therefore moderate) form of radicalism which existed in the port was rare elsewhere. Liverpool Constitutional

[92] W. Roscoe, *A Letter to Henry Brougham Esq on the Subject of Reform* (Liverpool, 1811), p. 15.

[93] S. Semmel, *Napoleon and the British* (New Haven, 2004), p. 24.

[94] Liverpool RO, 920 CUR 6, Currie to Creevey, 25 January 1801.

[95] *CMG*, 24 April 1802.

[96] Currie, *Memoir*, vol. 1, p. 362, Currie to Creevey, 21 May 1803.

Society ceased in 1795 but was resurrected as the Friends of Reform society in 1810. The path the Friends of Peace followed contrasted with the transition that occurred in Manchester, where the MCS were superseded by a new generation of radicals who organized the reform petitions and Hampden clubs in Manchester. This contrast reflected the different political outlooks and atmospheres in the two towns. The 1800s saw the Liverpool circle become actively involved in bourgeois economic campaigns against the Orders in Council, the slave trade, and the East India Company monopoly. It is significant that they did not in any way attempt to reignite the vigorous campaign of 1788–91 for the repeal of the Test and Corporation Acts, but vigorously supported Catholic relief in 1806–7. They maintained their prominence within and respect from the ruling local elite and Whig aristocracy while still opposing government. Their involvement in the peace campaign centred on publishing pamphlets and organising petitions, but they managed to maintain their respectability.

Another feature of their stance in the 1800s which distinguished this group from other radical circles was their mistrust of the 'mob' that emerged to support Sir Francis Burdett in Westminster and later supported the 'mass platform'. Disorderly or immoral working classes had no place in their bourgeois view of society (in direct contrast to Joseph Hanson's courting of and campaigning for the weavers over the minimum wage and peace issues in Manchester).[97] Unitarians favoured a patriarchal structure even when most enamoured of the free market. This was exemplified by the case of the Greg family at their factory at Styal, Cheshire, with its paternalistic hierarchy to control the activities of its workers. A desire to separate themselves from the mob influenced the moderate nature of their reform principles. It again suggests that, just as the loyalists' creation of 'vulgar conservatism' began to backfire on them in the 1800s, bourgeois radical activists had engendered a 'vulgar radicalism' among a minority of the working classes from which they would later shy away as the anti-corruption and peace campaigns revived from 1808. Rachel Eckersley has shown how later in the war both Burdett and Major Cartwright attempted to distance themselves from their mass following in Westminster and concentrated rather on parliamentary campaigning.[98]

[97] See Chapter 6.

[98] R. Eckersley, 'Of Radical Design: John Cartwright and the Redesign of the Reform Campaign, c.1800–1811', *History*, 89/296 (2004), 560.

In 1812, Roscoe wrote to Henry Brougham, the Whig-radical MP: 'I consider myself in some degree as a sort of connecting link between the more aristocratic and democratic friends of our cause, and if I were to give way to every popular impulse I should not only act against my own feelings, which revolt at all extremes, but do essential injury to the cause.'[99] His actions were influenced by this self-consciousness about his role and his desire to fulfil it. The bourgeois radicals in Lancashire not only mistrusted the Burdettite 'mob', but also expressed suspicion of Burdett and the other Westminster leaders. They thereby took a stand in opposition to the metropolis and asserted a respectable provincial and civic identity. In November 1806, Roscoe wrote to Lord Holland, who now led the Foxites within the parliamentary Whig party: 'I lament with your Lordship the extremes to which a good and virtuous man like Sir Francis Burdett allows himself to be carried; and fear that a line of demarcation between the firm consistent and temperate friends of liberty and those who allow their feelings on this subject to mislead their judgement, must ere long be drawn.' He argued: 'the rational friends of freedom should rely on their own efforts' rather than being associated with 'crude, inexpedient or injudicious designs'.[100] Roscoe was not merely pandering to Lord Holland; he was himself very much a Foxite Whig, as were his Liverpudlian colleagues, something which again made them somewhat distinct from other radical groups elsewhere. Dr Currie had written to Thomas Creevey in November 1802 about his pity for Charles James Fox's current position: 'to think of a man fit to make England and Europe listen and obey, being asked to lead the drunken mob of Sir Francis Burdett, or to fight election squabbles in a committee'.[101] Provincial Whigs must have been somewhat confused by the political philandering of the leader of the Whig opposition, who from the 1790s had divided his party with his absences from parliament and his resort to popular politics to maintain his influence. This appeal to opinion outside parliament may have seemed promising during the Association movement's campaign for reform during the 1780s, but seemed increasingly tired and dangerous in the new circumstances of 'vulgar reformism'. Reform for the Liverpool circle had little to do with emancipating the working classes. They were proud of their identity as members of an 'independent' middle class, but they did not refuse

[99] R. G. Thorne, *House of Commons, 1790–1820*, v (London, 1986), p. 45.
[100] BL, Additional MS 51650, fo. 92, Roscoe to Holland, 13 November 1806.
[101] Currie, *Memoir*, vol. 2, p. 360.

aristocratic links, and did not feel it their responsibility to push forward the specific needs of the working classes, with whom they had little contact.

J. E. Cookson's 'final analysis' concludes that the actions of the Friends of Peace were 'founded on their opposition to oligarchical society'. Hence their campaign against the war was 'a "symbolic" protest against a ruling class and the social system on which it depended'. Brian Lewis has also argued for a 'building of a bourgeois-radical narrative defined in opposition to an aristocratic state at the national level and to a developing Toryism at the local level'.[102] This may have applied to the Royton radicals and more republican strands such as the UE, although their aims were unclear or were bound up with the Irish issue. The Friends of Peace certainly chose not to put themselves in quite this position. They survived without arrest or even censorship precisely because they had close links with sympathetic elements among the aristocracy and cooperated with Tory–Anglican loyalist elites in civic institutions. Their behaviour and most of their rhetoric would suggest that they supported the existing hierarchy and wished for change only where there was corruption. They clashed with loyalist authorities during 1806–8, but on the whole, reaction to an aristocratic loyalism did not form an element in the making of their brand of radicalism. They and their friends may have resented the Corporation's hold on all the institutions of local government, but this attitude emanated from their inheritance from Rational Dissent, and their desire for freedom of expression rather than from an inherent hatred of the Tory–Anglican hierarchy; it reflected a wish for less state interference in personal religious and political affairs rather than a demand for immediate extension of representation and equality.

Members of the circle as an intellectual group remained respected members of Liverpool polite society. Roscoe's literary merits, as well as his wealth, helped him rise to the highest status. His most noted work was *Lorenzo di Medici*, first published in 1796 to international literary acclaim. Its standing was enhanced locally by the explicit analogies he drew between Venice and contemporary Liverpool, flattering the merchants' wealth and political position while also finding an acceptable and

[102] Cookson, *Friends of Peace*, p. 118; B. Lewis, '"A Republic of Quakers": the Radical Bourgeoisie, the State and Stability in Lancashire, 1789–1851', in A. Kidd and D. Nicholls (eds.), *The Making of the British Middle Class? Studies of Regional and Cultural Diversity Since the Eighteenth Century* (Stroud, 1998), p. 86.

indeed conventional way of explaining the potential of republicanism.[103] In January 1802, the freedom of the town was unanimously conferred on Dr Currie by the Corporation in acknowledgement of 'his very great attention, skills and abilities' as one of the physicians to the Infirmary.[104] Roscoe and Rathbone were especially prominent in helping establish many of the plethora of civic and intellectual institutions which were set up at this time of growing urban pride and wealth. Roscoe corresponded regularly with Lord Derby, the Duke of Gloucester, and Lord Holland, who patronized him in both his literary and political endeavours. This was reflective of how he could fit, when he wanted to, into Whig loyalism. Lord Derby wrote in February 1808 commending Roscoe's pamphlet calling for peace: 'the sentiments of which I heartily agree. I see nothing in the continuance of the war but misery and ultimate ruin.'[105] Despite becoming disillusioned with the Whigs after the Ministry of All the Talents, they maintained close relations with the 'Mountain' radicals among the Whig opposition. Thomas Creevey played the role of their faithful eyes and ears in the Commons, corresponding and meeting regularly with Currie, Roscoe, and Rathbone.[106] They involved themselves personally with the Whigs in campaigns against the Orders in Council and EIC monopoly. Cookson's anti-oligarchic characterization fits uneasily with the society in which Roscoe, Rathbone, and Currie mixed, particularly considering the contact and standing they had in civic institutions and the aristocracy.

The different radical groups of the UE, the Friends of Peace, the Manchester radicals, and other activists hardly constituted a united movement. Their aims stretched from achieving moderate parliamentary reform to revolution, their methods of achieving these aims and their internal organization differed wildly, and it is unlikely that their attempts to communicate with each other were fruitful or long-lasting. Nor did they form a 'radical underground' that carried the message of Paine over to the revival of popular radicalism at the end of the war. Their lasting significance was rather that they showed that loyalism did

103 Wilson, 'Culture and Commerce', pp. 77–8; W. Roscoe, *The Life of Lorenzo di Medici* (London, 1796).

104 Currie, *Memoir*, vol. 1, p. 343.

105 Liverpool RO, 920 ROS 1192, Derby to Roscoe, 9 February 1808.

106 Liverpool RO, 920 ROS 3060, Rathbone to Roscoe, 22 April 1807; 920 ROS 3061, Rathbone to Roscoe, 29 February 1808; BL, Additional MS 51650, f. 106, Roscoe to Holland, 1 February 1808; *Thomas Creevey's Papers, 1793–1838*, ed. J. Gore (Harmondsworth, 1948), pp. 8–11, 102–4.

not achieve total hegemony over popular politics during the French and Napoleonic wars. The response to the actions of the government in prosecuting both radicals and the war was not homogeneous. There were always opportunities for dissent, though in the period 1798–1806 only certain individuals translated this dissent into political activism, rather than into food rioting or trade union combination.

POPULAR RADICALISM

Committed radicals of all stamps were in the minority in Lancashire. The political culture in localities was essentially conservative. Radicalism survived within a sphere of reaction. E. P. Thompson acknowledged that the culture of Pennine handloom weaving villages was not inherently politically radical but embodied 'a unique blend of social conservatism, local pride and cultural attainment'. He presented the populace as clinging tenaciously to dialect, regional customs, and superstitions.[107] William Cowdroy recognized this essential reluctance by the majority of the population to become involved in disruptive activity. He complained in January 1800: 'A national torpor appears to pervade the great mass of subjects in this kingdom; otherwise petitions in favour of peace would immediately be sent from every part of the country.'[108] The peace issue was muted in 1801 as the general population quietly recovered from the atmosphere of loyalist suspicion that had reigned from 1795. The resonances from the repression by local and national government still dampened proclivities to act publicly in less staunchly radical areas. Robert Walker's main criticism of magistrates in *Plebeian Politics* was that they were over-zealous in their hunt for 'Jacobins', and had expanded the meaning of Jacobin to encompass anybody who opposed them, whether they had radical principles or not. This message was directed to a local audience as well as referring to the national situation. 'Whistlepig' recounted a tale of 'Warhawks' watching a 'Jacobin' risking his own life in rescuing the workers of a flooded cotton factory in Stockport on 17 August 1799. The loyalists Walker termed the 'rack of fools' responded to his courage with the ironic comment: 'it wur a theawsunt pittys ot sitch a mon wur a jakobin'. ['it was a thousand pities that such a man was a Jacobin'.] It is possible that this was based on

[107] E. P. Thompson, *The Making of the English Working Class* (Harmondsworth, 1968), p. 322.
[108] *CMG*, 11 January 1800.

a genuine incident with some exaggeration. Walker wished to portray real Church-and-King loyalist individuals in the hamlets of Cutler Hill and Wood Houses near Failsworth, with their prejudices against 'Jacobins' expressed in petty acts of hostility.[109] The local loyalists were well known to their immediate neighbours, as were those they berated as 'Jacobins', though beyond the local area they were anonymous. Nevertheless, Walker's stock characters would have been recognizable in the south-east Pennine towns and their neighbourhoods.

This conservatism did not preclude more heterogeneous expressions of radicalism at times of distress. Local populations opposed government intervention in their own affairs as much as innovation. They could, without internal inconsistency, be ensconced within the safer bounds of loyalism during more challenging times or revert to more radical tenets when activists roused campaigns that appealed to either their economic self-interest or their suspicions of compulsion by their social betters. Popular radicalism was often less a product of distinct or positive principles and more a matter of opposition to restrictions on the freedom of speech and assembly by government and local authorities. The suspension of habeas corpus expired in 1801. This provided a short opening for mass meetings to be held for the first time since 1795. The first major peace meeting in Lancashire was held on 5 April 1801 at Tandle Hill near Royton. Colonel Fletcher claimed that the meeting attracted 'upwards of two thousand persons at one time and the different persons who visited the ground during the course of the day might possibly be fourteen thousand'. Inhabitants of Oldham, Rochdale, Chadderton, Middleton, and their surrounds attended the meeting. Although crowd estimates were always inaccurate, Fletcher was unlikely to have wildly exaggerated the numbers to the Home Office as he sought to maintain his credibility as a magistrate. If his report can be trusted, then the attendance is testimony to a popular interest in moderate radicalism and peace resulting from a combination of factors: the state of economic distress felt during the winter of 1800–1, the reaction to the apparently unsympathetic attitude of manufacturers after the passing of the Combination Acts, war-weariness, and a general dissatisfaction that could not be explained solely in political terms.[110] Of course, not all the participants in the demonstration would have gone away convinced that the semi-Paineite, semi-constitutionalist demands would solve their

[109] Walker, *Plebeian Politics*, 18, 34–5.
[110] NA, HO 42/61/459, Fletcher to Portland, 6 April 1801.

problems, but the event cannot be dismissed as an aberration from a context of solid popular loyalism or as having had no effect upon the population. The magistrates became increasingly anxious about the size and scope of subsequent meetings. Revd Robert Hay estimated that over 5,000 attended the radical meeting at Buckton Castle on 3 May 1801, but 'we had no precise information of the object of the meeting'.[111] The large meetings ceased soon after the arrests at Rivington Pike in late May 1801, and Fletcher commented on the effects of the loyalist reaction:

These commitments of the seditious have considerably diseased the spirits of the disaffected in this neighbourhood and restrained their intemperate language and have encouraged several loyal masters who employ great numbers of servants in different branches of the cotton manufacture to examine into the political opinions of their workmen and discharge such as are known to be Jacobins from their employ.[112]

Throughout the Napoleonic wars, figures of local authority, primarily magistrates and clergy, were, more than manufacturers, the targets for attack in food riots, political gatherings, and Luddite agitation. This was only in part an obvious reaction on the part of an angry crowd when first approached by the face of authority. Most crowds were assembled for a purpose, either planned in advance or directed by activists, so attacks on justices were not merely unfortunate irrational expressions of overheated passions.[113] The food riots of the winter of 1799–1800 demonstrated certain aspects of this popular hostility. The Captain of the Ashton-under-Lyne Volunteers was defending a warehouse during a food riot on 3 February 1800, when 'the rioters laid hold of him and Mr Popit the Clergyman at Ashton and carried them away some yards'. The Captain also alleged that when magistrate Revd William Hay arrived, a member of the crowd shouted: ' "Now Lads this is the time Stone that devil to death", meaning Mr Hay.'[114] It is an interesting testimony to the crowd knowing its own limits in that no magistrates were actually murdered in this period, though their property was attacked without reserve. Workers in trade combinations similarly knew exactly whom to target: during the handloom weavers' strikes of 1808 in Rochdale,

111 NA, HO 42/62/11, Hay to Portland, 4 May 1801, HO 42/62/66, Hay to Portland, 13 May 1801.

112 NA, HO 42/62/145, Fletcher to Portland, 6 June 1801.

113 G. Rudé, *The Crowd in History, 1730–1848: a Study of Popular Disturbances in France and England*, rev. edn (London, 1995), p. 207.

114 NA, PL 27/7, examination of John Smith, 4 July 1800.

protestors 'collected opposite to where the Magistrates were assembled transacting public business', on the top of Yorkshire Street. The strikers then rioted outside the prison, eventually burning it down to release their fellow weavers imprisoned inside.[115] As part of an established ritual in protest, this had less to do with political radicalism and more to do with 'shared understandings' of common values.[116]

E. P. Thompson and later historians of popular protest concluded that the targeting of magistrates and clergy marked recognition of the destruction of the 'moral economy' of the eighteenth century and a politicization of the working classes. In short, social relations within local communities in the eighteenth century had been run along lines of reciprocity, in which there was an element of bargaining between the wishes of the crowd and magistrates or other authorities prepared to treat genuine grievances leniently.[117] Craig Calhoun and John Bohstedt linked the nature of protest to varying patterns of authority within territorial communities. They argued that propensity to disorder and radicalism increased with urbanization and industrialization, which destroyed cross-class community and therefore the bases of consensual authority. In this period, a middle ground was created in industrial villages and in small town and urban communities thronged by artisans and outworkers, where 'resident authority was weak but a sense of working-class autonomy was strong, enabling a greater degree of concerted collective action'.[118] It was among these communities that Thompson located the 'making of the English working class' and there that radicalism and other protests flourished. The social justice and egalitarian message of part II of Paine's *Rights of Man*, together with the massive economic and social disruptions caused by the French war and industrialization, apparently broke down this mutual understanding about the responsibilities of both parties. Hence magistrates, clergy, and landowners naturally became the targets of attack. From 1795, the cultural hegemony that Thompson believed to reside in the theatre of power of the assizes and quarter sessions and the 'equilibrium between

115 NA, PL 27/8, part 2, 'confession of John Shepherd', 20 June 1808; see Chapter 5.

116 C. Tilly, *Popular Contention in Great Britain, 1758–1834* (Cambridge Mass., 1995), pp. 46–7.

117 E. P. Thompson, 'The Moral Economy of the English Crowd in the 18th Century', *P & P* 50 (1971), 76–136; A. Booth, 'Food Riots in the North West of England, 1790–1801', *P & P* 77 (1977), 84–107.

118 C. Calhoun, 'Community, Class and Collective Action: Popular Protest in Industrialising England and the Theory of Working-Class Radicalism', D.Phil. thesis (Oxford, 1979), p. 102.

paternalist authority and the crowd' was subverted by the growth of this sense of independence. The 'great and undeferential popular agitations at the end of the French Wars' were therefore the product of an inherent independence among artisans newly freed from the cultural and ideological paternalism of the gentry class.[119]

Magistrates certainly felt that they were isolated targets. In March 1801, Thomas Ainsworth, JP of Bolton, described the reaction of the inhabitants of Bury to the arrest of seven people for stealing meal from a cart on its way to market in order to sell it at what they felt was a fair price. At Bury, 'the whole town was up' and Ainsworth believed 'the Prisoners seemed to meet with none but friends'. He intimated that this marked the end of the moral economy in so far as that entailed popular restraint in typically exaggerated but fearful language: 'I am sorry to say that what I have seen and heard today convinces me that the country is ripe for rebellion and in a most dangerous situation and I firmly believe that if provisions continue at the present high prices, a Revolution will be the consequence.'[120] An infamous handbill was pasted on New Bridge Tollgate in Manchester in November 1800, which associated magistrates and constables with national radical enemies:

> No peace, No King,
> To kill Billy Pitt it is no sin
> Likewise Justice Bayley and all his kin
> No forgetting Farrington, Leaf and Milnes,
> When they are hung we will have our fills
> Also Lloyd and Topping too.
> We will have a big loaf for a shilling
> Or else the Justices we will be killing.[121]

Republican rhetoric is evident in this, together with more traditional tropes of 'a big loaf'. Hostility to both Pitt and local magistrates reflected the connections made between local and national politics. Of course this was probably the work of an isolated individual, but it is important nonetheless that these connections were made.

Though the moral economy was disrupted in this period of intense scarcity and distress, it was not totally destroyed. Various methods and

119 E. P. Thompson, *Customs in Common* (London, 1991), p. 86; P. King, 'Edward Thompson's Contribution to Eighteenth Century Studies: the Patrician-Plebeian Model Re-Examined', *SH* 21 (1996), 222.

120 NA, HO 42/61/216, Ainsworth to HO, March 1801.

121 NA, HO 42/53, handbill enclosed in Bayley to Home Office, 30 November 1800.

tropes of popular political bargaining drew from a rich and continuous tradition. Ordinary inhabitants still had recourse to this tradition and used whatever was appropriate, just as the radical language was utilized from an extensive lexicon, depending upon circumstances. Food riots after 1800 were not replaced by, or as Alan Booth has contended, forced to merge with, more 'political' means of protest such as machine-breaking or petitioning. They continued in parallel, with their own specific objectives usually divorced from radicalism, although they became much less widespread by the 1820s.[122] Eighteenth-century protest moreover had always had a link with the national political sphere with its shared belief in the 'constitutional right' of addressing the king and parliament through a trusted intermediary. This very much remained the case throughout the eighteenth and nineteenth centuries, with the right interpreted in particular ways according to local disputes and grievances.

Nor can levels of popular disorder be linked deterministically to the social structure of urban areas. As Andrew Charlesworth has argued, this assumption underestimates the continued social mixing and lack of segregation and makes too sharp a distinction between artisanal and factory workers, particularly in Manchester.[123] Urban workers kept in regular contact with their semi-rural 'neighbourhoods' though travel. The reminiscences of Samuel Bamford illustrate how migrants, and thus many among the working classes, felt part of both urban and rural life. They contradict any notion of rural workers becoming 'proletarianized' or isolated from their background when they moved to a town in search of industrial employment. Workers living in cities and large towns maintained a strong connection with the countryside through rambles, bearing home, and helping with the hay harvest. While Bamford was employed at a printing warehouse on Peel Street in Manchester, he rambled through Hopwood and Middleton, as far as the 'wood-crowned Tandles'. He became a weaver in Middleton again in 1802 which gave him even more time to ramble and 'partake in country amusements with the other young fellows of the neighbourhood and frequently went out hunting'.[124] Nor were many of the growing Lancashire weaving and bleaching villages wholly devoid of paternalistic authority; feasts, charity schools, and soup shops supported by local landowners and lords of

[122] Booth, 'Food Riots in the North-West of England', 84–107.

[123] A. Charlesworth, 'From the Moral Economy of Devon to the Political Economy of Manchester, 1790–1812', *SH* 18 (1993), 205–17.

[124] Bamford, *Early Days*, pp. 276, 326.

the manor were still a feature of the lives of the general population in many areas throughout the Napoleonic wars, even if these were often a result of desperation and a desire to preserve order on the part of their supporters.[125]

The actions of crowds in food riots and other disturbances rather demonstrated their astute reaction to a situation where national orders and edicts were channelled through the magistrates. The Two Acts and Combination Acts were often experienced in their local context as being carried into effect by magistrates, in an atmosphere of repression heightened by the use of local spies paid by the government. Some of the towns and villages where magistrates were overtly 'active' were the very towns where radicalism or collective activity persisted because their inhabitants reacted against the magistrates, as has been seen in and around Bolton, Oldham, and Stockport.

E. P. Thompson's portrayal of the tensions within local societies remains true for some patterns of agitation in Lancashire. The region was composed of a patchwork of levels of authority, and some areas were particularly radically active because magisterial supervision was weak and jurisdictional boundaries were ambiguous. One part of the region most closely fitted these criteria: the area around the river Tame, including the towns of Ashton-under-Lyne, Mottram-in-Longdendale, and Stalybridge, and their neighbourhoods of hamlets, housing work-forces for the water-powered mills in the Pennines stretching down to Stockport and across to Huddersfield. Now known as Tameside, this district exhibited the most active popular politics in the region during the French and Napoleonic wars: UE, other forms of radical groups and meetings, peace meetings, combinations, strikes, and later Luddism and Hampden clubs.

'Tameside' was a highly unusual area within the Lancashire region as a result of various factors. Though these features in themselves did not determine the multifarious nature of protest in the area, the combination of all must have contributed to making popular unrest more likely there. Firstly, the population increased rapidly around the cotton spinning mills. Stalybridge was in essence a new town created in under twenty years. Though this did not mean that it had no sense of 'community', it did mean that new bonds and connections were being made by the immigrant inhabitants more quickly than elsewhere. Secondly, landownership was fragmented. The main landowner, the

125 See JRLUM, EGR 4/1, papers of 5th Earl of Stamford and Warrington.

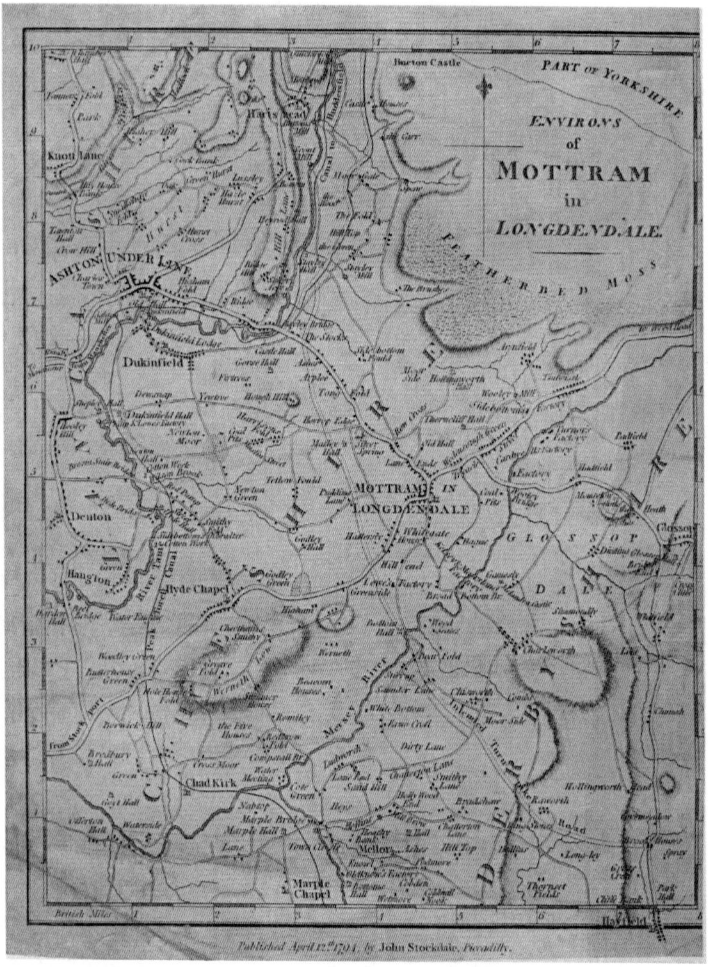

Map 3. 'Mottram-in-Longdendale', in J. Aikin, *A Description of the Country from Thirty to Forty Miles Around Manchester* (Manchester, 1794).

fifth Earl of Stamford (1737–1819), kept a close eye on building in Ashton-under-Lyne and the more rural parts of his demesnes, but in the new towns and villages, his hold slipped as manufacturers scrambled to buy up favourable plots along the river. Thirdly, its unique situation on the Pennine borders of Lancashire, Cheshire, Derbyshire, and the West Riding made jurisdiction ambiguous. Finally, it had religious peculiarities, indicating the role of industrialization, radicalism, and religion in binding together this unique local community.

No other area in Britain converted to the Methodist New Connexion (MNC) so wholeheartedly following Alexander Kilham's expulsion from the Wesleyan connexion in 1796. Kilham's supporters were regarded by Wesleyans as 'Tom Paine' Methodists who wished to break from both the Established Church and government, by supporting freedom of religious practice in 'lovefeasts', cottage meetings, and female preaching. Hence many were radicals, unlike 'Old Plan' Church Methodists and 'New Plan' Methodists, who supported a split with the Established Church but were suspicious of religious and political radicalism.[126] In August 1797, the majority of the Ashton-under-Lyne Methodist society, including almost all the leaders and trustees, agreed to join Kilham's New Connexion. The societies of the industrial villages of Red Hall, Mossley, and Mottram, and the townships of Stalybridge and Newton severed their links with the Wesleyans en bloc. The split revealed perhaps less about their radical political leanings and more about their community identity. It was exemplified by the successful resistance of the Kilhamite trustees of Mossley, Ashton, and Red Hall against outside Wesleyan attempts to regain physical and legal control over the chapels in 1810 and again in 1814.[127] Throughout the whole Methodist Connexion, only fifteen chapels seceded to the New Connexion and three of these were in Ashton parish. A receptive environment was created by the absence of the rector nominated by (and third son of) the Earl of Stamford and Warrington, and by the rapidly growing population and industry largely free from the Earl's control outside Ashton. Only in Huddersfield was there a comparable intensity of Kilhamite strength. This concentration also illustrates the cross-Pennine currents running between Huddersfield and Stalybridge (and the West Riding town can be regarded as integrally connected with the Tameside area, not least by the Ashton–Huddersfield Canal, opened in 1797). By 1812, the Ashton MNC circuit consisted of Ashton, Mossley, Failsworth, Mottram, Stalybridge, Red Hall, Middleton, and Oldham, with fourteen chapels and over 800 members.[128]

126 P. Stigant, 'Wesleyan Methodism and Working-Class Radicalism in the North, 1792–1821', *NH* 6 (1971), 103–4.

127 E. A. Rose, *The Story of Mossley Methodism* (Ashton, 1969), p. 12; JRLUM, Kilham papers (uncatalogued).

128 E. A. Rose, *The Story of Methodism in Ashton-under-Lyne* (Ashton, 1967), pp. 39–40; JRLUM, MA 9731, Minutes of conversations between travelling preachers and delegates from the People, 1797–1812.

Magistrates in the south-east of the region had precarious control over inhabitants' awareness of the non-urban environment and Tameside posed particular problems. Revd William Hay had previously mistaken turf-stacks on Ashton Moss for United Englishmen when attempting to disrupt a night meeting in 1801, as parodied in Robert Walker's *Plebeian Politics*.[129] Captain Hadfield lamented during the Luddite disturbances: 'There is only one magistrate within a distance of twenty miles and he is twelve miles from us and in another County.'[130] It appeared relatively easy to evade arrest by slipping over the border. In 1812, Ashton Moss and the surrounding moorland areas were the scene of nightly Luddite meetings. The roads and turnpikes over Hartshead, and by Mossley and Lees which connected the parish of Ashton with Yorkshire and Cheshire, were allegedly patrolled by bands of Luddites. Captain Raines recalled that one of his companies headed to Wednescough Green, often called 'Mottram Moor', where several Luddite drillings took place.[131] Revd Hay reported the difficulties the magistrates and cavalry had in responding to crowds' use of their environment. He wrote about the Buckton Castle meeting: 'I think it was nearly two hours before we succeeded in clearing the Hills immediately round and the people were no sooner driven from one than they took station on another hill and seemed to hold us at defiance.' Magistrates may have exaggerated the problems of counteracting moorland meetings because they were outside their sphere of knowledge or authority. The attendees were certainly acutely familiar with their surroundings and knew how to use them against the magistrates, who were either apparently less topographically aware or simply overwhelmed by the numbers. All Hay could do was 'to order three or four shots to be fired after different people with a view to prevent them from getting from one Hill to another'.[132] In part, this pattern of action was a deliberate attempt to evade the serious prospect of arrest.

Another less tangible reason for the preponderance of disturbances in the Tame area was the protection offered by the landscape. The Pennine villages and towns provided a psychological environment welcoming to protestors and strikers as well as a physical one allowing control and secrecy. The radical meeting atop Buckton Castle Hill on 3 May 1801

[129] Walker, *Plebeian Politics*, pp. 46–7.
[130] NA, HO 42/122/546, Hadfield to Beckett, 24 April 1812.
[131] W. Bowman, *England in Ashton-under-Lyne* (Ashton-under-Lyne, 1960), pp. 437–8.
[132] NA, HO 42/62/11, Hay to Portland, 4 May 1801.

exemplifies the use of a selectively chosen location which straddled local boundaries and was thus crucially jurisdictionally ambiguous. Rochdale magistrate John Entwisle described the place as 'a situation very high and where the counties of Lancaster, York, Chester, and Derby nearly meets [sic]'.[133] Attendees reflected in the very act of gathering a wider regional identity that did not heed administrative boundaries; the magistrates 'found at Buckton Castle people from Manchester which is a distance of twelve miles and from Stockport which is nine'.[134] These were most likely well-informed radicals, but the neighbouring semi-rural Pennine villages were not neglected: the magistrates heard a horn for two hours in different parts of Saddleworth, allegedly 'sounded for the purpose of calling the people together'. The location of the meeting had been moved to Buckton Castle Hill because the Volunteers had already been raised to guard Tandle Hill.[135]

Radicalism in Lancashire during the Napoleonic wars was a tense composite of various strands of political thought, built around disparate connections of individuals and embodying a variety of attitudes towards the role of working classes within the political nation. Its activity was however less circumscribed by these divisions than by the continued surveillance of the Church-and-King local elites. The ordinary population, usually acquiescent to loyalism, could be roused at times of distress to protest or engage in the 'moral economy'. Radical activists were disparate, silent, or hidden in their own communities, and focused their energies on less controversial campaigns or speaking out intermittently when the atmosphere of suspicion lightened. The range of radical opinions and rhetorical strategies was wide and often diffuse or conflicting, but all had in common a committed political opposition to Church-and-King loyalism locally and nationally. A sense of local identity and provincial independence also infused their actions on and off the political platform. Although amounting to no more than lone voices in the 1800s, their opposition to parliamentary corruption, loyalist repression and the war effort provided a solid basis for renewed popular agitation for reform from 1808.

133 HO 42/62/15, Entwisle to Portland, 11 May 1801.
134 HO 42/62/11, Hay to Portland, 4 May 1801.
135 HO 42/62/7, Gore to Portland, 3 May 1801.

5

Trade Unions and Combinations

All classes ostensibly shared in patriotic unanimity and the silencing of radicalism in the face of the Napoleonic invasion threats. Or at least this was the rosy picture envisaged in patriotic propaganda and by the paternalistic dinners given by employers to their workers at the celebrations of the peace of Amiens and the victory of Trafalgar. The reality of course was different. This period saw intensified activity among many trades and an increasing division between 'master' and 'servant'. Disputes between employers and trade combinations had occurred throughout the eighteenth century, but new political and economic circumstances placed collective action in a new light. Patriotism alone could not hide the heightened conflict around trade unions caused by the Combination Acts of 1799 and 1800. The acts were a landmark in trade union history in that they proscribed combinations but conversely encouraged resistance and more complex organization among workers until their repeal in 1824. This chapter charts some of the flashpoints between manufacturers and workers in Lancashire, including the major strikes of handloom weavers and cotton spinners during the Napoleonic wars.

EARLY TRADE COMBINATIONS

The founders of trade union history, the Webbs and the Hammonds, believed that 'genuine' trade unions could only have existed once the Victorian era of national, formal, and regular organization was established.[1] Historians have long since rejected this distinction. Combinations, trade

[1] S. and B. Webb, *The History of Trade Unionism*, rev. edn (1902); B. and J. L. Hammond, *The Town Labourer, 1760–1832* (London, 1917).

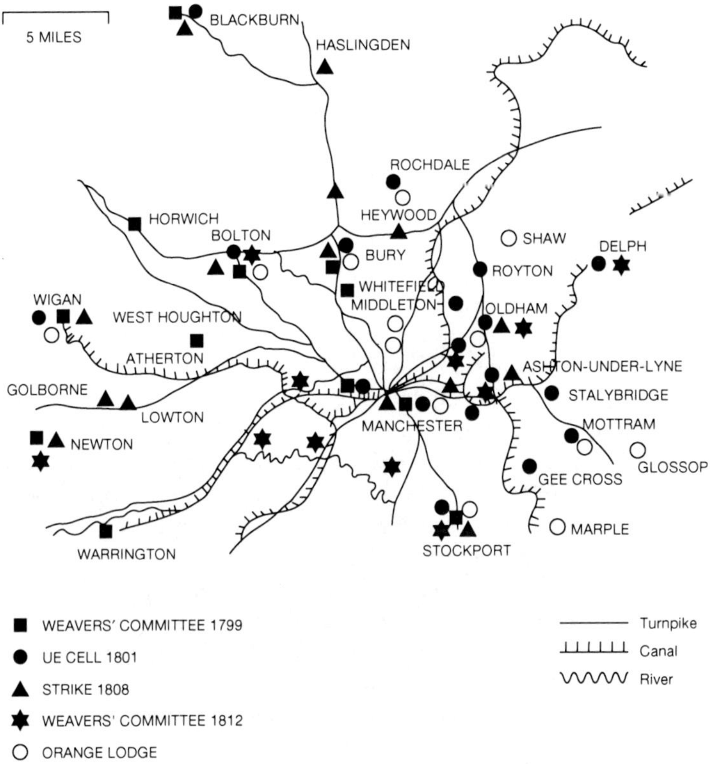

Map 4. South Lancashire agitation and Orange lodges, 1798–1815.

shops, and other forms of working-class collective action were part of a large and effective unionized repertoire well before the great general strikes of 1829 or 1842. Most trades had some sort of shop system, to be called into action as circumstances required, and negotiations and strikes had been a feature of working life throughout the eighteenth century. The ordinary working population often differed from the small number of skilled activists who held committees for negotiating with their employers, but most workers had the opportunity to become involved in some form of collective action, especially demonstrations and riots that often accompanied or merged into trade union activity.[2]

[2] J. Rule, *British Trade Unionism, 1750–1850: the Formative Years* (Essex, 1988).

Textile workers and colliers, amongst others, appropriated two forms of shared identity from the more skilled artisans and trades that were traditionally organized in guilds: firstly, identity linked to their specific locality (usually the town and 'neighbourhood') and secondly, to exclusion based on skill.[3] Most male workers positively related to what Malcolm Chase and John Orth have identified as the language employed by combinations, a long-established rhetoric of legal rights and protection of their economic interests and working conditions.[4] This translated itself into the banners, rules and regulations, organization during strikes, and restrictions upon and discrimination against the number of apprentices, day labourers, and women that journeymen would allow to be employed alongside them. These attachments were powerfully combined where certain trades were concentrated in particular localities.[5] The journeymen hatmakers, for example, were particularly strong in Stockport and held a General Congress to manage their strike in late 1808 to early 1809.[6] This identity also applied inter-regionally. The development of the textile, shipwright, and mining industries in particular areas of Lancashire gave their unions a distinct regional scope shaping their connections and patterns of action.[7] The mule cotton spinners, bleachers, and calico printers in south-east Lancashire maintained a strong geographical and trade identity and a shop system. This was not exclusive, as tramping artisans extended this network far beyond the limits of regional identity and thereby created the potential for pan-regional action. Closed shops could be achieved without a formal system of apprenticeship because short distance migration encouraged mutual trust and the emergence of friendly societies, which though not combinations in themselves, fostered an atmosphere of cooperation and self-help conducive to trade unions.[8]

[3] A. E. Musson, *British Trade Unions, 1800–1875* (Basingstoke, 1972), p. 13.

[4] M. Chase, *Early Trade Unionism: Fraternity, Skill and the Politics of Labour* (Aldershot, 2000), p. 66; J. Orth, *Combination and Conspiracy: A Legal History of Trade Unionism, 1721–1906* (Oxford, 1991), pp. 49–50.

[5] K. D. M. Snell, 'The Culture of Local Xenophobia', *SH* 28 (2003), 3.

[6] Cooper to Earl of Liverpool, 31 January 1809, in A. Aspinall, *Early English Trade Unions: Documents from the Home Office Papers in the Public Record Office* (London, 1949), pp. 104–5.

[7] H. R. Southall, 'Towards a Geography of Unionisation: the Spatial Organization and Distribution of Early British Trade Unions', *Transactions of the Institute of British Geographers*, 13 (1988), 466–86.

[8] Chase, *Early Trade Unionism*, p. 41.

The Combination Acts of 1799 and 1800 provided the touchstone to which unionized action constantly referred. The acts were the equivalent for workers of Pitt's anti-seditious legislation of 1795 for radicals. They pulled together a long sequence of acts relating to particular trades, and by this very means encouraged among workers a sense of facing a common threat. The first act enabled summary prosecution before one magistrate of anyone who attempted to strike or met with others with the purpose of improving wages and conditions, on the credible evidence of one witness. Levels of prosecution were low and the acts did not prevent such activity from taking place. It was rather their legislative existence that unionized workers saw as the problem, and the ways in which their spirit was translated into practice by local government to create an atmosphere of repression. The second act responded to opposition against summary jurisdiction and the evident bias in favour of employers, some of whom were magistrates. Two magistrates were henceforth required to try cases instead of one; employer-magistrates were forbidden from trying men in their own trade, but the act reiterated the illegality of combinations.

It is significant that the handloom weavers and cotton spinners reacted differently and had separate campaigns in response to the legislation and economic distress of 1799–1800. The petitions against the Combination Acts originated mainly from mule spinners, calico printers, and other more skilled trades. They were similar in language and style across the country, intimating some inter-regional as well as pan-trade coordination.[9] Those affected had fairly sophisticated unions and therefore felt threatened by their prohibition and the government's first comprehensive intrusion into their dealings with their employers. As Colonel Fletcher alleged in 1816, in a long summary of all the combination agitation that had occurred during the war:

> The classes of persons in the manufactures of this county that have been most formidable to their employers, by their combinations, are the calico printers and cotton spinners, who, labouring in large numbers together in print works or cotton factories under the same masters respectively, have for some years past been almost every year in some place or other in a state of combination against their respective employers.[10]

[9] Orth, *Combination and Conspiracy*, pp. 49–50.

[10] Fletcher to Beckett, 5 March 1816, in Aspinall, *Early English Trade Unions*, p. 214.

The cotton spinners took advantage of the more favourable economic circumstances during the peace of 1801–2 to sustain their strike activity. By contrast, the handloom weavers differed from spinners and printers in their outlook towards parliamentary legislation. An address from Bolton weavers printed in *Cowdroy's Manchester Gazette* (the Tory-loyalist newspapers *Manchester Mercury* and *Chronicle* refused to publish it) in May 1800 asserted: 'It is NOT the legislature we are contending against—we supplicate THEM for redress, but it is our employers we oppose.'[11] Furthermore, because of their tense relationship with the magistrates, they were more positive about finding a national or independent solution to their declining trade that might protect them from the whims of their employers. While sympathetic to the campaigns for repeal of the Combination Acts, therefore, their petitioning campaign focused on legislative intervention into their wage conditions and not on the acts themselves. It also reflected the fact that the weavers had less bargaining power and were keener to get outside help.

The two campaigns were significant in their attempts to use geography as well as rhetoric against their employers. Strikes were maintained for months, something partly made possible by financial support for the 'turnouts', but also by a careful exploitation of geographical knowledge. Geographical links and personal connections had already been solidified among handloom weavers 'bearing home' their cotton weft and among journeymen by tramping. These factors were exemplified in one of the most potent forms of collective action: the 'rolling strike'. This was a tactic of targeting selected individual employers and sustaining the strikers with a subscription from a network of shops or friendly societies, which would then spread the agitation across the region. The rolling strike had been used successfully by calico printers in 1795, and was employed to its fullest geographical extent by handloom weavers in 1803 and mule spinners in 1810.[12] Most trades were blighted by intermittent strikes during the French wars, on account of the general upwards trend in prices putting pressure on wage levels. Peaks of activity, however, correlated more closely at times of economic upturn, when workers could more freely support the subscriptions involved in rolling strikes. In 1810, the Manchester-based General Congress of cotton mule spinners elected to concentrate their efforts in two towns: Stalybridge

[11] *CMG*, 3 May 1800.

[12] Anon, *The History of the Combination of the Journeymen Calico Printers* (Manchester, 1795), p. 20. A. J. Kidd, *Manchester* (Keele, 1993), p. 83.

and Preston. The chosen targets were about thirty-three direct miles from each other, but in travelling terms, much further. They also differed in size and in structure of industry and landholding. As has been seen, Stalybridge had rapidly expanded as a direct result of manufacturers building spinning mills alongside the river Tame. Preston was more gradually transformed from being a centre of gentry leisure to becoming the manufacturing empire of the Horrocks brothers, with a population of over 17,000 by 1811.[13] The object of the strike was to raise wages in the 'country' districts to the higher levels earned by Manchester spinners. The Congress chose to call out only a few mills at a time in both towns, until each master should agree to the Manchester terms. In total, 8,000 to 10,000 allegedly turned out in Stalybridge and Preston.[14]

The scale of the spinners' strike was impressively pan-regional; geographical links contributed to its initial success. James Frost, a Mancunian spinner activist, provided the 1824 parliamentary select committee enquiring into combinations with a list of receipts received from those shops towards subscriptions in the week beginning 2 June 1810. The importance of Manchester was again in evidence in the amount—over £600—that they raised for both Preston and Stalybridge. Preston received more contributions from Oldham, Stockport, Macclesfield, Manchester, and Carlisle, while Stalybridge was funded by Bolton, Chorley, and other smaller places in the south-east.[15] Some cross-trade cooperation was suggested, although this cannot be verified; woollen workers from the West Riding may have supported the subscriptions and the judge at the Manchester Quarter Sessions alleged: 'it had appeared in evidence at the West Riding sessions, that a combinations of cutlers in Sheffield had been supported by contributions from cotton-spinners in Manchester'.[16] The spinners' strike maintained momentum for three to four months while its subscription fund enabled the Congress to make weekly payments of twelve shillings to the strikers. The failure of the strike was attributed less to employer repression than to a decline in subscriptions as the renewed depression of winter 1810–11 set in.[17] This suggests that the spinners, already

13 T. Burke and M. Nevell, *Buildings of Tameside: a History and Archaeology of Tameside* (Manchester, 1996); N. Morgan, *Vanished Dwellings: Early Industrial Housing in a Lancashire Cotton Town, Preston* (Preston, 1990).

14 PP 1824, V, *Report on the Combination Laws*, p. 393.

15 *Ibid*., p. 604.

16 *Blackburn Mail*, 23 May 1810.

17 H. Tufnell, *Character, Object and Effects of Trade Unions with Some Remarks on the Law Concerning Them* (1834), p. 14.

better paid than weavers, were sufficiently prosperous in the summer of 1810 to maintain each other's standard of living. Nevertheless, the effectiveness of strikes by spinners and calico printers amongst other apprenticed trades was dampened by the economic instability when war returned; whereas handloom weavers were more consistently active throughout the war period as their position progressively declined.

Most handloom weavers were unable to tramp as they usually owned or hired their looms, which were permanent fixtures in their houses. They have therefore often been erroneously perceived as more disorganized than the traditionally unionized textile trades of hatters, bleachers, and mule spinners, who could build up connections on the tramp. Women, children, and casual labour furthermore undertook a large proportion of weaving work. Unskilled workers seemingly lacked the ability to transcend geographical boundaries in trade terms and their attachment was predominantly to their parish or immediate locality.[18] Duncan Bythell has argued strongly that the handloom weavers should never be regarded as skilled full-time craftsmen who fell from a high position into abject poverty, but rather as always being on the edge economically, profiting when times were good but quickly declining in times of shortage.[19] The Bolton weavers complained that in 1792 a man received 22 shillings for 44 yards of cloth, but by 1799, 'instead of 44 yards they have increased the length to 60, and give him only 11s for it'.[20]

Yet just as radicalism consisted of a committed activist leadership supported by a less politicized and active mass, similarly among handloom weavers a unionized minority acted as they believed fit on behalf of the majority of weavers. Unionized activists were usually male, full-time, and often weavers of fine cloths requiring some skill. James Draper, President of the Weavers' Association formed in Bolton in 1799, had worked for thirty years as a muslin weaver for Thomas Ainsworth, Robert Peel's partner and one of the largest Bolton manufacturers.[21] Most towns had some fine weavers, but they were especially concentrated in Bolton, Stockport, and Manchester, and this helps explain why unionized activity was especially virulent in those towns and their neighbourhoods. Check weavers in Manchester had formed a combination as early as the

[18] Snell, 'Culture of Local Xenophobia', 3.

[19] D. Bythell, *The Handloom Weavers: A Study in the English Cotton Industry During the Industrial Revolution* (Cambridge, 1969), p. 60.

[20] 'Association of Weavers to the Public', in Aspinall, *Early Trade Unions*, pp. 21–3.

[21] PP 1803, III, part 4, *Select Committee into the Masters and Servants Act*, p. 17.

1750s.[22] Despite not having a tradition of well-enforced apprenticeship, the unionized weavers of the region employed the rhetoric of skill and legality as established by their peers in other textile trades and other artisans, and took similar collective action to defend their status.

The Secretary of the Weavers' Association, James Holcroft, illustrated the extent of erudition on the part of the unionized weavers. He had been both a fine and coarse weaver for fifteen years before becoming a putter-out (the middleman who took in the woven cloth from the weavers) for Joseph and Jeremiah Crooks of Bolton. He played a major role acting as arbitrator between manufacturers and their employees to the prodigious number of over three hundred times under the provisions of the new Arbitration Act of 1802. Holcroft was thus among a small group of leaders who acted almost as professional representatives, being paid two shillings a case by the committee of the Weavers' Association in some disputes.[23] Despite high turnover rates in many trades, there was some continuation at the level of leadership amongst skilled workers involved in unionized activity. Richard Needham was a committee signatory to weavers' addresses and petitions from Bolton in both 1799 and 1808, an arbitrator to about a hundred cases of weavers negotiating with their employers over wages in 1801–2. He testified to various parliamentary select committees from 1802 to 1824.[24] The fact that parliament set up select committees to investigate many trades' demands and grievances in response to their petitions perhaps showed some element of concern about the state of the working classes as well as the poor (this paternalism was evident among the Lancashire MPs, particularly Thomas Stanley, who ran the enquiries), although the witnesses were aware that such events were often a sop to prevent further petitioning or more parliamentary bills.

Continuous leadership of the kind Needham provided, however, was not, as the Webbs assumed, a prerequisite for successful action. Local and regional geographical networks again contributed to weavers sustaining action relatively successfully throughout this period. From April 1799, the General Committee of the Weavers' Association directed the campaign for parliamentary legislation to provide for an arbitration system to raise piece rates and later to enforce a statutory minimum wage.

22 Chase, *Early Trade Unionism*, p. 45.

23 PP 1803, III, part 4, p. 17; NA, HO 42/61/176, Bancroft to Portland, 1 March 1801.

24 Bolton Archives, Holden diaries; PP 1803, III, part 4, p. 3; PP 1824, V, *Report from the Committee on. . . Artisans and Machinery*, p. 543.

The origin of the delegates to the committee indicated the proportionate importance of fine weaving in the various towns in the region. Six delegates represented Bolton and 'neighbourhood' and there were three delegates from Manchester and Salford. Stockport, Oldham, Wigan, and Bury sent two each, as did towns further out of the circle: Blackburn, Chorley, Newton, and Warrington. The villages of Chowbent, New Chapel (four miles from Bolton), and Whitefield sent one delegate each.[25]

The Weavers' Association used the ostensible form of a friendly society for their central organizing body. John Holden believed that sixty-three members had entered a society at the Jolly Tailor Inn in March 1799 explicitly 'for the purpose of regulating the price of muslins'.[26] Lancashire had the highest rate of friendly society registration in England under Rose's Act of 1793, and also had the largest proportion of its population enrolled in registered friendly societies. Bolton was unusual in comparison with many Lancashire manufacturing towns in that it fostered many single-trade friendly societies.[27] Although most societies, particularly those under the treasuryship of manufacturers, denied direct links with unionized committees and refused to fund them, Francis Place later believed the connections with unions were obvious.[28] The president of the association, James Draper, corresponded with magistrate Revd Thomas Bancroft in April, deferentially but assertively proclaiming their legality and loyalism and that they were not dependent on the friendly society to legitimize public pursuit of their real aims.[29] At a meeting on 13 May, the collected delegates produced a broadside entitled 'The Association of Weavers etc to the Public', which clearly stated their names and origins and asserted forcefully their loyalty to Church and State in order to convince 'the public' of the legality of their 'applying to the legislature of the country for such further regulations'. As large proportions of workers belonged to friendly societies, there were undoubtedly many who would have been active in strikes and who

25 NA, HO 42/47/3, Singleton to King, 27 May 1799; Aspinall, *Early English Trade Unions*, pp. 21–3.

26 Holden diaries.

27 M. Gorsky, 'The Growth and Distribution of English Friendly Societies in the Early Nineteenth Century', *EHR* 101 (1998), 502; NA, FS 1/239–45, 2/1, Lancashire friendly societies rules.

28 BL, Additional MS 27798–9, Place papers, Proceedings for the Repeal of the Combination Acts, 1824–5; PP 1824, V, *Report from the Committee on. . .Artisans and Machinery*.

29 NA, PC 1/44/A155, J. Draper *et al.* to T. Bancroft, 16 April 1799; PC 1/44/158, evidence on weavers' combinations, 1799.

would have come into conflict with the more conservative members of their friendly societies over their involvement and respectability. Magistrates' spies alleged that the weavers' committee persuaded the friendly societies to advance money to weavers on strike in 1808, though they admitted that little was collected and 'it has been a bone of contention ever since with those that were opposed to it, who declare there shall never be any more money but for the purposes it was put in for, viz. to relieve the sick and bury the dead'.[30]

By spring of 1800, the weavers' petition had allegedly collected 23,000 signatures and was presented to parliament by Colonel Stanley. The weavers' demands were not met by parliament, which passed the Arbitration Act as a compromise measure. The act allowed for a system where weavers could negotiate wages with their employers, under the arbitration of a magistrate.[31] In February 1802, the weavers again petitioned, seeking to amend the act. The majority of major cotton manufacturers of Manchester, led by the German merchant and former boroughreeve Charles Frederick Brandt, held a series of meetings to oppose what they saw as too great an intrusion into their relations with their employees.[32] In response, the weavers' committee demonstrated the use they could make of geographical connections. They tested a loophole in the act in the township of Pilkington, near Bury. Manufacturers in Whitefield within Pilkington were presented with over 900 arbitration demands in one day, in an attempt to force the wages up comprehensively in a specific area. Similar demands were made to two manufacturers in nearby Stand; the manufacturer James Ramsbotham reported that 108 notices of arbitration were delivered to him in one day, 'principally from heads of families where we had two to four people employed, and those were all brought us by one man'. The Pilkington arbitration cases could not have occurred spontaneously and indicate the extent of organization and regional awareness of the weavers in towns connected with the committee. Holcroft denied any connection with the instigation of the tactic, but his claim is implausible as Whitefield had a delegate to the committee and Holcroft admitted to yet another parliamentary select committee that he had been asked immediately to arbitrate many of the cases.[33] Pilkington may have been chosen by the committee as a target because of its

30 Warr to Fletcher, 1 March 1816, in Aspinall, *Early English Trade Unions*, p. 215.

31 J. Bohstedt, *Riots and Community Politics in England and Wales 1790–1810* (Cambridge, Mass., 1983), p. 140.

32 *Blackburn Mail*, 2 March 1803.

33 PP 1803, III, part 4, pp. 40, 33.

socio-economic structure. Most of the land in Whitefield was owned by the Earl of Derby (taken to be to some extent sympathetic to workers) but was overseen by local manufacturers. This contrasted sharply with neighbouring Prestwich, which was closely supervised by the Earl of Wilton (an Orangeman) at Heaton Hall, and was seemingly inactive in the field of weaver agitation. The Unitarian branch of the Philips family were the most prominent landowners in the area and the existence of a Unitarian chapel there may have been significant. Whitefield had a tradition of political and social polarization from Jacobite times and would continue to do so. Luddites were to be active in the area; Whitefield men were prominent in the attack on Burton's mill in Middleton in April 1812.[34]

What the weavers' agitation of 1799–1803 demonstrated, along with the opposition of other textile trades to the Combination Acts, was a drawn-out process of thought about the role of parliament and the state in the economy of the provinces as well as in labour relations. The situation was complex and strained, and most workers maintained a faith in the power of parliament to do good. It was the employers who sensed an increasing distrust of the intrusion of the state in what they regarded as their private affairs. This distrust was to reignite more seriously during the economic blockade from 1806, as evidenced in the bitter accounts of their financial difficulties that the manufacturers and merchants related to the select committee into the petitions against the Orders in Council in 1807 and in 1812.[35]

The largest collective action by handloom weavers during the war occurred in 1808, following renewed petitioning to parliament from many towns for a statutory minimum wage. The agitation again demonstrated the regional scope of action, although the locus of the campaign had shifted from Bolton to Manchester and Stockport and the committee began to lose control of the wider repercussions of its actions. The economic situation, after some respite during the peace of 1801–2, had deteriorated. Colonel Fletcher reported to the Home Office that the wages of handloom weavers had fallen from an average of 2 shillings 4½ pence a day in June 1805 to 10½ pence a day in January 1808, in the context of rising food prices and unemployment.[36] The strikes were

[34] J. F. Wilson, *A History of Whitefield* (Whitefield, 1979), pp. 17–18; NA, HO 42/122/600, Manchester Police Office to Ryder, 27 April 1812.

[35] PP 1808 (181), X, *Minutes of Evidence upon Taking into Consideration Several Petitions Presented to the House of Commons Respecting the Orders in Council*.

[36] Fletcher to Hawkesbury, 24 February 1808, in Aspinall, *Early Trade Unions*, p. 95.

not, however, a blind reaction to distress but rather entailed calculated cooperation amongst unionized weavers across the region based upon hope for legislation from parliament. Hence only after government had half-heartedly introduced a minimum wage bill and then withdrawn it on 19 May 1808 did strikes occur. This indicated continued heightened awareness of the role and impact of government legislation. News reached Manchester of the rejection of the bill on 22 May, but no disturbances occurred there until a committee at Stockport took the lead in organization and began the strike on the following day.[37]

The climax of the agitation occurred on 24 and 25 May 1808, when mass meetings were held to draw up a petition for parliamentary legislation to enforce minimum wage levels. The scale of these meetings should not be underestimated, particularly in a period when such large gatherings were automatically suspected to be seditious. They formed the largest meetings of working people in pursuit of a single aim that took place in the region until after the war. The most numerous gatherings of handloom weavers were held in fields on the immediate outskirts of Manchester and Stockport, with smaller meetings in other towns. It was clear that Manchester was the central event and the regional centre. It alone attracted 'ten to fifteen thousand' calling for minimum wage legislation.[38] The meetings were precursors to Peterloo not just because the cavalry were sent in to disperse the crowds but also because of the choice of meeting place by the participants. The changing urban environment affected the nature of protest, in particular the opportunity to make use of fields for large meetings was being eroded in areas swamped by residential and industrial development. The Manchester weavers' committee may have made a conscious decision to hold the meetings on St George's Fields, an area which had probably not been used for meetings or demonstrations before. The weavers thus explored the potential of assembling in great numbers not on the streets but in a large space they could claim symbolically as their own. St George's Fields were off Newton Lane, opposite the newly laid out streets of workers' houses in Ancoats. They were easily accessible for weavers from north Manchester and the neighbouring villages. By contrast, the weavers and others who lived in Chorlton Row and south Manchester would have

[37] *The Whole Proceedings on the Trial of an Indictment Against Joseph Hanson* Esq (1809), p. 30; R. Glen, *Urban Workers in the Early Industrial Revolution* (New York, 1984), p. 160.

[38] NA, TS 11/836, King vs Joseph Leah *et al.*, 27 May 1808.

had to cross the town to get there. This crossing of districts may have had visual and psychological consequences for both weavers and for the middle classes who witnessed them passing their houses and workplaces.

The strikes were enforced by large groups of weavers taking away the shuttles from weavers reluctant to lend support in their homes and workshops in and around Rochdale, Bolton, Wigan, Stockport, and other Pennine satellite towns. Most began on Monday 30 May, which, as 'Saint Monday' was still observed, would not have been a day of work. Removing and sequestering shuttles indicated a determination not to commence work, and the strikes continued in a ritualized way throughout the week, usurping the manufacturers' usual control of space and time. The Mayor of Wigan wrote to the Home Secretary, Lord Hawkesbury:

> We have within the borough 3000 weavers. The rejection of the Bill introduced into Parliament to fix a minimum of the wages to be paid to weavers in those manufactures immediately created universal discontent amongst them. And on Monday, 30 May, many of them from the adjacent villages entered the town in different parties and expeditiously collected as many shuttles from the weavers residing here as they could obtain, which they marked with the owners' names and locked up near the places from whence they were taken.[39]

The magistrates appear to have arrested a few scapegoats to stand in for the 'hundreds of divers persons' they could not charge. The actions of the crowds, as described by the magistrates, appear organized and involved almost a programme of various forms of intimidation, but the weavers' committee did not officially countenance the direction of the active gangs and it is unclear exactly who their leaders were.[40] During the evening of 30 May, stones were thrown at the magistrates in Rochdale police office and, in an attempt to release arrested strikers and reclaim confiscated bundles of shuttles, the rioting weavers burnt down Rochdale prison.[41] The strikers' aims and actions became more diffuse and more violent the more distant they were from the committees at Stockport and Manchester. Prosecutions of weavers from Blackburn, Haslingden, and other towns heading up to the calico-weaving district were numerous but the depositions of witnesses indicated that these disturbances involved general rioting more than organized combinations

[39] Mayor of Wigan to Hawkesbury, 15 June 1808, in Aspinall, *Early Trade Unions*, pp. 102–3.

[40] HO 42/95/274, Farington to Home Office, 25 May 1808; Holden diaries.

[41] Rowbottom diaries; Drake and Entwisle to Hawkesbury, 4 June 1808, in Aspinall, *Early Trade Unions*, pp. 99–100.

or the removal of shuttles.[42] By the beginning of June, the negotiations with the manufacturers appear to have split the committee between those who were satisfied with the deal offered of an increase of 20 per cent and those who wished to go further for the 33 per cent originally demanded, and it seems that the legacy of these splits plagued the organization of the weavers into the Luddite agitation.[43] Whatever the ambiguities of the structure of activity and individual support for opposition to the shuttle-takers, the ordinary workers of each town or village were likely to have been complicit in the strikes and in maintaining strikers' anonymity when faced with the magistrates; the Mayor of Wigan and his colleagues claimed that they 'endeavoured to identify the persons who had taken the shuttles, but all the owners (except one) pretended that they did not know any of the offenders'.[44]

It is the amalgamation of the two worlds, urban-industrial and rural, in action occurring in the 'neighbourhoods' of the expanding towns that stands out in unionized action in this period. The geographical expansion of communications did not inhibit protest but conversely facilitated its spread beyond local 'communities' while still leaving smaller and more established connections at the heart of the action. Patterns of agitation controvert John Bohstedt's argument that textile workers were 'new groups of workers in 1790' and thus, lacking the 'long traditions' of other types of workers, 'had to organize themselves on the basis of regional and industrial, rather than local and communal, solidarity'.[45] Rather, cotton spinners' organization and rhetoric built upon the centuries-old 'repertoires' of guilds, while the handloom weavers were constantly in touch with their environment and communities. The weavers and spinners' strikes exemplified connections established by 'bearing home', friendly societies, and religious meetings, all prominent elements of quotidian life in the 'neighbourhoods' of Pennine manufacturing towns. James Holcroft 'put out work two days in a week, at a place called Chowbent, five miles from Bolton, and the next magistrate is about a mile beyond Bolton'.[46] This perhaps indicates why the small village of Chowbent had a delegate to the 1799 weavers' committee. The

[42] Lancashire CRO, QJC1, MF10/139; *Blackburn Mail*, 7 September 1808.

[43] Farington to Hawkesbury, 1 June 1808, in Aspinall, *Early Trade Unions*, p. 97.

[44] Mayor of Wigan to Hawkesbury, 15 June 1808, in Aspinall, *Early Trade Unions*, pp. 102–3.

[45] Bohstedt, *Riots and Community Politics*, p. 126; A. Charlesworth, 'From the Moral Economy of Devon to the Political Economy of Manchester, 1790–1812', *SH* 18 (1993), 205.

[46] PP 1803, III, part 4, *Select Committee Report*, p. 33.

participants' awareness of routes and locations, fostered by mobility and migration, influenced patterns of action. The road on which Samuel Bamford 'bore home' between Middleton and Manchester was prominent in weavers' disturbances throughout this period. The deputy constable Joseph Nadin 'received information that a considerable body of weavers were on their way from the villages of Blakeley and the Neighbourhood round the town of Manchester to join the mob' at St George's Fields. After the dispersal of the demonstration, the military scoured the countryside, allegedly breaking up smaller meetings in the villages of Blackley and White Moss, in Middleton and on Kersal Moor.[47] Samuel Bamford commented on the route in his recollections of the Luddite attack on Emmanuel Burton's factory and house in Middleton on 20–21 April 1812. He met individuals on the road from Middleton going back to Manchester, bringing back pieces of mahogany that they had raided from the remains of Burton's house.[48]

The location of this wider district and its communications network embodied in particular roads were therefore integral to encouraging participation in the attack. The magistrates, as during the radical meetings of 1801 and the demonstrations for peace in 1808, felt helpless as workers appropriated times of day and spaces that were normally occupied by manufacturers or forces of order; this was especially the case when weavers paraded the streets for hours or Luddites took control of Pennine routeways. The strikes of 1808 were suppressed only when military backing arrived, and even then the authorities' command over places was tenuous. R. A. Farington wrote on 9 June about how handloom weavers could only continue working if they were guarded along their putting-out route: 'the avenues to Manchester are patrolled by dragoons and special constables to protect people bringing in and taking out their work'.[49]

The strikes of 1808 also illustrated the close geographical identity amongst diverse trades in the Westhoughton mining district. The rise of population in tandem with the distance from Bolton and Wigan appear to have made this district less manageable for the magistrates than elsewhere. Most unionized action by textile trades occurred within areas where skilled workers were concentrated and geographical connections could be maintained by delegate systems. John Holden stated in his diary

[47] NA, TS 11/657/2075, King vs Hanson, 1808, prosecution brief; E. Little, 'Joseph Hanson: "the Weavers' Friend" ', *MRHR* 5 (1991), 28.

[48] S. Bamford, *The Autobiography of Samuel Bamford: Early Days*, new edn, ed. W. H. Chaloner (London, 1967) p. 300.

[49] Farington to Hawkesbury, 9 June 1808, in Aspinall, *Early Trade Unions*, p. 101.

that striking weavers who demonstrated in Bolton on 25 May dispersed to Leigh, Chowbent, and Tildesley.[50] These townships had patterns of authority contrasting with those of Bolton itself, suggesting that either large groups of protestors were most likely to come from these outlying areas or that those who dispersed outwards included Boltonians who knew family or friends in the wider 'neighbourhood' who would support them there. Leigh, Chowbent, and Tildesley were rapidly expanding weaving and mining townships. Chowbent was renowned for the size of its Dissenting population. Patterns of action were thus established which would be reflected in the more amorphous collective disturbances of 1812. Some of the Luddites arrested at Westhoughton in 1812 came from Chowbent, Atherton, and Tildesley and appear to have known each other.[51] The Holdens of Hag End were prominent among those arrested and appear to have been accustomed to associating with the other prisoners who worked in handloom shops of Hag End or the Great Lever bleachworks of Thomas Hulme and Co. Colonel Fletcher's informant, Joseph Lomax, a cropper from Darcy Lever who worked for Messrs Cooke and Hulme, claimed that he had met others at Tanner's Hole, went to Dean Moor and then called upon his friend 'Arthur Holding' [Holden] at Hag End.[52] It was these sorts of personal connections based on geography more than trade that enabled activity to occur.

The disruption the strikes caused was not just to manufacturers but also to the quotidian patterns of life in the towns and villages affected, on which they had a much more profound effect than radical agitation did. Farington wrote on 28 May 1808 about the state of Manchester: 'the whole of the town and neighbourhood, so far as the weaving branch is concerned, are in a state of confusion. No work is carried on, and the well-disposed families, who are inclined to pursue their labour, are prevented doing so by the threats and intimidation held out to them.'[53] The manufacturers and merchants perhaps gleaned some sense of shared identity in cooperative efforts against their employees. Many addresses were published throughout this period stressing their united stance against agitation. Ironically, the employers combined themselves in order to defeat combinations. The mule spinners' strike was only

50 Bolton Archives, Holden diaries.

51 NA, TS 11/980, Trial of the Westhoughton Luddites, 1812, briefs for prosecution.

52 V. I. Tomlinson, 'Letters of a Lancashire Luddite Transported to Australia, 1812–16', *TLCAS* 77 (1967), 121; NA, HO 42/122/522, examination of Joseph Lomax, 15 May 1812.

53 *Ibid.*

broken in late 1803 after the major Manchester manufacturers had raised a fighting fund of £20,000 to pay for the military and legal expenses.[54] In 1808, Farington reported that the merchants and manufacturers of Manchester and the wider region 'have formed a committee with a view to assisting the civil power and devising some mode of meeting the claims of the weavers'.[55] What the workers had achieved was to add a particular geographical awareness to their repertoire of tactical skills and a sense of bitterness against the inability or unwillingness of their employers and parliament to concede to what they regarded as rightful demands.

LUDDISM

The Luddites undoubtedly caused the greatest social disorder in Lancashire during the wars. The historiography of Luddism ranges far and wide, from Marxist interpretations of the machine-breaking as class conflict, to dismissive accounts of its reactionary nature, to more balanced accounts evoking the working-class response to severe economic distress, high food prices, unemployment, and seemingly interminable war.[56] More recently, historians have viewed the disturbances within a wider context of working-class culture and mythology. Luddism was not just about reactionary machine-breaking. The disturbances as a whole encompassed most forms of collective action, including food riots, radical meetings, threatening letters, and secret cells; the connections among all forms were ambiguous and fluctuating.[57] The language of Luddite ballads and texts as well as of threatening letters suggests a wider culture in which legal rhetoric was appropriated by the combinations. Luddites had similar forms of networks to the United Englishmen cells, if only as a means of maintaining anonymity against the spies. Lancashire again demonstrated its peculiarity in that Luddite texts evinced a much wider economic knowledge than did those of Yorkshire or the East

[54] *CMG*, 22 October 1803.

[55] Farington to Hawkesbury, 28 May 1808, in Aspinall, *Early Trade Unions*, p. 96.

[56] B. Bailey, *The Luddite Rebellion* (Stroud, 1998); R. Reid, *Land of Lost Content: the Luddite Revolt, 1812* (London, 1986).

[57] K. Binfield, *The Writings of the Luddites* (Baltimore, 2004); A. Randall, *Before the Luddites: Custom, Community and Machinery in the English Woollen Industry, 1776-1809* (Cambridge, 1991); J. R. Dinwiddy, 'Luddism and Politics in the Northern Counties', *SH* 4 (1979), 33–63.

Midlands.[58] This suggests the legacy of Paineite ideas, though actual links with radicals were tenuous; it at least tied in with the political economic principles of unionized workers counterpoised to the laissez-faire orientation of their employers. The rituals of Luddite action also revealed in extreme the impact of the war upon the ordinary populace. Luddites drilled in military style, led by an imaginary 'General Ludd'. These rituals were not simply a means of organization and defence; they represented workers' cathartic reaction in physical form against the pressures of militarization and the economic scarcities.[59]

Luddism in Lancashire started in March 1812, long after the original outbreaks in the East Midlands. There is evidence that it spread from Yorkshire but the attacks reflected the regionalization of industrialization in that the target was steam powerlooms rather than cropping machines or stocking frames. Luddism in Lancashire was different as it was integrated with an exceptionally varied set of disturbances, ranging from food rioting to strikes, and both magistrates and historians have found it difficult to separate out the different threads. Machine-breaking was much less prevalent in Lancashire than in the other regions. Luddites concentrated on 'set-pieces', attacking a factory on Oxford Road in Manchester, the Burtons' factory at Middleton, and finally in the most violent clash at Wroe and Duncroft's powerloom mill at Westhoughton near Bolton. There were strong suspicions at the time that the last, if not all, were instigated by spies and it is likely that Lancashire workers would not have gone to such extremes without some provocation.[60] John Holden's account of the misunderstandings at Westhoughton suggests between the lines that something was afoot. He wrote that about one o'clock on 24 April 'Information was received here of the Factory at Westhoughton being on fire'. The cavalry arrived at the scene but believed it was 'a complete Hoax!' as the Luddites 'were dispersed and lay concealed behind Edges a few fields below the Factory'. The Luddites attacked the mill after the cavalry left, but among the twenty-four arrested, 'their ringleader turned Kings Evidence a Man of the name of Halliwell who manufactured goods in or near Chowbent'.[61]

[58] Binfield, *Writings of the Luddites*, p. 42.

[59] This is explored in K. Navickas, 'The Search for General Ludd: the Mythology of Luddism', *SH* 30 (2005), 282–95.

[60] R. Taylor, *Letters on the Subject of the Lancashire Riots* (Bolton, 1812), p. 9.

[61] Bolton Archives, Holden diaries.

Luddism in Lancashire and Cheshire involved a more complex pattern of activity than previous strikes by handloom weavers because the agitations were not solely under the control of unionized committees. Although Luddite activities often resulted from a breakdown in negotiations, they were not explicitly directed by the weavers' committees. Conversely, reports from spies suggested that dissensions within the committees stimulated outbreaks of machine-breaking. At an executive committee meeting in Salford on Sunday 5 April 1812, delegates arrived from Bolton, Stockport, Failsworth, Saddleworth, Oldham, and Ashton-under-Lyne.[62] It constructed a deal with the manufacturers for a 20 per cent increase in wages but its more moderate approach isolated some delegates, who then appear to have deliberately acted alone. According to spy reports, the committee decided that on the following Thursday simultaneous attacks should be made on factories at Bolton, Stockport, and Manchester. Yet representatives from the Manchester districts rejected the plan and delegates were sent to Bolton and Stockport to countermand the operation. From this point, as J. R. Dinwiddy suggests, the Bolton committee and its Chowbent subsidiary seem to have proceeded independently from Manchester.[63] 'Bent', Colonel Fletcher's appropriately-named spy, reported that a committee meeting was held at Ardwick Green on 20 April 1812. Representatives attended from townships in Manchester's southern neighbourhood and Tameside, but significantly, no delegate from Bolton was present and the Manchester committee threatened to disassociate itself from the committees of other towns.[64] It was perhaps no coincidence that the day after the Bolton delegates missed the Ardwick Green meeting, attacks began on the factory and house of Daniel and Emmanuel Burton in Middleton, followed by the pitched battle at Westhoughton on 24 April. The scale and organization of the Westhoughton attack was probably unique, reflecting activities in Bolton being separate from the Manchester committee organization. The other Luddite attacks, on factories in Stockport and Middleton, were also unlikely to have been part of a directive plan from the committees but rather were the result of local initiatives combined with pressure from the spies. Inter-trade committee sympathy was also strained at this point. John Buckley, a Dissenting preacher and weaver, called on the spinners and tailors in

62 Dinwiddy, 'Luddism and Politics', 42; NA, HO 40/1/1/48.
63 Dinwiddy, 'Luddism and Politics', 45; HO 40/1/1/47.
64 Glen, *Urban Workers*, p. 178.

Manchester to contribute money but they 'refused to pay anything to the weavers'.[65]

Wider inter-trade and cross-community participation was achieved therefore not via unionized committees but through direct action shaped by a more extensive regional identity. Luddism encompassed both the local bases of food riots and the geographical connections of previous unionized activity. A characteristic of the Lancashire Luddite disturbances was participation by workers from outside the 'neighbourhood'. Bands of colliers were especially prominent among the Luddite 'regiments'. This was exemplified at the disturbances at Middleton, which combined attacks on machinery, manufacturers, and food rioting. The magistrate William Chippindale reported that agitation began in Oldham market place on 20 April, where a crowd assembled, 'chiefly from Saddleworth and Hollinwood'. He identified the latter inhabitants as 'almost all colliers'. He termed the Saddleworth inhabitants 'rude' and 'uncultivated', which perhaps reflected town magistrates' perceptions about the semi-rural villages on their outskirts. The crowd then walked the few miles to Daniel Burton's powerloom factory at Middleton.[66] William Rowbottom's description confirms this account and the origins of those shot or arrested at the scene. He wrote of a 'great number' from Oldham heading for Burton's factory on 20 April. Magistrates estimated that about two thousand people gathered round the factory, when Burton's workers who lay in wait fired upon the crowd, killing five and wounding eighteen. The next day, he observed that a 'large mob again assembled at Middleton armed with Guns and Pistols and a very large number of colliers arrived with picks no doubt for the purpose of destroying the weaving factory'. After they had attacked Emmanuel Burton's house and the homes of workers loyal to their employer, a troop of Scots Greys retaliated, killing another five people.[67] Similarly, the Luddite disturbances at Stockport in March featured colliers from Denton and elsewhere, having apparently assembled in the 'neighbourhood of Gee Cross' (two miles south-east of Denton and five miles east of Stockport) before descending into the town.[68]

The participation of colliers in the agitation demonstrated the uniquely strong bonds formed on the south-west Lancashire coal belt

[65] Dinwiddy, 'Luddism and Politics', 45.

[66] B. Hall, 'Luddite Riots in Middleton', *Lancashire Local Historian* (1985), 9.

[67] Rowbottom diaries; NA, HO 42/122/515–17, Chippindale to Chippindale, 21 April 1812; Binfield, *Writings of the Luddites*, p. 180.

[68] NA, King's Bench trials, KB 8/90, King vs John Jackson, 1812.

and their sympathy with other trades. The colliers and their families were bound together by tight kinship connections, Catholicism, unionization, insecurity, and migration along the belt.[69] Why they felt so strongly as to take part in the Luddite disturbances on the north-east fringe of the coal district is, however, difficult to establish. The conscious decisions made were significant: to leave their place of work, travel a distance from the coalfield, and maintain anonymity in large groups in disguise. These tactics aided communities where magistrates would recognize local participants and it also involved a collective distancing from an individual sense of self associated with daily arduous working life. Miners had a long and solid history of striking and also of radical activity. In the same area, colliers had taken part in United Englishmen agitation during 1799–1801. Of the twenty-one UE arrested at Rivington Pike in 1801, the most prominent were employed at Orrell colliery. The UE members appear to have known each other well. For example, John Houghton and Ralph Wood left home and travelled the twelve miles to Rivington. Revd Thomas Bancroft wrote that Houghton was 'suspected of being a delegate from the colliery at Orrell where it is said there are many United, Mr Blundell the proprietor having frequently reproved and warned them upon the subject'.[70] In attacking powerloom factories, colliers perhaps saw their role as enforcing a wider political economy out of a sense of inter-trade solidarity.

Luddites were thus not solely handloom weavers attacking their employers' machinery. Lancashire Luddism involved the 'neighbourhood' in a brief trades alliance. Various trades from the surrounding 'neighbourhood' and further afield, particularly hatters, were also involved. After two days of pitched battles around Burton's factory and house in Middleton, those shot by the military included a joiner and four hatters from Oldham. The Manchester executive committee had both spinner and tailor representatives on it, although as has been seen, these connections would later be strained by the weavers' demands for money.[71] The oath takers at many places appear to have been cotton spinners, such as in Tameside, where at Dukinfield spinners took oaths on a coal pit hill.[72] Powerloom factories were not the only workplaces to

[69] J. Langton, 'Proletarianisation in the Industrial Revolution: Regionalism and Kinship in the Labour Markets of the British Coal Industry from the Seventeenth to the Nineteenth Centuries', *Transactions of the Institute of British Geographers*, 25 (2000), 42.

[70] NA, HO 42/62/111, Bancroft to Portland, 27 May 1801.

[71] Rowbottom diaries; Dinwiddy, 'Luddism and Politics', 45.

[72] F. R. Raynes, *An Appeal to the Public* (1817), p. 90.

be attacked; John Pilkington of Bolton reported an attempt to set fire to 'a very large spinning factory on the north side of the town' belonging to Roger Holbourn and Co. on 18 April.[73]

The origins of those arrested for rioting or attempting to 'twist in' soldiers or weavers who turned out, handily for the authorities, to be spies perhaps did not accurately reflect general patterns of participation. Luddism may have had attracted a wider range in terms of class and geography than what was recorded. In their arrests following incidents, magistrates and constables appear to have targeted specific places within towns. In Bolton, magistrates focused on the newly built streets of working-class housing. John Holden noted on 28 April 1812: 'Tuesday night the local out all night and constables—and took up during the night and Wednesday morning in Howell Croft, Spring Gardens and Bengall Sq 25 men.'[74] The men tried for administering the illegal oath to the spy Holland Bowden were indeed mainly weavers from Bengal Square (the complex of workers' cottages, warehouses, and workshops built for Robert Peel in 1795), and Howell Croft, Can Row, and Silver Street, inhabited by textile workers. The streets were built on the land released by the enclosure of moorland outside the old town.[75] After Westhoughton, the local militia arrested men in raids on the town and in Chowbent and Tildesley. The sphere of arrest after the attack on the Burtons' mill and house in Middleton was wider. According to William Rowbottom, the Manchester deputy constable and notorious 'thief-catcher', Joseph Nadin, arrived at Middleton on 5 May and arrested a few suspects there, before moving on to Royton, then Oldham, and finally at 'Thorp Clough he attempted to take two persons but failed'.[76]

Lancashire Luddism thus did not involve a case of local communities of weavers reacting against isolated employers and powerlooms. It involved different levels of demonstration and varied targets. The ordinary populace participated in the riots or coalesced in the threats. It should not be assumed, however, that the situation was so clear-cut as to array the 'neighbourhood' united against the magistrates and manufacturers. In some townships, the situation approached almost a local civil war. Those who were not involved as sympathizers became special constables.

[73] NA, HO 42/122/44, Pilkington to Beckett, 26 April 1812; see Binfield, *Writings of the Luddites*, pp. 172–4, for more examples of spinners' Luddism.

[74] Bolton Archives, Holden diaries.

[75] Bolton Archives, ZAL 327, plan of Bengal Square.

[76] Bolton Archives, Census of Great Bolton, 1811; Rowbottom diaries; NA, TS 11/980, trial of Westhoughton Luddites, 1812.

The Home Office had enforced this situation by initially insisting that no extra troops were available to suppress disorder; the magistrates felt the necessity to be so great that they overcame their misgivings about the loyalties of the general population. Their change of mind was vindicated by the response. Colonel Fletcher wrote on 1 May that in the Bolton division alone they had 'sworn in Special Constables the number of about 1000—being after the proportion of two to every hundred inhabitants—or about a tenth part of the adult males'.[77] Rowbottom indicated that there were many willing to serve under the magistrates in Oldham on 27 April, together with two hundred Oldham Local Militia called on duty.[78]

The eventual military response approved by the Home Office indicated how officials both within and outside the region believed that Luddites shared a common regional identity, whether or not this was the case in practice. The magistrates and Home Office had already suspected this when some volunteer corps had refused to put down food riots in 1800.[79] After failing to obtain military reinforcement to repress food riots on 20 April 1812, Revd Hay anxiously pleaded with Colonel Silvester in Manchester for troops, but specified that 'the *Militia* regiments from which the force should be selected should be those of the underline *Southern* counties, unconnected with manufacturing districts'.[80] General Maitland was eventually sent by the Home Office from the south to take control of events. He intended to be free from local bias. John Holden recorded that on 29 May, 2,000 soldiers were encamped in tents in the Bolton district, possibly on the moor. There were three regiments: one southern English (Buckinghamshire militia), one Irish (Louth), and one Scottish (Stirling).[81] The Home Office's perception of the necessity for a 'British' force is significant, as is the deliberate exclusion of a northern regiment.

Northern Lancashire was somewhat removed from events. William Fleming, magistrate of Ulverston, feared potential copycat disturbances in his area between late-April and mid-May 1812. He feared more serious disorder as a result of the high prices and low wages. The incidents that did occur were relatively minor, including minor arson in barns and threatening letters sent to the owners of Stonecross, the town mill, and

[77] NA, HO 40/1/1/71, Fletcher to Beckett, 1 May 1812.
[78] Rowbottom diaries.
[79] NA, HO 42/61/213, Bancroft to Portland, 12 March 1801.
[80] HO 42/122/22, Hay to Beckett, 21 April 1812, his emphasis.
[81] Bolton Archives, Holden diaries.

some factories. Fleming noted that the situation was kept under control by the instigation of watch and ward, but it appears that the disturbances were typical reactions to economic distress in a semi-rural area and on nothing like the scale or with the organization associated with Luddism in the south-east of the region. Indeed, Fleming wrote about how the judicial authorities recognized that Lonsdale 'north of the Sands' was separated from the rest of Lancashire in both jurisdiction and identity:

> 23 May–the judges will arrive at Lancaster for the special purpose of trying the Rioters who have made great disturbance for some time in the lower parts of this county and probably there will be an example made of some of the leading men. The greater part of the jurors are summoned from this side of the sands, those from the south part not being safe already from the vengeance of the mob who have threatened to shoot the judges and the witnesses too if any of their comrades shall be convicted for the enormous crimes which have been wantonly and cruelly committed.[82]

The Grand Jury at the trials at Lancaster was decidedly southern and composed of most of the major manufacturer-magistrates of the region.[83]

The geography of the Luddite disturbances had also a more sinister explanation reflecting variable patterns of repression by magistrates and other forces of order. The magistrates announced an amnesty for those who had taken the Luddite oath on 9 July. That offer met with little response until it was publicized in *Cowdroy's Manchester Gazette* on 22 August, another reflection of that paper's wide circulation and influence among the working classes.[84] Those who came forward to take the oath of allegiance which formed part of the amnesty, however, were almost exclusively from those parts of the region where Captain Frederick Raynes and his troops had been continually harrying the local population, that is, Stockport and north-east Cheshire. Raynes later noted that 'not less than 300 persons were assembled in the outskirts of Newton to set off to Stockport for the purpose of taking the oath of allegiance', whereas 'the Luddites at Stayley Bridge did not shew a disposition to return to their allegiance'.[85] Few Mancunians or others in Lancashire came forward. John Lloyd, magistrate of Stockport, was known to have brutally interrogated arrested suspects, which suggests the difficulties of assessing the extent to which the witness statements were invented to forestall more of Lloyd's rough treatment. For example,

82 Cumbria RO, Diaries of William Fleming of Rowe Head.
83 *MM*, 2 June 1812. 84 Glen, *Urban Workers*, pp. 186–7.
85 Bailey, *The Luddite Rebellion*, p. 80; Raynes, *An Appeal to the Public*, p. 60.

to avoid more torture by Lloyd, Corporal Barrowclough invented information about those involved in the murder of the manufacturer William Horsfall of Marsden in the West Riding of Yorkshire, in April 1812. Lloyd was furthermore embroiled in a bitter dispute with Joseph Radcliffe in Huddersfield over the boundaries of each other's spheres of authority in the Pennine-Tameside area.[86] As E. P. Thompson suggested, the relative severity of magisterial repression and of responses to them played a part in determining the pattern of Luddism.[87]

There were many places in Lancashire which saw neither unionized nor radical agitation. Prominent campaigns or major strikes did not feature in the histories of the smaller towns in the north of the region, where the textile industry was less invasive and the population more dispersed. Yet there were towns with many of the same economic and social characteristics as the disturbed areas which also did not experience any major disturbances. Warrington provides an interesting example, apparently unaffected by food riots or by radical activity of any kind. It produced no petitions for peace or reform and was seemingly unmoved by Luddism. Iain Sellers attributed much of this quiescence 'to the social composition of the town, the absence of factories and its dispersed, politically unawakened working class, with a middleclass small and insignificant'. He also pointed to the 'heavy hand of the junta' (local Anglican clergy, Botelier grammar school, the lord of the manor) 'interrelated by marriage, engaged in all kinds of commercial enterprises'.[88] The sail-making and heavy industries in Warrington were busy in wartime and this perhaps also satiated its inhabitants. Glossop, which expanded its population and industry on a scale approaching that of its neighbours Dukinfield and Hyde, also did not share any of the disturbances which blighted social order in these places. Unrest cannot therefore be mechanically attributed to the destruction of what John Bohstedt regarded as a paternalistic moral economy.[89] Perhaps it can only be surmised that the reasons lay in a peculiar local temperament, character, or identity which engendered contentment or acquiescence with the status quo in some areas, while areas including the Westhoughton district, Middleton, and Tameside

86 Reid, *Land of Lost Content*, pp. 176, 191.

87 E. P. Thompson, *The Making of the English Working Class*, (Harmandsworth, 1968) p. 536.

88 I. Sellers, 'Prelude to Peterloo, Warrington Radicalism, 1775–1819', *MRHR* 3 (1989), 17.

89 Charlesworth, 'From the Moral Economy of Devon', 205–17; Bohstedt, *Riots and Community Politics*, p. 126.

contained particularly radical or oppositional inhabitants willing to take the considerable risks involved.

A handful of the many arrested during the disturbances of 1812 were executed, including John Bromilow, aged 15, and Abraham Charlson, aged 16, for their part in the Westhoughton riot, and Hannah Smith, aged 54, for allegedly leading a food riot at Bank Top, Manchester on 29 April. Others were transported, including four members of the Holden family of Bolton, among whom Thomas wrote a series of moving letters home from Australia.[90] Luddism was a product of desperation, but it also demonstrated the rich variety of forms of protest and organization available to inhabitants of Lancashire, based on their semi-rural communities and relationships between these communities. Many of these tactics had been learned from unionized workers and continued to be used into the post-war period.

UNIONIZED MYTHOLOGY

James Epstein and other historians have underlined the significance of ritual and festival in radical activity during the French wars. The rich symbolism of banners, toasting, and 'caps of liberty' constituted a form of visual contestation of rights pitted against an admittedly similar culture of loyalism. Both went far beyond what might have been achieved by textual propaganda alone.[91] These forms of symbolic challenge were also integral to trade union action. One striking example occurred during the weavers' strikes of 1808. John Holden wrote in his diary on Wednesday 25 May: 'all that day the mob continued to assemble on Bolton Moor and to parade the streets with the effigy of Sir Robert Peel and they took off to Chowbent, Tidlsley Banks and Leigh'. They assembled the next morning and 'carried the effigy of Thomas Ainsworth'.[92] The elder Sir Robert Peel and his business partner, the magistrate Thomas Ainsworth, achieved a certain infamy in the town and across the region where the weavers had been on strike since 22 May. Reports of attacks on individual manufacturers' factories and homes across agitated districts are plentiful throughout the war,

[90] Lancashire CRO, QJC 1, Calendar of Prisoners held in Lancaster. Tomlinson, 'Letters of a Lancashire Luddite', 97–127.

[91] J. Epstein, *Radical Expression: Political Language, Ritual, and Symbol in England, 1780-1850* (Oxford, 1994), p. 70.

[92] Bolton Archives, Holden diaries.

but this kind of ritual or symbolizing appeared specifically in reports of the strikes of 1808. In late June, the *Manchester Mercury* alleged that weavers in Manchester were assembling in large numbers, stopping looms and burning effigies of 'several respectable manufacturers, whom they deem inimical to their claim'.[93]

The burning of effigies, together with other common tactics including threatening letters and machine-breaking, did not merely represent 'bargaining by riot'. They rather subverted the loyalist modes of action, especially the Paine-effigy burnings that those very manufacturers had condoned in the 1790s.[94] It was indicative of the complex identity of towns and villages still dominated by domestic production but increasingly aware of their wider role in a new industrial age. The ritual expressed provincial opposition to both local and national figures and institutions who local inhabitants believed had betrayed them by siding with the tide of economic laissez-faire. This involved what E. P. Thompson would have seen as a rebellious but conservative popular culture reacting against the very independence it enjoyed.[95] The strikers were well aware of the reciprocal obligations of parliament; hence their use of effigies of Robert Peel. Peel was the enemy on both a local and national scale because of his antagonism towards his employees in the region and in parliament against minimum wage legislation.[96] Striking weavers furthermore apparently regarded themselves as loyalists and were probably genuine in their denunciation of radicalism; they saw themselves as conducting their protest within the loyalist repertoire of action.[97] There was no direct 'progression', as Charles Tilly models it, from local and specific aims to direct and national appeals to parliament. The weavers' agitation of 1799–1802 demonstrated both elements, and while the mule spinners regretted parliamentary legislation, the weavers actively sought it, going over the heads of the local authorities. As their committee wrote in their address of May 1799: 'Are you afraid that we should approach the Government, and there tell the truth?'[98]

Prisoners provided another focus for many different campaigns and each ensured that its martyrs were celebrated publicly with much show: during the weavers' strike in Stockport, sixty weavers were brought into

93 *MM*, 28 June 1808.

94 F. O'Gorman, 'The Paine Burnings of 1792–1793', *P & P* 193 (2006), 111.

95 E. P. Thompson, *Customs in Common* (London, 1991), p. 76.

96 *Hansard*, XI, 19 May 1808, p. 426.

97 See NA, PC 1/44/A155, Draper *et al.* to Bancroft, 16 April 1799.

98 Aspinall, *Early Trade Unions*, pp. 21–3. C. Tilly, *Popular Contention in Great Britain, 1758–1834* (Cambridge, Mass., 1995).

custody on 14 June 1808. The prosecution claimed: 'The Prisoners were considered champions of the cause and were hailed as such. An assembly took place of such as appeared desirous of being made prisoners.'[99] On 19 September 1809, two Oldham hatters were freed from the Salford New Bailey after being imprisoned for remonstrating about the employment of women, a common source of contention among unionized journeymen. Rowbottom reported that they returned 'in a chaise [and] when the[y] arrived at Coppice Nook the hatters took the horses out of the carriage and drawed them in great triumph through every publick place in Oldham'.[100] Again the emphasis was on the reappropriation of space and forms of civic ritual. Occupation of the streets during times when the middle classes and gentry should have had control over them was a similar tactic. John Holden noted in horror the discipline of the demonstrations in the 1808 weavers' strike after the Bolton manufacturers refused to offer the deal agreed by their Manchester counterparts: 'on Friday they paraded the streets very quietly to the number of several Thousands and they are determined not to go to any work till s[ome]th[ing] is done for them'. This parading 'by file of three in a Breast' continued each day until the following Tuesday when the manufacturers went to the market place to offer the higher Manchester prices for their cloth but the weavers were dispersed by the cavalry.[101] The cumulative effect of this sight repeated over and over, without noise or riot, must have shaken the confidence of the local notables and the employers, who had to rely on the military to regain their control of space and time.

This sense of foreboding about the weavers' 'quiet' parading resurfaced in 1812. The tumults were however seen by some manufacturers and magistrates as being caused by 'strangers'. Participation in agitation outside one's 'neighbourhood' may have been a means of evading recognition, and therefore arrest, on the part of inhabitants of other towns, who travelled in on different routes from the bearing-home roads. Jeremiah Bury, a major manufacturer from Stockport whose factory was attacked, claimed when examined by the 1812 select committee into the petitions against the Orders in Council that he did not believe the riots were caused by 'the resident weavers, I mean those brought up in the country', a significant distinction. Rather, they were caused by 'persons who come from a distance', of whom he knew 'very little'. He

99 NA, TS 11/836, Chester Assizes, September 1808.

100 Rowbottom diaries.

101 Holden diaries.

testified to the good behaviour of the resident weavers and stated: 'I believe they have the system of leaving their own neighbourhood when they intended to riot.'[102] Although some of these reports may have reflected manufacturers' wishes to hide the possibility that their own workers may have been involved, the existence of such rumours also reflected the irrational, almost millenarian atmosphere surrounding the events of 1812. On 22 April, Revd Hay gave his account of the attack at Middleton to the Home Office, which corroborated Bury's opinion:

> The outrage which was very considerable was committed for the most part by strangers and therefore their proceedings being complete, they were no more heard of. This method of supplying strangers to commit such riots is generally resorted to and is one amid many other circumstances to prove that the insurgents act under an organized system.[103]

The magistrates shared these fears. Revd Hay's call for troops from the southern counties intimated his anxiety that the whole of Ashton-under-Lyne and its neighbourhood was against him. The emphasis on strangers may have been a delusion on the part of the overwhelmed authorities and forces of order, who certainly exaggerated the situation or perhaps wished to hide their incapacity to control the situation. It is possible on the other hand that there was some organization involved when inhabitants of other districts travelled to disturbances, and that the strangers were colliers. On 24 April, Hay, John Silvester, and Ralph Wright at the Manchester Police Office (set up a few years previously as an attempt to manage the increased demands placed upon magistrates by the rising population) wrote mysteriously:

> In the course of Sunday and Monday some thousands [of] seemingly strangers resorted to this town. They were all of awkward description—yesterday these people who very many of them had bundles and newly cut sticks totally disappeared.[104]

This delusion or scapegoating perhaps also indicates why the magistrates and many others placed much of the blame on Irish weavers, although few Irish were among those arrested.

Both radical and unionized protestors consciously manipulated confusion and overheated imagination as a means of disguise and method

[102] PP 1812, III, *Minutes of Evidence on. . .Petitions. . .Respecting the Orders in Council*, p. 269.

[103] NA, HO 42/122/592, Hay to Ryder, 22 April 1812.

[104] HO 42/122/546, Hay, Silvester, and Wright to Ryder, 24 April 1812.

of action. Exaggeration about the extensiveness of agitation and the existence of a movement rather than of isolated groups was initially a useful tactic in maintaining morale. Hyperbole developed into a common tactic among all types of protestors who wanted to invoke an image of collective strength. It then became a mythology, with a wider variety of meanings for participants and supporters. The leaders of the Weavers' Association during the strike of 1799–1803 envisaged a unified, although federated, northern weaving identity. Although the practical spread of the association was cast among skilled delegates within relatively easy reach of Bolton, the committee claimed to work 'in conjunction with the cotton weavers of the several counties of Chester, York, Derby, and Lancaster'.[105] Although this was a rhetorical device designed to persuade the legislators, the repetition of such tropes perhaps created a belief among activists and supporters that united action was possible. James Holcroft of Bolton was asked by the 1803 parliamentary select committee: 'Was it the favourite wish, in Whitefield, there should be a regulation of wages?' He proclaimed with confidence: 'It was not only the favourite wish of the People at Whitefield, but the favourite wish of the four counties of Lancaster, Cheshire, Yorkshire and Durham.' Again, this was an obvious generalization to convince the Commons that the demand for a minimum wage prevailed over sectional interests and regional boundaries, but his reply illustrated the pan-regional identity envisaged by the Committee. Holcroft's thinking was utopian compared with the practical horizons of the ordinary weavers he led. It is hard to judge what the Bolton weaver Thomas Thorpe actually knew about the extent of support for a new Arbitration bill, when he proclaimed before the 1803 select committee:

> I believe the whole Body of Mechanics are anxious for it at large . . . generally speaking, the whole Body wishes it to be done. What I speak of are in Lancashire, and a great number in Yorkshire, that I know are anxious for the Bill.

When asked, however, 'Are they anxious about it at Blackburn?' he replied: 'I do not know much about Blackburn'. The reason for this ignorance may have been that he had no personal contacts there, though he possibly did in other places, as he assured the examiner that 'there are a great many anxious about it at Chorley and Preston . . . and at Wigan too'.[106]

[105] BL, Additional MS 27835, Place papers on the Combination Acts.
[106] PP 1803, III part 4, pp. 34, 13.

Like the unionized workers, the United Englishmen, Luddites, and some radicals exaggerated their pan-regional and national spread to rally their supporters, give wider legitimacy to their campaigns, and intimidate their opponents. Their much more imaginative narrative about their enemies and leaders contrasted with the direct and legislation-oriented appeals to parliament made by the unionized workers. Although using many of the same legalistic tropes as the unionized workers, for Luddites these formed less of a common rhetoric and more of a mythology, shared not only by its participants but also by their would-be suppressors, who served to further develop the narrative. Pan-regional networks may not have worked in practice, but perceptions of them were crucial.

The influence of popular campaigns against corruption and for peace and reform infused its way into Luddite mythology. Luddites therefore came to share a still broader perception of the extent of connections and delusions targeted upon London. A prisoner of the Stockport magistrate J. S. Lloyd spoke of the Westminster radical Sir Francis Burdett as destined to become the first president of the Commonwealth when George III and the Prince Regent had been dispatched.[107] The Whig-radical MP Henry Brougham was also a major figure in inspiring ideas of wider connections. He acted as a defence lawyer for the 'Thirty Eight', arrested in Manchester in May 1812 during a meeting to discuss reform and also defended the Luddites against over-zealous magistrates and their spy system in the Commons debate over the select committee report into the disturbances.[108] Knowledge of these links with London personalities were evolved by extremists and other activists into plans for a rising reliant upon Burdett and the other London reformers. On 29 April 1812, a gaoler at Lancaster Castle found a letter in the pocket of a Bolton cloth worker written by James Burdett on 16 April, which mentioned his brother Francis and linked him with the cause of the Bolton committee.[109] That those Luddites who were not directly involved in moderate reform meetings took up the idea of support from London again demonstrated the intricate web of connections and ideas circulating within Luddism. Their support might come from Ireland, and France was still a hope, but the Luddites demonstrated their recognition of parliament's increasing centrality to their aspirations and of London radical leaders in furthering their demands. This may indeed

[107] Reid, *Land of Lost Content*, p. 176.
[108] *Liverpool Mercury*, 22 May 1812.
[109] Reid, *Land of Lost Content*, p. 146.

have been a consequence of the increasing size and effectiveness of the petitioning movements for peace and reform.

The consistency of unionized committees' strategy varied with the current economic situation, relative levels of repression by local forces of order and the progress of bills in parliament. Conflicting aims and strained connections altered the location and activities of committees. This did not mean that concerted action was impossible in this period. Nor did that require either a formal permanent structure or shared class-consciousness to be effective. The campaigns for peace and reform were able to cut across local boundaries; the strikes and petitions by weavers and spinners were pan-regional in scope. Furthermore, the rhetoric of Luddism revealed wider aims and extended links and bonds among communities. Luddism did not just consist of reactionary machine-breaking; participants were well aware of the traditions of unionized action and its relationship with parliamentary legislation. The language and mythology of Luddism illustrated that wider horizons were important both regionally and in terms of orientation towards London. Shared attitudes helped to consolidate the movement without the need for unified organization. Collective action by the working classes relied on geographical identities as well as class consciousness to sustain aims and solidarities. The connections built up during the war provided strong foundations for the much more extensive and pan-regional strikes of 1818 and 1826.

6

The Revival of Radicalism, 1807–15

On 4 June 1807, a celebration of the birthday of George III was held on Ardwick Green, an affluent village that was rapidly becoming a bourgeois suburb of Manchester. Superficially, all elements of the usual display, annually ritualized by local governing elites, were present. Several volunteer corps mustered, speeches were made, and the event was followed by a dinner with toasts. The celebration was sincere but the immediate appearances of loyalist patriotism were deceptive. The procession was led by Lieutenant-Colonel Joseph Hanson. The toasts at the dinner included:

> Lord Milton and the Independent Electors of Yorkshire;
> Mr Roscoe and Independent Liverpool Plumpers;
> Fox and the memory of Pitt;
> Colonel Hanson and the independent plumpers of Preston.[1]

The toasts thus celebrated contests by the independent candidates of Lord Milton, William Roscoe, and Hanson himself against Pittite-Tory borough elites in the elections of 1806 and 1807. They marked the public beginnings of the anti-corruption campaign that Sir Francis Burdett had revived in Westminster and which was becoming popular across the country. The toasts subverted ownership over the concept of loyalism. They reclaimed the 'true' memory of William Pitt the Younger, his original attachment to parliamentary reform in the 1780s, as opposed to the new and false memory of his anti-Jacobinism and anti-Catholicism fostered by Pittite Tories after his death.[2]

[1] *CMG*, 6 June 1807.

[2] J. J. Sack, *From Jacobite to Conservative: Reaction and Orthodoxy in Britain, c.1760–1832* (Cambridge, 1993), p. 133.

Such a brazen public demonstration would have been unthinkable only a couple of years earlier. The event was another form of the 'radical dining' which James Epstein has identified as a means of anti-loyalist meeting and protest in the 1790s.[3] It also exhibited some elements of electioneering satire and theatre, which Hanson may have picked up from his recent experience of narrow defeat while contesting the borough of Preston. The location was also significant, in that Ardwick was both the fashionable residence for aspirant Mancunian merchants and bore a Jacobite legacy in the form of its mock corporation. Hanson and his supporters partook in a radical act, but they deliberately displayed an alternative loyalism, which imitated then subverted loyalist tropes and symbols.

This story of the revival of radicalism has already been covered in detail by Peter Spence, Philip Harling, and Martin Ceadel amongst others, especially in relation to Westminster politics.[4] What this chapter examines are the consequences of these events for the development of radicalism in Lancashire. Two aspects have not been emphasized enough. Firstly, there is the sheer scale of the campaigns for peace and parliamentary reform from 1808. Hundreds of thousands of inhabitants met in mass meetings and assented to petitions to parliament. The agitations could no longer be suppressed as the brief burst of activity in the 1790s had been, but instead formed the essential preparation for the post-war mass platform, both in organization and leadership, and in sustaining ideas about the means of redress. Times had changed since the dark days of the late 1790s. There were new leaders and personalities on the political scene, new forms and principles of radicalism, and new opportunities for action. Secondly, public incidents involving bourgeois radicals were only one indication of something wider happening in the relationship between the provinces and Westminster politics. Though inspired by Burdett and Cartwright, local leaders consciously maintained an aloofness from metropolitan politicians. In so doing, they created their own distinctive brand of anti-corruption patriotism and constitutional radicalism, with important consequences for splits within the post-war radical movement.

[3] J. Epstein, 'Radical Dining: Toasting and Symbolic Expression in Early Nineteenth Century Lancashire: Rituals of Solidarity', *Albion*, 20 (1998), 271–91.

[4] P. Spence, *The Birth of Romantic Radicalism: War, Popular Politics and English Radical Reformism*, 1800–1815 (Aldershot, 1996); P. Harling, *The Waning of Old Corruption: The Politics of Economical Reform in Britain, 1779–1846* (Oxford, 1996); M. Ceadel, *The Origins of War Prevention: The British Peace Movement and International Relations, 1730–1854* (Oxford, 1996).

RADICALISM REVIVED

Two factors facilitated the change of direction in parliamentary and popular politics from 1806. The first was the general elections of 1806 and 1807, in which the abolition of the slave trade and Catholic relief were widely debated. The second was the reaction by the middle and lower classes, loyalist and radical alike, to the economic distresses caused by Napoleon's blockade of trade, and the government's response in the form of the Orders in Council. Both resulted in a revival of popular interest in national politics and the economy that in turn allowed the peace and reform campaigns to revive on a much greater scale than seen before. Challenges to the meaning and ownership of 'loyalism' flourished from 1806, led by the Friends of Peace, but opening the way for a new generation of radicals.

A specific combination of domestic and international events contributed to this new beginning. Firstly, after the death of Pitt the Younger, politics in parliament lost the relative stability it had sustained under the threat of French invasion. The Whig coalition of 1806–7, the 'Ministry of All the Talents', promised much for those among the radicals who clung to the memory of the glory days of Foxite Opposition, and even to recollections of the reforming Pitt of the 1780s. Its effects upon popular politics were both positive and negative. The ministry's failure to pass substantial parliamentary reform rankled many. Nevertheless, the brief hopes raised by its commitment both to abolition of the slave trade and to Catholic relief inspired a renewal of all forms of political expression: in the press, contested elections, public meetings, petitions to parliament, and by subverting civic patriotism. Patriotism was changing in response to the new international situation. After the British naval victory at Trafalgar in October 1805, the immediate sense of elation quickly faded in the face of Napoleon's increasing grip on the Continent and Britain's consequent slide into an isolated war of attrition. The unity fostered by the invasion scares similarly dissipated as Napoleon shifted to economic warfare with his Berlin Decrees of November 1806.[5] The Duke of Portland's response, in the form of the Orders in Council, became a major source of grievance for manufacturers and merchants. The British economic blockade was even more important in that it

[5] M. Turner, *The Age of Unease: Government and Reform in Britain, 1782–1832* (Stroud, 2000), pp. 126–8.

brought previously 'loyalist' merchants and manufacturers into the fold of opposition, together with their employees, now suffering from a drawn-out period of high prices, low wages, and short-time working.

This parliamentary instability that made it difficult for ministers to master the situation might have been overcome by a stronger ministry, but the Duke of Portland could not fill the gaping hole left by Pitt's death. Not that the Whigs were united in opposition either, after Fox had been taken away from them at last. Whig factionalism, though initially a problem to their supporters outside parliament, proved useful for radicals from 1808. The 'Mountain' group of younger radical Whigs gave a much needed boost to the anti-corruption campaign, and provided inspiration for radicals out of doors by calling for more extensive reform. Samuel Whitbread, Thomas Creevey, and their circle linked parliamentary with popular politics. Spence has argued that what solidified mass support for anti-corruption and reform was a conscious decision by the Mountain and their supporters to distance themselves from all vestiges of Paineite radicalism of the 1790s, particularly their former Francophilia and pacifism. From 1807, while loyalist Pittites were shifting towards neo-Toryism, the Westminster circle and the Friends of Peace shifted towards a more moderate platform of anti-corruption. They were able to reclaim some hold over the meaning of patriotism from the Church-and-King loyalists by connecting the corruption in government with Britain's poor conduct on the Continent. They attacked the failures of Canning's 'gunboat diplomacy' (primarily the Copenhagen, Convention of Cintra, and Walcheren debacles between 1807 and 1809) while avoiding the old imputation of sedition.[6] This was paralleled by a series of scandals over aristocratic corruption, climaxing in 1809, when Colonel Wardle, an obscure Welsh MP, exposed the Duke of York, commander-in-chief of the army, as having profited from illicit commissions sold by his former mistress. Outrage spread throughout the nation and the affair appeared to prove the radicals' accusations that financial corruption was connected to military failure.[7] This sense of unease about the state of the constitution that they were able to create culminated in May 1810, when Thomas Brand moved for a committee to 'inquire into the state of the representation of the people

[6] P. Spence, *The Birth of Romantic Radicalism: War, Popular Politics and English Reformism, 1800–1815* (Aldershot, 1996), pp. 22, 136.

[7] P. Harling, 'The Duke of York Affair (1809) and the Complexities of War-Time Patriotism', *HJ* 39 (1996), 963.

in parliament'. The old constitutionalist Whig demands reappeared in more radical terms: triennial parliaments, householder franchise, and redistribution of seats from rotten boroughs to the large unrepresented industrial towns.[8]

The elections of November 1806 and May 1807 provided an important stepping stone between the closed radical silence of the 1790s and the open debates of the later part of the war. National issues were now at the forefront, with local issues taking a secondary role in many constituencies. Frank O'Gorman has identified seven contested counties and fifteen contested boroughs in England which concentrated their elections around three major national issues: the pledge demanded of the ministry by the king, the abolition of the slave trade, and the Catholic relief bill of 1807.[9] The strength of feeling about these matters, reflected in speeches and electoral squibs, testified to their prominence in political debate across the country at this time. Electorates judged their sitting members and their landowning or corporation backing according to their positions on the national matters of importance rather than being swayed by patronage and local issues.

In Liverpool, the 'Friends of Peace', as always, took the lead. In 1802, Joseph Birch (1755–1833), a local West Indies merchant esteemed in Dissenting circles for expressing 'his opposition to the late administration and the war', began the 'independent' ball rolling.[10] Sir Francis Burdett's tumultuous attempts to gain a seat at Middlesex in 1804 and 1806, before succeeding in 1807 at Westminster, provided a model that could be imitated elsewhere. William Roscoe stood for election in 1806 and, to the dismay of the anti-abolitionist Corporation, was elected with a total of 1,151 votes, including 867 'plumpers', or electors who had given both their votes to him. General Isaac Gascoyne kept the seat he had long occupied while the infamous adventurer and Pittite General Banastre Tarleton lost. Roscoe wrote to Lord Holland after his election victory about his surprise that 'a friend to liberty and toleration and open and proclaimed enemy to the African Slave Trade should be returned for this place'. He optimistically attributed the result to the 'liberality, spirit and independence of my Townsmen'.[11] The reality was

[8] Turner, *Age of Unease*, pp. 124–8.

[9] F. O'Gorman, *Voters, Patrons, and Politics: the Unreformed Electoral System of Hanoverian England* (Oxford, 1989), p. 298.

[10] Liverpool RO, Roscoe papers, 920 CUR 9, Currie to Creevey, 9 July 1802.

[11] *History of the Election for Members of Parliament for Liverpool*. . . (Liverpool, 1806), p. 29; BL, Additional MS 51650, f. 92, Roscoe to Holland, 13 November 1806.

probably that the result had been achieved both because professionals and American merchants desired change, a wish brought about by the end of the Pittite regime, and by Roscoe's considerable personal expenditure on the campaign. In Preston, the 'independent' party was initially led by an attorney, a timber merchant, and a banker. Joseph Hanson came up from Manchester to fight the Whig–Tory coalition in 1807. Cowdroy resorted to hyperbole in his report of the contest: 'a closely pent-up borough, considered to be the almost unalienable property of a noble family, bursting as it were, into an effort of emancipation, scarcely to be paralleled . . . another attack and it must fall'.[12] Hanson failed to win a seat but received a total of 1,002 votes, including 960 plumpers, mainly from weavers and the professional middle classes, particularly attorneys.[13] Both results indicated a new atmosphere and activity among Whig-radical artisans and discontented members of the middle classes. The elections also illustrated the importance that special interests, particularly Tory-Anglican West Indies merchants, placed on national issues. Roscoe was forced by pro-Corporation violence to stand down from his candidacy in the 1807 election because of his votes in parliament for abolition and Catholic relief.

The activities of bourgeois radicals in the elections and renewed petitions to parliament did not necessarily imply an unenfranchised middle class was attempting to gain direct control over local government or representation. Rather, the anti-corruption and peace campaigns revolved around eroding the political hegemony local loyalist elites had acquired over freedom of expression and, in particular, over the meaning of the term 'loyalism'. The definition of loyalism was questioned and reclaimed by moderate radicals. Epstein argues that 'it was following the war that radicals attempted to counter the partial closure of meanings effected during the past two decades, boldly seeking to reappropriate and refashion visual and gestural symbolism' that drew on both the Glorious and the French Revolutions. However, this process had already begun in text and in action among the Lancashire radicals as early as 1807.[14] Imitation and subversion of loyalist ritual emerged as an effective tactic for sustaining a sense of radical purpose and identity in changing political circumstances. Contesting loyalism was itself a means

12 *CMG*, 23 May 1807.

13 *The Whole of the Addresses, Squibs, Songs and Other Papers Circulated During the Time of the Contested Election in Preston* (Preston, 1807), appendix.

14 J. Epstein, 'Understanding the Cap of Liberty: Symbolic Practice and Social Conflict in Early Nineteenth Century England', *P & P* 122 (1989), 91.

of regaining freedom of speech. The *Liverpool Chronicle* criticized General Gascoyne's speech after his 1807 election victory because it implied that 'all opposition to his being returned' was 'rebellion'. It cried ironically: 'Have General Gascoyne and his party a patent for monopolising by prescription all the loyalty of the town of Liverpool?'[15] The newspaper also printed a series of 'letters to the Freemen of Liverpool' by 'M.N.', probably as usual Matthew Nicholson, a member of Roscoe's circle. He meditated on the 'abuse of the word Loyalty', proclaiming that it should not be represented by the narrow definition favoured by Tory-Anglican elites. He accused the Corporation of regarding 'loyalty as an excuse for the malignancy of their tempers, and as a very convenient passport into the Custom-House, and the Excise Office'.[16] William Roscoe similarly disputed General Tarleton's Anglican view of loyalism during his final speech at the poll in 1806, while also expressing his own religious liberalism:

> Sorry I am to have heard some improper language used and to have seen bills posted with the words Church and King. We are all Church and King, but whether the Church of England—the Church of Scotland—the Church in St Ann's Street—or the Church in Paradise Street—is a matter that belongs in every man's bosom.[17]

High Anglican suspicion of Dissent provided one source of ideological complexity in the conflict. Church-and-King intolerance was so strong that Dissenters had already sensed that it would be futile to renew their campaign to repeal the Test and Corporation Acts. Tarleton criticized the Liverpool peace petition in the House of Commons in March 1808, bearing 'testimony to the respectability of Mr. Rathbone, the delegate from Liverpool, but he did not like his sectarian principles'.[18] Some of the anti-Roscoe squibs were framed in terms of loyalty; a call to support Gascoyne to repeal the African bill promised 'the victory of loyalty (over disloyalty and those who wish to triumph over His Majesty's Crown and Dignity)'. 'The True Meaning of Certain Phrases Used at Elections' was a revealing electoral squib produced by the pro-Generals camp in 1807 and equally remarkable was the pro-Roscoe retort. Both expounded in

[15] *Liverpool Chronicle*, 20 May 1807.

[16] *Liverpool Chronicle*, 10 June 1807; F. Nicholson, *Memorials of the Family of Nicholson* (Kendal, 1928), p. 75.

[17] *An Impartial Collection of the Addresses, Songs, Squibs. . .of the Election at Liverpool* (Liverpool, 1806), 14; *CMG*, 17 November 1806.

[18] *Hansard*, X, 3 March 1808, p. 892.

imitation of a dictionary the respective meanings which were attributed to common tropes. The loyalist pro-Generals squib included:

> *No popery*–That glorious Constitution in Church and State . . . the Watch Word of Loyalty and Patriotism against the Spirits of Turbulence and Disaffection.
> *The Generals*–A National Contest between Religion and Infidelity, the King's Prerogative against turbulent and disappointed Ambition; the purity of Protestant principles against the Fanaticism of Superstition.

The pro-Roscoe squib retorted:

> *The King*–The Chief Magistrate . . . may he govern all his good and loyal Subjects . . . by *equal laws*, and *grant them equal Rights and Privileges*, that they may *rally round his Throne* . . .
> *Slave Trade Restored*–This cannot be explained, having no meaning whatever, except Insanity.[19]

The pro-Generals' squib stressed how each stood for loyalty to an unreformed Anglican Hanoverian state; the pro-Roscoe squib focused on religious liberty and purging of parliamentary corruption to guarantee the stability of the constitution. Although the highly exaggerated language of the election propaganda was probably extreme even by the standards of their writers, they demonstrated that the subversion and manipulation of meanings in political rhetoric was a live issue.

Conflicts over the meaning of loyalism did not occur just in abstract debates in newspapers or tracts. Bourgeois radicals and their supporters saw opportunities to challenge the local loyalist elites over actual physical place, symbols, civic rituals, and forms of patriotic discourse. Contesting loyalism involved ritual on both sides. Local elites drew up loyalist addresses and petitions, always legitimized by a 'public' meeting. Their opponents requested the boroughreeve and constables or Corporation to call another meeting to draw up an altered petition. The local elites would refuse and usually retaliate with a counter-meeting and counter-petition. Often two opposing addresses or petitions were produced, each claiming to represent the views of the majority. This charade was well established: for example, it had been acted out during the Regency crisis in December 1788 when a public meeting in Manchester resulted in such turmoil that the chairman terminated the proceedings.[20] Implicit was a conflict

19 *An Impartial Collection*, 6, 43–4.

20 J. Bohstedt, *Riots and Community Politics in England and Wales, 1790–1810* (Cambridge, Mass., 1983), p. 104.

as to who had the right to represent the town's views to parliament or the king using the medium of meetings and petitions or addresses.

The Friends of Peace took the lead in these counter-rituals. In March 1808, Liverpool Corporation held a meeting to draw up a loyal address to the king. William Roscoe believed that the West Indies merchants within the Corporation had called the meeting specifically because they were aggrieved at the American merchants' campaign against the Orders in Council. During the meeting, Roscoe proposed an amendment to the address, calling for peace with France and the maintenance of amicable relations with America. The new address questioned Church-and-King domination over the term 'loyal'.[21] Cowdroy reported: 'He appealed to the meeting whether it was fair to say that the *generality* of the town of Liverpool were loyal—he would object to that expression in the Address—he would say that *all* the people of Liverpool were loyal.'[22] This was a direct challenge to claims of authority over the meaning of loyalism, offered from within the discourse of the elites rather than from outside it: Roscoe was anxious to stay within the bounds of bourgeois respectability and therefore proclaimed his tolerance towards the opinions of his opponents.[23] He nevertheless attempted to break the constraints which the Tory-Anglican definition of loyalism had placed upon his supporters, charging the self-proclaimed loyalists with 'the impropriety of imputing disloyal motives to those who might differ'.[24] A similar rhetorical battle was waged by the Royton radicals. After a mass meeting to draw up a peace petition was held on Oldham Edge on Christmas Day 1807, the Oldham constables issued an address in the Manchester newspapers accusing the participants of Jacobinism. The Royton spokesmen Henry Whitaker and James Kershaw published a counter-address, turning this rhetoric against the constables. They sardonically admitted to the charge of being 'enemies to the Government' because they believed the government had degraded and impoverished the country by pursuing the war: 'It is true that the Royton people have uniformly opposed both this and the last destructive wars! And if that entitles them to the epithet of enemies to the Government, they freely and gladly submit to it.'[25] Cowdroy

[21] Liverpool RO, 920 ROS 1755, Roscoe to Gloucester, 17 March 1808.

[22] *CMG*, 19 March 1808.

[23] M. Steinberg, 'Culturally Speaking: Finding a Commons Between Post-Structuralism and the Thompsonian Perspective', *SH* 21 (1996), 193.

[24] *CMG*, 19 March 1808.

[25] Chetham's Library, Hay MS, Mun A.3.10, Scrapbook 4, p. 110.

accompanied the address with his typically sardonic editorial expressing radical patriotism:

> Strange, that men who profess but one object . . . namely, our King's and Country's good—shall differ so widely about the means of obtaining that end: through war and blood, says one—through peace, commerce and manufactures, says another:—which are to be preferred, we leave history, policy, morality and above all Christianity to answer.[26]

In Bolton, the boroughreeve chaired a public meeting to draw up a loyal address to the king on 21 December 1807. Colonel Fletcher reported that a group of Unitarians were present who 'more than once attempted to introduce the subject of a petition for Peace, but this the Chairman repressed as it was not the object of the meeting'.[27] These protestors were probably led by Dr Robert Everleigh Taylor. Another meeting was held in February 1808. Fletcher described the 'conflict over the meeting room': 'a hundred petitioners burst in, refused to let the boroughreeve speak, crying, "*Peace, Peace, Peace*' ".[28] The views of the radical Dissenting intellectuals had gained open support from a wider section of the local middle classes. A letter by 'Verax', possibly Dr Robert Taylor, to *Cowdroy's Manchester Gazette* complained that the group of tradesmen and manufacturers 'who on former occasions have distinguished themselves by what is commonly called loyalty' were ignoring the voice of 18,000 pro-peace signatures by drawing up the town's loyal address. Cowdroy commented on the symbolism of place in the conflict: 'The opposers of peace at Bolton after experiencing a disappointment in not being able to obtain access to their intended place of meeting adjourned to the shambles—a situation not ill chosen for the friends of Slaughter.'[29]

Radicals similarly claimed control over the symbols of patriotism during the Napoleonic War, mainly those associated with George III and Pitt the Younger. Alternative celebrations of the king's birthday became an established means of opposing those arranged by the loyalist local notables elsewhere. The day of 4 June was commemorated in Bolton in 1810 by a dinner headed by the Unitarian radical Dr Robert Taylor. Toasts were raised in honour of Samuel Whitbread, Sir Francis Burdett, Lord Sheridan, Colonel Wardle 'and all the enemies of corruption', and with reference to the recent parliamentary reform bill: 'Mr Brand and

26 *CMG*, 2 January 1808.
27 NA, HO 42/91/963, Fletcher to Hawkesbury, 27 December 1807.
28 HO 42/95/1, Fletcher to Hawkesbury, February 1808.
29 *CMG*, 20, 27 February 1808.

may a timely reform prevent the danger of a revolution'. The alternative celebrations of 4 June were both national and local in context and scope. The toasts expressed elements of 'romantic' or 'reactionary' radicalism, as they adopted Burdettite tropes, especially an execration of Pittite corruption, constitutional reformist language and offered support for the metropolitan radical leaders.[30] As with Hanson's supporters, anti-Pittism was also a key theme of Roscoe's intellectual circle. Liverpool Corporation instigated annual civic celebrations of Pitt's birthday from 1810. Revd William Shepherd's scrapbooks contained a satire on such loyalist celebrations of Pitt's birthday. Among the toasts, the satire postulated, were 'Middling Classes of Society annihilated' and 'Sources of Corruption deepened and enlarged'.[31] The Liverpool 'Friends of Reform', the new incarnation of the Friends of Peace, met on 16 June 1810 in direct response to the anniversary. The toasts focused on Pitt's apparent betrayal of his Whig reforming past.[32]

These events exhibited how a shift away from the polarization and secrecy of the 1790s. As Peter Spence has argued, from 1806, radicals were able to use patriotism to gain the moral high ground from loyalists.[33] The national political upheavals and unsuccessful electoral challenges created wider ripples within the waters of popular politics. The Ministry of All the Talents had made it possible to speak about parliamentary reform, even if the divisions among the coalition Whigs had prevented any measure of reform being passed. The elections also focused popular attention on the state of the war and its effects upon the economy at a time when the unifying threat of invasion had faded. There were renewed opportunities for oppositional activity in the provinces, although in an altered and still tense milieu. As in 1801, the campaign for peace was slower to emerge in Lancashire than in the West Riding: mass meetings for peace were held in Sheffield and Leeds as early as October 1807.[34] Once again, radicals and their supporters decided that petitioning parliament was the easiest way of gathering hesitant public opinion and raising the profile of the campaign. Through the peace petitioning campaign, a mass popular movement was engendered, which did not have to be formally federated to be genuine or to gather significant support.

30 *CMG*, 9 June 1810; Spence, *Birth of Romantic Radicalism*, p. 33.
31 Harris Manchester College, Oxford, Shepherd MS, IX, p. 27.
32 *CMG*, 16 June 1810. 33 Spence, *Birth of Romantic Radicalism*, p. 47.
34 *Preston Journal*, 31 October 1807.

One new development was that in both Lancashire and the West Riding, radicals recognized that it would be more effectual for regions to combine their efforts and choose regional leaders to take the campaign to parliament. A few hundred inhabitants from Oldham, Ashton, Stockport, and Saddleworth attended a meeting in Ashton-under-Lyne on 23 November 1807. The Tameside inhabitants, or at least the organizers, radical schoolmaster William Clegg and Richard Partington, envisaged a regional campaign headed by Joseph Hanson as a pan-local leader, rather than just drawing up their own petitions, as Oldham and Stockport had done autonomously in 1800. They resolved to request Hanson and 'other gentlemen of rank and respectability in Manchester and its neighbourhood' to raise the petition. The resolutions further expressed a provincial identity in stating that the war was affecting the economic position of the 'lower and middling classes of manufacturing districts of Lancashire, Yorkshire and Cheshire'.[35]

Joseph Hanson was regarded as the most suitable 'gentleman leader' by the artisans across south-east Lancashire wishing to petition for peace and reform. He had publicly disagreed with Lord Milton, who was seen as having reneged on his Whig-radical stance when he argued that the Yorkshire peace petitions should not be presented to parliament. Hanson gained respect from petitioners across the Pennines. A letter in *Cowdroy's Manchester Gazette* in December 1807 from 'a woollen clothier' thanked Hanson 'at the request of a number of respectable distressed tradesmen in the West Riding'.[36] Hanson attempted to arrange for a meeting in Manchester to draw up a peace petition but was prevented from doing so by the authorities. It was well publicized by Cowdroy and must have influenced, if not inspired, meetings and petitions across the region. Hence Colonel Fletcher alleged in February 1808 that the Bolton peace campaigners knew 'they should fail to obtain such a meeting in the same manner as Mr Hanson Lieut. Commander of the Rifle Corps and his abettors had failed to obtain the call of a meeting'.[37]

Hanson then published *A Defence of the Petitions for Peace*, a pamphlet which contained strictures against the Manchester elites for their repressive actions against the working classes particularly, as its title suggests, their petitioning activity. His peace pamphlet was concerned primarily with the effects of the war on the weavers, stating his belief that the duty lay with the government to prevent starvation by negotiating

[35] *CMG*, 28 November 1807. [36] *CMG*, 5 December 1807.
[37] NA, HO 42/95/1, Fletcher to Home Office, February 1808.

for peace. It is an interesting example of middle-class awareness of the economic changes shaping their own class, in tension with their sense of paternalism for the workers. Hanson accused the parliamentary and local gentry, Whigs included, of prejudice against the middle classes: 'Talk of the distresses of manufacturers and others, they instantly refer you to the sudden rise and extravagance of commercial men.'[38] He criticized the failures of the Whig opposition, suggesting particularly that they had aligned themselves with the peace petitioners solely to gain votes. The great disappointment felt by the Liverpool circle over the failures of the Ministry of All the Talents was more rancorously expressed by Hanson. He announced his independence from 'party' much earlier than the Friends of Peace and maintained this stance, although this was eventually to prove to his detriment.

These challenges were not taken lightly by loyalist local elites. The coalition of magistrates and Tory manufacturers solidified under pressure. In March 1808, a Manchester counter-petition against peace raised 400 signatories, including the largest manufacturers, magistrates, and clergy. It again claimed to represent the genuine loyalism of the city against the peace petition which was characterized as seditious for admitting Britain's military weaknesses and desperate situation.[39] John Leigh Philips composed broadsides and wrote draft pamphlets censuring Hanson and his supporters.[40] Perhaps deliberately, at the 1808 celebration of the king's birthday, the boroughreeves and constables led the procession from the Bridgewater Arms to Ardwick Green, thereby reasserting Church-and-King control over the ceremony and route.[41]

Hanson's most infamous moment occurred on 25 May 1808, during the mass demonstrations of thousands of weavers on St George's Fields in Manchester. He had previously met with the Manchester weavers' committee and promised financial support, but it appears that his decision to address the crowd was more spontaneous than premeditated. Together with his subsequent arrest, trial, and imprisonment, the event secured his popularity amongst the working classes of the region and beyond.[42] He was not alone in addressing the striking multitude. On the

[38] J. Hanson, *A Defence of the Petitions for Peace* (Manchester, 1808), pp. 15–16.

[39] *MM*, 22 March 1808; MCL, BR f. 942.7389 Sc 13, Scrapbook.

[40] MCL, broadsides, 'Plain Truth' (1808); M84/3/5/21, Philips MS, volume of draft articles.

[41] *CMG*, 7 June 1808.

[42] NA, Treasury Solicitor papers, TS 11/657, Rex vs Hanson, Lancaster Assizes, 1809; E. Little, 'Joseph Hanson, "Weavers' Friend" ', *MRHR* 4 (1991), 22–30.

very same day as the St George's Fields demonstration, a large assembly of weavers gathered in Stockport was addressed by manufacturer William Dawson, who was subsequently arrested. A William Dawson Esq. had chaired a meeting in Wakefield to petition the king for peace in January 1801, although it cannot be proved that this was the same Dawson as at Stockport.[43] There is other evidence of middle-class, possibly radical, sympathy for the striking weavers; 120 rioters were bailed for riot in Stockport on 14 June 1808, some of whom at least must have received outside financial support.[44]

No more was heard of Dawson, but Hanson's popularity rose to new heights. The handloom weavers of Preston wrote to him while he languished in the King's Bench prison, calling for him to re-stand for election after his release and raising a subscription for his legal expenses. He politely declined both offers, so William Rowbottom noted in his diary: '39,600 weavers subscribed a penny each and bought a superb gold cup and salver w[h]ich they made him a present of the weavers from Bolton, Manchester, Ashton and Stockport'. A public presentation of the cup was cancelled for fear of a riot.[45] Hanson eventually answered the Manchester weavers' committee's request to represent them at the 1811 parliamentary select committee into the petitions from Manchester and Bolton about their economic distress.[46] He died soon afterwards and thus did not take his place among the litany of 'gentlemen radicals' headed by Henry Hunt in the post-war mass platform.

Hanson's predicament reflected in part the nature of radicalism in Manchester but also his own temperament. He did not and could not lead the sort of vibrant and supportive intellectual Dissenting circle that the Friends of Peace enjoyed. He was isolated politically in the 1800s. He apparently made little if no attempt to coordinate his political activities in Manchester with his friends Francis Astley Dukinfield (the prominent Unitarian landowner of Dukinfield near Ashton-under-Lyne and Stalybridge) and (possibly his brother-in-law) Joseph Kershaw, after

43 W. Dawson, *Stockport Flim-Flams* (Manchester, 1807), 7–8. The MCL copy is from John Leigh Philips's collection of tracts. Sheffield Archives, Wentworth-Woodhouse MS, WWM F/45/30, Wakefield broadside, 30 January 1801; there are no records of his trial—acknowledgements to Robert Glen for this information.

44 NA, Palatinate of Chester, CHES 24/183, Chester County Sessions, trial of Stockport weavers, 1808; See MCL, ballads, BR f. 824.04, BA 1, 1, p. 117, 'A New Song in Praise of Colonel Hanson'.

45 Rowbottom diaries; *Preston Journal*, 6 May, 18 November 1809.

46 PP 1810–11, II, *Minutes of Evidence from the Report on Petitions of Weavers from Manchester and Bolton*; *CMG*, 27 July 1811.

their support of the United Englishmen, although he shared their mercantile, volunteer, and Unitarian associations.[47] These, amongst other merchants and gentlemen, testified for Hanson at his trial in 1808, but apart from William Cowdroy and the attorney Frederick Raynes (who would later defend the Luddites and the 'Thirty-Eight' radicals tried in 1812), they were otherwise politically inactive in the 1800s.[48] Hanson's isolation sprang from his situation. His family attended Stand Chapel in Pilkington and so may not have had much contact with Roscoe's friends in the more socially respectable Liverpool and Manchester chapels. Most Manchester Unitarians were keen to disassociate themselves from his overt radicalism: the merchant Samuel Hibbert-Ware discontinued his friendship with Hanson in 1808 because of the latter's involvement in the peace movement. Hibbert-Ware wrote sardonically, in a counter-pamphlet to Hanson's peace pamphlet: 'He has quitted that circle of youth, loyalty and patriotism, to assume the more honourable character of a popular leader of petitioners.'[49] William Roscoe's Mancunian friends, for example the merchant William Parr Cresswell of Denton, shared Roscoe's views rather than those of the more radical Hanson, and even so they remained publicly silent.[50] Hanson thus became relatively neglected in the history of Lancashire radicalism, what reputation he had built up being rapidly overtaken by that of the new generation of post-war radicals.

Popular Petitioning

Peter Spence and J. E. Cookson have characterized the revival of popular petitioning from 1807 as part of the revival of 'romantic' patriotic radicalism, forged by economic distress and war-weariness.[51] This development was certainly apparent in Lancashire, though again regional particularities coloured the ways in which inhabitants responded to radicals' efforts to mobilize their political feelings. The first open mass gathering for peace in Lancashire recorded in the newspapers occurred

[47] Little, 'Joseph Hanson', 27; Lancashire CRO, WCW/1812, will of Joseph Hanson of Strangeways Hall.

[48] NA, Treasury Solicitor 11/657/2075, King agt Hanson, 1808; *The Whole Proceedings on the Trial of an Indictment Against Joseph Hanson Esq* (1809), p. 109.

[49] S. Hibbert-Ware, *A Reply to the Real Writer of a Pamphlet, April 1808* (Manchester, 1808), p. 38.

[50] Liverpool RO, 920 ROS 1865, Creswell to Roscoe, n.d., 1809.

[51] Spence, *Birth of Romantic Radicalism*, p. 81; J. E. Cookson, *The Friends of Peace: Anti-War Liberalism in England, 1793–1815* (Cambridge, 1982), p. 213.

in Rochdale on 7 December 1807.[52] This was followed on Christmas Day by a much larger event on Oldham Edge, high common land overlooking Oldham and Royton. Up to a thousand people reputedly attended, the largest number since the radical meetings of 1801. The event appears to have been arranged and led by the Royton radical circle. They probably authored the petition to parliament calling for peace, which was brought to the meeting for popular ratification. It was presented to the House of Commons in February 1808 and contained an estimated 13,000 signatures, from a population total of about 12,000 in the centre and 36,000 in outlying townships and district.[53] The number of signatures may have been exaggerated, but the number stated to have signed other peace petitions at that time suggests that a total of several thousands signed. Manchester's petition, for example, was stated in parliament to have 50,000 signatures. Cowdroy also claimed Stockport had collected 12,000 and Bolton 18,000. Liverpool also raised a large petition.[54]

A larger section of society was thus moving towards making strident demands for an end to the government's war of attrition against Napoleon and the economic blockade. At base, the rising levels of distress among large sections of both working and middle classes motivated the high proportion of signatures across the region. The earlier patterns of peaks and troughs in prices and wages were no longer characteristic. The average price of wheat and oats in Lancashire rose steadily from 1808–12 to the levels reached in 1800–1. Wheat was at the highest level of the war, at 163s 10d per quarter, in the week ending 29 August 1812; oats reached their highest price at 72s 5d per quarter.[55] The select committee reports of 1808 and 1812 concerning petitions against the Orders in Council charted the manufacturers' reactions to the trade restrictions and the weavers' increasing distress. They all indicated that the economic situation was much more serious than it had been when they had been interviewed about the Masters and Servants Act in 1801. Although both periods were marked by high prices, unemployment and low wages were more widespread from 1808. Jeremiah Bury, a major muslin manufacturer of Stockport, claimed he had turned off 500 to 600 weavers and was paying one third of the

52 Chetham's Library, Hay mss, Mun. A. 3.10, Scrapbook 4, pp. 109–10.

53 *CMG*, 27 February 1808; PP Census Abstracts, 1801.

54 *Hansard*, X, 18 March 1808; *CMG*, 20, 27 February, 12 March 1808.

55 *Manchester Chronicle*, various issues.

wage levels of 1803.[56] The effects were again voiced most clearly in the observations and lamentations of William Rowbottom in his diaries. He intimated a wish for peace for the first time in the winter of 1807–8, although not in overtly radical terms: 'Uncommon gloomy appearances for Christmas for the weaving Trade in all its Branches in the lowest Ebb wich as put the poor into a very deploreable situation and there is no hope of better times until a General Peace takes place.' This provides the specific context for the mass attendance at the meeting at Oldham Edge, but his comments also indicate more generally why the peace campaign spread in the rest of the region. On 3 April 1808, he lamented:

> The poor at this time are in a wretched situation such as was seldom known before all sorts of work Both scarce and a very little for working it and all sorts of provisions at an Enormous price makes the state of the poor to be miserable behind [beyond] description and a great deal of poor familys in a state of actual starvation.[57]

Rowbottom punctuated the rest of his annals with similar comments about the state of the poor and the economic effects of the war. Crucially also, the economic position of manufacturers and other middle-class elements was turning desperate on a greater scale than previously. Jeremiah Bury for example claimed that eleven out of the sixteen muslin manufacturers in Stockport had failed within the past twelve months.[58]

Economic distress alone could not have popularized widespread calls for peace. The war, especially in its phase of trade blockade, heightened interest in economic, geographical, and political affairs among the working and commercial populace. In his pamphlet of 1808, *Considerations on the Causes, Objects and Consequences of the Present War*, William Roscoe commented that public interest in the government's conduct of the war had reawakened and that this stemmed from the shift in the British perspective as the war changed from posing a physical threat of invasion to economic warfare:

> These circumstances, added to the threatening aspect of public affairs, have at length excited the dormant feelings of the people; and a suspicion, not wholly groundless, begins to prevail, that if they sleep much longer they may awake only to their destruction. Subjects of the greatest importance to their interests begin again to be discussed.[59]

[56] PP 1808, II, *Report from the Committee on the Petitions of Several Cotton Manufacturers. . .*, p. 2.

[57] Rowbottom diaries.

[58] PP 1808, II, *Select Committee Report*, p. 2.

[59] W. Roscoe, *Considerations on the Causes, Objects and Consequences of the Present War. . .* (1808), p. 2.

The population readily gleaned from the newspapers the increasingly isolated position Britain was in after losing its allies at Austerlitz, Jena, and Friedland. This situation, in which there was genuine doubt about whether victory was attainable, persisted from 1806 to 1813.[60] Napoleon's economic blockade inevitably put an extra strain on British manufacturing and trade, especially in Lancashire. The region was certainly not alone, but it reacted to the changes distinctly. The key conceptual connection many of the population began to make was between the seeming mismanagement of the economy by Portland's government and its foreign policies. Although this critique was initially conducted within the outwardly neutral framework of 'independence' or evangelical humanitarianism, it nevertheless shook the general torpor of the preceding few years. Pamphlets by William Roscoe and Joseph Hanson, and William Cowdroy's editorials were amongst the literature that politicized the distress and channelled it into campaigning for peace.[61] Radical patriotism was again the best means for reclaiming loyalism.

This is not to imply that all the population were immediately converted to a radical stance. Though Hanson's and Roscoe's pamphlets of 1808 were printed in great numbers and William Cobbett was increasingly scathing about government foreign policy in his *Political Register*, the loyalist spirit of Trafalgar was not completely or immediately erased among ordinary inhabitants. The bitter criticisms of the war by William Cowdroy and the editor of the *Liverpool Chronicle* similarly did not reflect public opinion at this point, judging by their frequent complaints about public indifference. Cowdroy lamented on 3 October 1807: 'Our countrymen, we fear, are too much infatuated by the splendour of military glory, if that can be called glory which is a terror to humanity, and utterly inconsistent with Christianity, to wish for peace.' In October 1808, he called for his readers to address the king but with a hint of resignation: 'we fear that our countrymen are more impressed with warlike than peaceful sentiments'.[62] Enthusiasm was shown for the revolutions against Napoleon on the Peninsula; radicals hoped that government and loyalists' tentative support for these popular displays of liberty would lead to renewed demands for reform in Britain.[63]

60 Cookson, *Friends of Peace*, p. 182.

61 W. Roscoe, *Occasional Tracts Relative to the War Between Great Britain and France* (1810), preface.

62 *CMG*, 29 October 1808.

63 S. Semmel, *Napoleon and the British* (New Haven, 2004), p. 138; Spence, *Birth of Romantic Radicalism*, pp. 92–7.

Yet this soon waned. Cowdroy felt that the situation had worsened in February 1809: 'The public mind, which only a few months ago was so enthusiastically excited in favour of Spanish liberty, has rapidly sank into a state of desponding indifference.'[64] It would take the parallel efforts of radical activists and discontented merchants to focus general discontent onto the government and towards parliamentary reform.

What spurred the petitioning of 1807 and 1812 was not a surge of 'radicalism', but rather a certain level of provincial opposition to metropolitan intrusion into the terrain of economic life. The Orders in Council touched even the most 'loyalist' of the commercial classes, and the petitions raised testify to the involvement of loyalists in methods of protest more associated with radicals. Loyalist Methodist preacher Charles Hulbert wrote in his memoir that he had been one of the 50,000 signatories to the petition against the Orders in Council from Manchester: 'No English Law was ever more injurious to the Trade and Manufactures of the country.'[65] The manufacturers and merchants keenly felt the direct impact of the shift in government tactics against the French and consequently against America. The introduction of an income tax in 1799 had already fuelled ideas that the government was profiting from war contracts and the hard-won profits of the industrious middle classes.[66] The peace petitions from 1807 gave great prominence to the ruinous economic effects of the government's foreign endeavours, the French and American blockades, increased taxation, and the growth of the national debt. Lancashire merchants were examined at the 1812 select committee into the petitions against the Orders in Council where they all bitterly related verging on bankruptcy as their trade with America through Liverpool had collapsed. Many nonetheless did not sign the petition itself, perhaps from lack of faith in its efficacy. James Kay, a major manufacturer in Bury, claimed in front of the select committee: 'I am no politician, and only came to point out the distresses of the country.'[67]

The issues of opposition to government and indeed Church-and-King loyalism were thus no longer the preserve of committed radicals in 'hotspots' such as Royton. The anti-slave trade campaign had provided an important precursor, demonstrating that the line could be crossed

64 *CMG*, 11 February 1809.

65 C. Hulbert, *Memoirs of Seventy Years of an Eventful Life* (Shrewsbury, 1832), p. 135.

66 Ceadel, *Origins of War Prevention*, p. 182.

67 PP 1812, III, *Minutes of Evidence. . .on Petitions Presented to the House of Commons Respecting the Orders in Council*, p. 195.

when provincial attitudes conflicted with those of government policy. Other examples of this can be seen in the campaign by Dissenters and Evangelicals against restriction of the Toleration Act in 1811. These outbursts of popular activity made it harder for petitioning to be seen as disloyal in itself, however much the Church-and-King loyalists argued about the seditious nature of the process of petitioning for peace. The middle-class reaction against the Orders in Council fused with the Whig-radical campaign against 'Old Corruption'. Like the issue of the Orders in Council, the reaction against the Duke of York's involvement in selling army commissions in 1809 straddled the boundary between loyalist and radical principles. In bringing the charges to light, Colonel Gwyllym Wardle became a national figurehead for the anti-corruption movement.[68] In Manchester, a war of rhetoric about the issue in handbills and broadsides erupted in late April. The fact that 2,000 names could be published in full on a broadside calling for a meeting in support of Wardle indicated how criticism of monarchy and government could now be expressed in the open.[69] Most names however did not appear on other petitions for more oppositional questions of peace and parliamentary reform, suggesting that even local loyalists felt incensed by the scandal.

The polarization of opinion between Church-and-King loyalism and Jacobin radicalism, enforced by loyalist elites after the French Revolution, had left those wishing to maintain their status in local government in a difficult position, one that they had created for themselves. Popular campaigns against 'Old Corruption' in parliament and in the monarchy posed more complex political decisions than the more clear-cut issues of peace and parliamentary reform. Some who might have agreed with the premise of the anti-corruption campaign nevertheless felt obliged to take sides on the basis of their previous positions and because of the stance they had taken against peace and reform petitions. This confusion of political stances was evident in Preston. The mayor refused to call a meeting to draw up a congratulatory address to Colonel Wardle. The front page of the *Preston Journal* for 20 May 1809 carried two columns of addresses and signatures for and against the mayor's decision. Controversy was heightened by the fact that the borough's two MPs, Lord Stanley and Samuel Horrocks,

68 Harling, *The Waning of Old Corruption*, p. 103.
69 MCL, BR f. 942.7389 Sc 13, Scrapbook, 1808–24.

had both voted for Wardle's motion in parliament and thus were also included in the proposed address of thanks. The local elites had significantly to shift their political perspective towards an acceptance of a more general loyalism. The counter-request sent to the mayor, although advising him not to call the meeting, nevertheless stated that Colonel Wardle's 'Conduct may deserve Approbation and applause and however [sic] we may with others lament and reprobate those corrupt Practices which have too plainly appeared'.[70] This counter-request was signed mainly by the clergy and gentlemen of the town and neighbourhood. Most of the signers of the pro-Wardle request who can be identified from the 1807 polls were artisans and skilled workers, but only a few had plumped for Hanson in that year.[71] Notably, the esquires who signed the counter-request can be identified as having been listed in a sequence that mirrors their places of residence. This suggests that the counter-request was carried door-to-door for the gentlemen to sign, in contrast to most pro-Wardle petitions and others calling for peace and reform or against corruption, which were left at printers, Unitarian chapels, and specified houses for people to visit voluntarily.

The peace petitions and mass meetings of 1808 were eclipsed by the anti-corruption campaign of 1809, in part because of greater middle-class support for the latter. The Hammonds contended that the rejection of the peace petitions by parliament in 1808 turned the working classes towards unionized action or radicalism.[72] The shift of focus in 1809 however marked only a temporary hiatus in the peace campaign. In summer 1810, Manchester and Salford raised a peace petition to the Commons containing 18,000 signatures. This rose to a total of 40,000 'manufacturers and artisans' in May 1811 together with 7,000 'weavers, spinners and artists' [sic] from Bolton.[73] Peace petitioning continued in parallel with the work of reform committees. John Holden recorded that another peace meeting occurred in Bolton in March 1812, where a petition was signed by over 11,000 weavers and subsequently presented to the Commons by the Earl of Derby.[74] In Manchester and surrounding towns, reformism became an active movement among the working classes from 1808. In Liverpool, there appears to have been much less radical activity amongst the working

70 *Preston Journal*, 20 May 1809.
71 *The Whole of the Addresses, Squibs, Songs. . . 1807*, appendix.
72 J. L. and B. Hammond, *The Skilled Labourer, 1760–1832* (London, 1919), p. 85.
73 *CMG*, 30 June 1810; *Hansard*, XX, 30 May 1811.
74 Holden diaries; *CMG*, 7 March 1812.

classes. The reform campaign there remained bourgeois with the same leaders as in the 1790s, centred on Roscoe and Rathbone.

Petitions for economic relief were submitted to parliament in 1811 from various Lancashire towns. They differed from those of 1808 because they were products of cooperation with manufacturers who would generally have considered themselves avowed loyalists. They briefly embraced a position oppositional to government as a result of two influences, the economic strains of war and evangelical Christian impulses. This indicated the extent of the toll the war was taking on most of the population. On 14 February 1811, according to John Holden, the 'Committee of Weavers called a meeting of the merchants and manufacturers and landholders etc of Bolton at the assembly room' to draw up a petition to the Prince Regent calling for economic relief. It was the loyalist manufacturer and commander of the Bolton cavalry, John Pilkington, rather than the weavers themselves, who drew up the petition.[75] The Blackburn petition 'respecting the state of Public Affairs' presented to the Commons on 20 March 1812 was in effect a middle-class petition against the Orders in Council and East India Company monopoly. Its major complaint was 'the gradual disappearance of the middling classes, which are fast melting down into the lower orders of the community'.[76]

A whole range of issues and interests thus spurred a wide range of people to meet and petition parliament from 1807. Of course, much of the support for the campaign against the Orders in Council was economically self-interested, and the economic distress of these years undoubtedly pressed individuals to act who would normally have been acquiescent. Neither did all towns in Lancashire send petitions; Cowdroy intimated that local efforts were often stalled by the opposition of loyalist corporations and notables who still regarded such action as seditious or did not wish to associate their town with discontent. What is certain is that a broader spectrum of opinion could now find voice, and radicals could legitimize their campaigns for peace and reform in terms of principles previously annexed by loyalism, that is, in terms of patriotism. The revived rhetoric of Old Corruption was highly influential in shaping the change in public perceptions of Britain's role in the war and on the Continent. Regional interests, principally economic, were also prominent, combined with a shared

[75] Holden diaries; NA, HO 42/117/520, Pilkington to Derby, 12 November 1811.
[76] *Blackburn Mail*, 4 March 1812; *Hansard*, XXII, 20 March 1812, 212.

sense of provincial opposition to intrusion from London. This was not just reactionary radicalism or the idealism of the Friends of Peace but also contained hints of the legacy of Paineite radicalism from the early 1790s. This synthesis formed a distinctive Lancashire stance which ran through the peace and reform campaign. The next section will explore that synthesis in more detail.

FROM OLD TO NEW RADICALS

Radicalism in Lancashire drew freely from both constitutionalism and Paineite egalitarianism according to circumstances. It was regionally distinctive, imbued with a particular patriotism tailored to its geographical identity. E. P. Thompson conjectured that popular politics in the north of England differed from that of London in this period because of its reliance on secrecy, oaths, and the 'radical underground'. Hence he believed that metropolitan leaders were distanced from the mass of the English working classes, claiming: 'Until 1815, neither Burdett nor Cobbett meant much in the heartlands of the Industrial Revolution'.[77] In some senses, this was correct, but John Belchem and Peter Spence have provided an alternative picture of the 'radical overground' across the country rallying behind the leadership of Sir Francis Burdett.[78] The reform campaign from 1810 indeed had the definite feel of a national movement, with petitions to the Commons sent from across the country, and much emphasis was placed upon Burdett's activities in the local press and in petitions and toasts. Yet, as in relation to other forms of opinion and identity, northern radicals did not accept Burdettite tenets or leadership wholesale. Radicalism became popular through the filter of provincial identity and needs.

The petitions from 1809 and other broadsides and addresses were different from those of the 1790s because of their adoption of Burdett as a focus for national leaders. This was partly a result of the popularity of Colonel Wardle's anti-corruption drive, which centred attention on the London radicals. In many places support for Wardle was contiguous with the peace campaign. William Rowbottom noted on 20 March 1809: 'a very numerous meeting took place on Boardman Edge to

[77] E. P. Thompson, *The Making of the English Working Class* (Harmondsworth, 1968), pp. 509, 514.

[78] J. Belchem, *Industrialization and the Working Class: the English Experience, 1750–1900* (Aldershot, 1990), p. 69; Spence, *Birth of Romantic Radicalism*.

petition for peace'.[79] This was followed on 3 April by 'a very numerous meeting at Tandle Hills and came to a resalution [sic] to petition for Peace and to return Collonal Wardle and Sir Francis Burdett thanks for careing [sic] the charges up to the Duke of York'.[80] A Liverpool reform petition of May 1810 avowed the 'expediency of summoning Sir F. Burdett to assist in the deliberations' for reform and cited him in the context of their rhetoric against parliamentary corruption.[81] Radical John Knight wrote a letter of 4 June 1810 addressed to Burdett which was left for signatures in various places in Manchester and Salford.[82] There had been no comparable adoration of a reformer since the days of John Wilkes in the 1760s, though even then, the 'friend to liberty' was not as popular in Lancashire as elsewhere.

Provincial radicalism was thus influenced by national radicals, but it should also be stressed that it was organized on the ground by a new generation of local leaders. Hanson and his contemporaries were gradually overtaken by new personalities, who would later help to organize post-war mass-platform radicalism. Their political education took place during the years of the Napoleonic War. They had neither the experience nor sense of identity of the veterans of the 1790s. They had been nurtured less directly on Paine and more on Cowdroy and Cobbett. One member of the new generation, John Edward Taylor (1791–1844), indeed began contributing to Cowdroy's *Gazette* from about 1812. They had first witnessed radical leadership in the heady battle of meetings and words between the survivors from the 1790s radicals and loyalist authorities in 1806–8. Their post-war political activities, particularly their participation in the Hampden Clubs and at Peterloo, have been examined in detail by Michael J. Turner and Louise Edwards and therefore will not be discussed in detail.[83] What is surveyed here are the events leading up to the Exchange Riot of 1812 which brought them into the public light.

In Bolton, a meeting on 7 May 1809 appears to have marked the birth of their new reform committee. A fortnight later, a request signed by 225 names called for a pro-Wardle meeting after the boroughreeves and

79 A hill overlooking Lees, south east of Oldham.

80 Rowbottom diaries.

81 *Hansard*, XVII, 21 May 1810, 117.

82 MCL, BR f. 942.7389 Sc 13, Scrapbook, p. 15; *MM*, 30 June 1810; J. R. Dinwiddy, 'Luddism and Politics in the Northern Counties', *SH* 4 (1979), 38.

83 M. J. Turner, *Reform and Respectability: the Making of a Middle-Class Liberalism in Early Nineteenth Century Manchester*, Chetham Society, 3rd ser., 40 (1995), p. 16; L. Edwards, 'Popular Politics in the North West of England, 1815–21', Ph.D thesis (Manchester, 1998), p. 72.

constables had failed to reply to their original request. The signatures included the Bank Street Unitarian Chapel bourgeoisie, including prominently the physician Dr Robert Everleigh Taylor and the cotton manufacturers Joseph Heywood and Jeremiah Crook.[84] Other names had not been evident in earlier agitation and indicated a new generation of radicals gradually coming to prominence. One new person who signed the notice, John Ormrod, was a 'currier' from the working-class area of Spring Gardens; he appeared as one of the committee of four who organized the Bolton peace petition of 1812. Ellis Yates of King Street was another name on both petitions. He may have been the Ellis Yates who was later overseer, muslin manufacturer, and owner of much property in the town.[85] The informant James Lomax implicated his employer, the bleacher Thomas Hulme, during his examination about the Luddite disturbances at Westhoughton. He claimed he 'was sometime back Chairman of a meeting for Parliamentary Reform', and that 'many of his men have been found to have attended the late seditious meetings'. Spies were prone to exaggeration, but at least some suspicions can be verified. Hulme indeed joined Major Cartwright's Union for Parliamentary Reform in 1812 and was to be a Hampden Club delegate in 1817.[86]

Manchester again served as the focus for new leadership. Two Manchester scrapbooks survive (now in the Central Library), containing handbills advertising political meetings to draw up addresses from 1809. John Shuttleworth (1786–1864) compiled one scrapbook and the other may have been put together by Archibald Prentice (1792–1857).[87] Shuttleworth was a leading new name among the 2,000 signatories in Manchester who called for a meeting to address Colonel Wardle on 3 May 1809.[88] Some were Unitarians, including Ottiwell Wood (1760–1847), who headed the list. Wood was a merchant and a trustee of Cross St Chapel and his son John became a prominent

84 Bolton Archives, Heywood papers, ZHE 5/9, Bank Street Chapel subscription of 1809.

85 Bolton Archives, 1811 Bolton census return; MCL, BR f. 942.7389 Sc 13, Scrapbook, p. 11; R. Dryburgh, *Individual, Illegal and Unjust Purposes: Overseers, Incentives and the Old Poor Law in Bolton, 1820–1837*, University of Oxford Discussion Papers in Economic and Social History, 50 (2003), 24–5.

86 NA, HO 40/1/1/115, Fletcher to Home Office, 15 May 1812; Dinwiddy, 'Luddism and Politics', 59.

87 MCL, BR f. 942.7389 Sc 13, Scrapbook, 1808–24; BR f. 324.942733 S3 and Sh1, Shuttleworth Scrapbooks.

88 MCL, BR f. 942.7389 Sc 13, Scrapbook, p. 5.

campaigner for Reform in the 1820s.[89] The Manchester merchants, Thomas Slater and George William Wood, also signed. The former was a trustee of Cross St. Chapel, while the latter was trustee of both Strand and Platt Chapel, future president of the Manchester Chamber of Commerce and later MP for Kendal.[90] The manufacturer Robert Philips was a Lit and Phil member and father of the first MP for Manchester. William Washington made his first public appearance chairing a meeting in the Manor Court Room in Manchester on 29 April 1811, held to petition parliament for redress for economic distress.[91] Dissent formed part of these men's identity and principles, though not all were Unitarians. Joseph Brotherton was a member of Revd William Cowherd's congregation of Bible Christians in Salford. The sect had great faith in the 'march of intellect' and the post-war Peace Society was one of its offshoots. He became overseer of the poor in Salford in 1811. Samuel Bamford had been brought up as a Wesleyan Methodist. Absalom Watkin was a lay preacher for the Methodist New Connexion.[92]

The new radical leaders were in age a new generation, mainly born in the late 1770s and 1780s. John Shuttleworth was 22 or 23 at the time of the pro-Wardle address; the attorney Fenton Robinson Atkinson, who defended the Luddites, the 'Thirty-Eight' radicals in 1812 and the Blanketeers in 1817, was only a couple of years older. They were therefore too young to have had the chance to participate in the radicalism of the 1790s. Some of the infamous 'Thirty-Eight', arrested in Manchester while meeting to draw up a reform petition in June 1812, were in their early twenties: James Knott, a hatter of Hyde, Charles Smith, a Manchester fustian cutter, and Charles Wooling, a Manchester cotton spinner, were only 21; Aaron Marvel, a weaver of Mottram and John Howarth, a fustian cutter of Salford, were 22.[93] The prosecution at their trial indeed expressed doubt that people of such an age were capable of discussing constitutional rather than revolutionary reform. Of the 'Thirty-Eight', twenty-two lived in Manchester, with the rest coming from the immediate satellite towns, including Ashton, Oldham,

89 T. Swindells, *Manchester Streets and Manchester Men*, vol. 2 (Manchester, 1906), pp. 116–17.

90 T. Baker, *Memorials of a Dissenting Chapel* (1884), pp. 93, 107.

91 *CMG*, 4 May 1811.

92 Ceadel, *Origins of War Prevention*, p. 157; *The Diaries of Absalom Watkin: a Manchester Man, 1787–1861*, ed. M. Goffin (Stroud, 1993).

93 NA, TS 11/1059; Lancashire CRO, MF 10/139, Lancaster Assizes indictments.

Droylsden, Hyde, Stalybridge, and Hadfield in Derbyshire.[94] Some of the new generation were newcomers from outside the region and had not therefore even seen the political events or the older radical personalities of the 1790s in Lancashire. The Potter family came from Tadcaster, Yorkshire, in 1801; John Edward Taylor was born in Illminster, Sussex, and moved to Manchester in about 1805. Fenton Robinson Atkinson was born in Leeds and Joseph Brotherton moved to Manchester from Chesterfield in 1789.[95]

There were differences of political perspective between the old and new radicals and the general population, which though not impermeable were still apparent. This can be seen in the conscious separation between Samuel Bamford and his father's generation. The young Samuel must have imbibed an openness towards radical ideas from his father and uncle's Middleton radical circle, but he appears to have considered their political beliefs as part of the old world of the 1790s. He rather attributed his political education to reading Cobbett's *Political Register* at work in the later 1800s, and only became deeply involved in the new radicalism following Major Cartwright's tours of the North in 1812–13.[96] Bamford's late entry into radical activism was comparable to that of his colleagues. During the summer of 1811, Absalom Watkin formed the Literary and Scientific Club in Manchester with Richard Watson, a Methodist preacher and a business friend, William Makinson, possibly as an alternative to the now Tory-dominated Lit and Phil. Watkin emerged into prominence after the Exchange Riot of 1812, when he read a provocative paper to the Club on the needless prolongation of the war. He only became fully involved in the public eye when he went to an anti-corn bill meeting in February 1815, where he met with J. E. Taylor, Archibald Prentice, Shuttleworth, and the Potter brothers.[97]

The new generation used the metropolitan radicals and sympathetic Mountain Whig MPs as patrons, but it was a reciprocal process. In 1811, the reform committee in Bolton corresponded with Samuel Whitbread who advised them to petition both parliament and the Prince Regent for peace.[98] Henry Brougham was also a significant

[94] *The Trial at Full Length of the Thirty Eight Men from Manchester, 27 August 1812* (Manchester, 1812), p. 41.

[95] P. Shapley, 'Joseph Brotherton (1783–1857)'; A. C. Howe, 'Thomas Bayley Potter (1817–1898)', *Oxford Dictionary of National Biography.*

[96] S. Bamford, The Autobiography of Samuel Bamford: *Early Days*, new edn, ed. W. H. Chaloner (London, 1967), p. 282.

[97] *Diaries of Absalom Watkin*, pp. 9–12, 21.

[98] Dinwiddy, 'Luddism and Politics', 39.

contact, presenting the peace petition from Chorley, amongst others, to parliament in 1812. Major Cartwright corresponded with Shuttleworth, Atkinson, Potter, and Walker. By 1812, Lancashire men borrowed and disseminated rhetoric from the London radicals, particularly from the set of resolutions moved in February by City radical Robert Waithman. The petition submitted to a reform meeting in Manchester on 11 June was to have been presented to the Commons by Burdett. It included a number of romantic radical or 'liberal' grievances that Burdett had already emphasized in his address to the Prince Regent: the burden of taxation, the spread of army barracks across the country and the use of 'ex officio informations' to control the press.[99]

The Lancashire reform movement nevertheless had a regional stamp firmly impressed over any wider influences. The metropolitan radicals provided inspiration and renewed radical ideas, but the new generation of local leaders brought these into practice. While E. P. Thompson underestimated the impact of Burdett and the metropolitan radicals on provincial radicalism, Philip Harling and others have conversely neglected the role of local leadership on the ground in their explanations for the renewal of interest in parliamentary reform before the rise of the post-war mass platform.[100] The Manchester reform committee led by William Washington still put their trust in the leadership of Joseph Hanson, deputed to represent them at the Commons Select Committee into the petitions for economic relief in 1811.[101] The new generation remained in contact with old local radicals after Hanson's death. Major Cartwright wrote to John Shuttleworth, asking him to forward a paper to Dr Taylor in Bolton. Manchester veteran Thomas Walker sent subscriptions to Shuttleworth for the defence of the 'Thirty Eight' in August 1812 'from a friend of Peace and Reform', and they cooperated with Cartwright to this end.[102] Radicals occupied themselves especially with locally pressing issues, even if in conjunction with national leaders. Deputies were sent by the 'Friends of Freedom' of Bolton to the parliamentary select committee on the Luddite disturbances, though they were not examined. They communicated their concerns to Henry Brougham; in response, he made an accusatory speech in the Commons against the

99 *Trial at Full Length of the Thirty Eight*, pp. 124–5; Dinwiddy, 'Luddism and Politics', 62.

100 Harling, *Waning of Old Corruption*, p. 103; see R. Eckersley, 'Of Radical Design: John Cartwright and the Redesign of the Reform Campaign, c.1800–1811', *History*, 89 (2004), 560–80.

101 *CMG*, 11 May 1811.

102 MCL, BR f. 324.942733 Sh1, Shuttleworth loose leaves, no. 5.

Peace Preservation Bill on 13 July 1812, using Robert Taylor's evidence about the magistrates' spy system. The Bolton Friends of Freedom presented 100g of plate to Dr Taylor in that month for his efforts in exposing the spies' activities.[103] The Liverpool Friends of Reform by contrast rejected organization from London. Spence argues that the opposition among metropolitan leaders to Cartwright's attempts to revive the tradition of grand reform dinners was because 'one half of romantic reformism had derived from popular loyalism and as such distrusted the political strategies of the patriot reformers'.[104] In 1812, Roscoe twice refused Major Cartwright's requests to be a steward at the reform meeting of the 'Committee of Friends of Parliamentary Reform'.[105]

The new generation of radicals were eager to assert their own local identity and leadership of the growing movement. Both committed radicals and their supporters refused to accept Burdettite radicalism unconditionally, adapting London resolutions to their own prejudices and identity. The Manchester resolutions of 11 June 1812 went beyond Burdett's programme of moderate reform. While they asked for an extension of suffrage 'as far as taxation', they did not repeat Burdett's demand for the enfranchisement of those subject to direct taxes; rather, they specifically requested 'that each man, not insane nor confined for crime, be entitled to vote for his representative'. Manhood suffrage had been an intermittent theme among many Lancashire radicals from 1789 and now the opportunity had again arisen to demand it. This prefigured the success of Samuel Bamford and others in substituting this claim for a more restrictive proposal at the Hampden Club convention of January 1817.[106]

Provincial radicalism had moved on. The key radical–loyalist battles of the 1790s do not appear to have been commemorated or mythologized in the 1800s. This may have been impossible because of loyalist control of ritual or radicals may have celebrated them in private. Yet none of the toasts or rhetoric during radical dinners or meetings from 1808 mentioned such definitive incidents as the attack on the *Manchester Herald* or the 1795 petition against the Two Acts. Nor did the writings of later radicals dwell on the significance of these wartime struggles. The surviving scrapbooks compiled by post-war radical leaders charted

[103] *Hansard*, XXIII, 13 July 1812, 1021; R. Taylor, *Letters on the subject of the Lancashire Riots* (Botton, 1812), p. 5.

[104] Spence, *Birth of Romantic Radicalism*, p. 162.

[105] Liverpool RO, 920 ROS 759, Roscoe to Cartwright, 9 February 1809.

[106] Dinwiddy, 'Luddism and Politics', 62.

only recent radical events from 1809 in shaping and affirming their radical identity.[107] Archibald Prentice did summarize the conflicts in 1790s Manchester in his *Personal Recollections*, but only as a historical prelude to the efforts of his own generation and the role of 1815 in shaping post-war radical sentiment.[108] This indicated the desire of a new generation of radicals for a clear break from the difficulties of coordination their predecessors experienced during the war. Their priorities and sense of history were different from the radicals of the 1790s. The Mancuno-centric nature of the surviving evidence about radical events is also attributable to this bias, with most post-war radical organization in the region dependent upon the town. Hence there remains no indication of wartime radicalism in for example Lancaster or further north in Lancashire, though the presence of radicals there, active or not, cannot be discounted.

The Last Years of War

William Rowbottom made a prophetic observation in his diary in January 1812:

> 1812–the old English hospitality is nearly Extinguished in every family at this time the lower class of people who have a family of small children are absolutely short of the common necessaries of life and a deal of familys have not left off work at all . . . to all appearances if there be an alternation of times it must be for the Better except there be commotions or civil wars wich [sic] God grant may never happen in this country or Kingdom.[109]

His comment marked the start of the most tumultuous year of the wars for Lancashire. If ever there was a serious threat to public order and social stability, it was not in the post-French Revolution years of 1792 or 1795, nor even during the United Englishmen conspiracies and food rioting of 1798–1801, but in 1812, which was the year of nemesis for loyalist ruling elites. They witnessed and attempted to deal with a complex range of problems including: the Regency, widespread rioting, serious economic distress, Luddite disturbances, the assassination of the

107 MCL, BR f. 942.7389 Sc 13, scrapbook, 1808–24; BR f. 324.942733 S3 and Sh1, Shuttleworth Scrapbook.

108 A. Prentice, *Historical Sketches and Personal Recollections of Manchester*, 2nd edn (1851).

109 Rowbottom diaries.

prime minister by a Liverpudlian merchant, the success of the campaign to repeal the Orders in Council, and the first mass radical meeting, which began to build up momentum for the post-war popular radical movement.

The changing popular political atmosphere had reopened the scope for debate, particularly about the relationship between local and national issues. The tangible increase in the national political content of election material that had been first evident in 1806 culminated in the general election of 1812. Roscoe noticed that the increased importance attached to the function of representation could be seen in the conduct of electoral candidates who 'find it necessary to state, more at large than was formerly done, the nature of their political opinions, and the grounds upon which they solicit the suffrages of the electors'.[110] It was exemplified by the candidacies of national figures in Liverpool. Parliamentary allies of the Friends of Peace, Thomas Creevey and Henry Brougham, were pitted against the West Indies merchants' controversial choice of the pro-Catholic Emancipation George Canning. They thereby turned the borough into an arena representing the national conflict between the Mountain Whigs and Pittites. One election squib was adamant against 'this political Chameleon', Canning, denouncing his infamous duel with Lord Castlereagh and calling upon Liverpudlian freemen to vote for Brougham and Creevey, 'the Friends of Peace and Reform'.[111] Canning's courting of the merchant interest with promises of economic relief and castigations of the radical histories of his opponents won him a large majority. Roscoe was outraged and published a vicious critique of his campaign.[112] Preston was contested by Joseph Hanson's younger brother Edward. The squibs similarly highlighted issues unspoken in previous elections, in language reminiscent of a decade's worth of Cowdroy's editorials. A letter by 'an old Freeman' lamented the effects of the 'blood-stained sword of desolation' with hints of Gothic millenarianism: 'Cast a retrospective glance over your country; see her in the midst of a vortex of difficulties; groaning under an immense load of debt—her unparalleled taxation—her commerce almost annihilated . . . her mechanics and artificers starving.'[113]

[110] W. Roscoe, *A Review of the Speeches of the Right Hon. George Canning* (Liverpool, 1812), p. 3.

[111] *Impartial Collection of Addresses, Songs, Squibs* (Liverpool, 1812), p. 6.

[112] Roscoe, *A Review of the Speeches.*

[113] *Complete Collection of Addresses, Squibs, Songs etc. . .at the Election at Preston* (1812), p. 16.

Cowdroy's editorials returned almost to previous levels of detailed, bold, and vitriolic spleen against the corruption of ministers and the conduct of the war. The founding of the *Liverpool Mercury* marked the culmination of the freeing of debate . The newspaper was published from 5 July 1811 by Egerton Smith, an abolitionist, poet, and later founder of the Mechanics' Institute.[114] He deliberately set out to propagate constitutionalist radical and 'liberal' themes from the outset. 'Peace, freedom and improvement' were announced to be the leading objects that would be advocated in its pages. The first issue contained Roscoe's letter to Henry Brougham in support of parliamentary reform. It was supportive of the Friends of Reform in Liverpool but avowed some independence from them. The editorial stated the paper's approval of Roscoe's opinions and asserted: 'It is not violence, but firmness, not virulence of language but clearness of reasoning, which distinguishes the reformer from the revolutionist, the friend of liberty from the partizan of anarchy.'[115] Meanwhile, Hampden clubs began emerging after the model promoted by Major Cartwright. It is clear therefore that moderate radicalism had grown in strength and confidence.

March–June 1812 was the period of greatest activity among the myriad committees and groups across the region. Petitions from Blackburn, Manchester and Preston concerning the Orders in Council, East India Company, peace, reform, and economic relief were 'laid on the table' in March. The language if not the background organization of the various peace and reform petitions converged, indicating closer sympathy and cooperation among radicals and the ordinary population. The Preston petition reiterated the new form of romantic patriotism that straddled the divide between loyalism and radicalism in its paternalist concern for the state of its artisans and the attritional nature of the war: 'This anxiety . . . they beg to assure the House, is not created in them by any dread of the enemy; but being unacquainted with any desirable object, to the attainment of which a prosecution of the war will be conducive.'[116] The petitions from Chowbent and Chorley to the Commons of May 1812 also suggest a revived network among the weavers' committees and more tentatively, their links with reformers' committees. The Chowbent petition was signed by 1,900 individuals, predominantly weavers. The two petitions employed very similar formats and rhetoric, which

[114] T. Baines, *History of the Commerce and Town of Liverpool* (1852), pp. 545–6.

[115] *Liverpool Mercury*, 5 July 1811.

[116] *Hansard*, XXII, 23 March 1812, 212.

indicates that the individuals or communication used and adapted the same template in their initial composition. Chowbent and Chorley had raised delegates to the weavers' committees in 1799 and 1808 and were only a few miles from each other. The petitions indicate that local identity remained paramount in the mobilization of popular politics. They were different from the Manchester and Bolton petitions drawn up at the same time and therefore may not have been subject to any dictates from the Manchester executive weavers' committee. Both petitions repeated anti-corruption complaints prevalent in Cobbett's *Political Register* and *Cowdroy's Manchester Gazette*, concerning sinecures and public money spent on Sicilian and Portuguese courts, German refugees, Catholic clergy, and laity rather than on starving weavers. They regarded this expenditure as disrupting opportunities either for negotiation for peace or for bringing the war to a satisfactory conclusion. Both called on government to conciliate neutral nations. Each nevertheless expressed slightly different aims reflecting their distinct identities. The Chorley petition claimed to represent more than one opinion, an alliance of loyalist middle classes and more radical weavers over economic grievances: 'Some were against the East India monopoly, others against the Orders in Council and a third class against the Orders and also against sinecure places and pensions.' It was therefore headed against sinecure places, while that from Chowbent was specifically from 'Englishmen' for peace.[117]

Liverpool had its own circle of action around the two campaigns against the Orders in Council and East India Company monopoly. The Chancellor of the Exchequer furthermore spoke out against the wave of petitioning, spuriously linking the agitation to sedition and Luddism.[118] It climaxed in a dramatic debate in the House of Commons between General Banastre Tarleton and Thomas Creevey, MP for Thetford, who contested but failed to win the Liverpool seat. Creevey accused Tarleton of misrepresenting the genuine state of commerce in the port in order to further his own position in the eyes of the Corporation.[119] This suggests strongly that Liverpool merchants at least, if not many more among the Lancashire middle classes, identified their region and their sense of Britishness with their economic role, and were thus concerned about how their position might be (mis)conceived by MPs.

[117] *Hansard*, XXIII, 13 May 1812, p. 180; *Hansard,* XXII, 4 May 1812, p. 1156; Dinwiddy, 'Luddism and Politics', 46.

[118] *Hansard*, XXII, 22 April 1812, 1058, 1064.

[119] J. R. Harris (ed.), *Liverpool and Merseyside: Essays in the Economic and Social History of the Port and its Hinterland* (London, 1969), pp. 113–14.

The Blackburn petition of March 1812 offered a vision of Britain similar to that of Liverpool, as an international hub of commerce and manufacture operating in a system of mutual respect for other nations. Although stamped decisively with middle-class grievances, it also exemplified the petitioners' acceptance of multiple identities. Thus 'as natives of a country professing the Christian religion, they deplore the moral effects of war', while 'as men, they lament the miseries of their fellow creatures' and finally 'as Britons, they feel convinced that war is inimical to their interests' commercially.[120] Bolton radicals by contrast addressed the Prince Regent and were thus more obsequious in their rhetoric. They therefore provided less abstract reasoning about the war but a more graphically vivid account of its role in causing the distress of the working classes: 'Their pale and ghastly countenances—their squalid and ragged clothing . . . might possibly beget a doubt in your Royal Breast whether the most glorious results of war and victory abroad would be sufficient to compensate for such a mass of wretchedness at home.'[121] All petitions expressed severe doubts about the state of British foreign policy before 1813; middle-class economic and paternalist identities were a strong undercurrent, but the concerns of the working classes managed to shine through in parts.

Discontent culminated with the Manchester Exchange riot of 8 April 1812. This was the most significant event in the history of Lancashire popular politics during the Napoleonic wars. All the annals and diaries from Lancashire in this period expound on the repercussions of the riot, some in detail. The boroughreeve and constables had called a meeting in the new Exchange to draw up a petition to the Prince Regent, expressing satisfaction that he had decided to retain the Tory ministry in power. Handbills were put up across the city calling for inhabitants to attend the meeting to protest that this did not represent their genuine opinion. Sensing trouble, the authorities cancelled the meeting, but the protest ensued regardless. The riot was not an intentional act by the new radical committees, but on the contrary was a result of sheer numbers of attendees slipping out of their moderating control. The riot witnessed the protestors' appropriation of the commercial civic centre of the new Exchange and the loyalist parade ground of St Ann's Square. The violence escalated throughout the day. According to R. H. Whitelock at the Post Office, the crowds assembled at ten o'clock in the morning, taking possession of the Exchange for two hours until

120 *Blackburn Mail*, 4 March 1812.

121 *CMG*, 2 May 1812.

they 'began to riot'. Agitation outside the building apparently lasted until one o'clock, when the windows were smashed and the most violent entered the building and destroyed its furniture.[122] James Weatherley wrote in his diary:

Scarc[e]ly a whole Pane of Glass was left in the room, and the whole len[g]th portrait of Colonal Stanley painted by Sir Thomas Lawrence it was Presented by Colonal James Ackers of Lark Hill and Placed in the Exchange the Picture was nearly ruined but fortunately restored and replaced the Soldiers had to come before the mob dispersed, the Streets were throng'd that same night the People Inclined to riot.[123]

Many of the reports of the riot picked up on the defacing of the portrait of Colonel Stanley, one of the Whig MPs for the county, as it was believed that the rioters mistook him for George III and thereby proved their disloyalty. It is more likely that the picture was attacked as a symbol of the wealth of the merchants who owned and used the Exchange and were seemingly unresponsive to the demands of the populace.

The riot demonstrated how radicalism had evolved but also suggested the tensions within the future mass-platform movement. Firstly, it confirmed the magistrates' suspicions that the loyalist mobs they had countenanced in the early 1790s were long gone and that Church-and-King was now solely the preserve of the local authorities. This was also the observation made by post-war radicals. Archibald Prentice claimed that Thomas Kershaw, a calico printer who had associated with Thomas Walker in the 1790s, had asserted:

The occurrences of that day, however, indicated a turn in the current of popular opinion. Previously to that 'Church and King' was the favourite cry . . . but subsequently the old dominant party appeared to feel that they had an opposition to contend with and they became less arrogant in their conduct.[124]

The riot did not illustrate the fickleness of the crowd or their inherent radicalism. Rather, it was a product of a wider loyalism, which encompassed previously radical elements, in the context of which participants vented frustration at the nadir of the war and economic distress. Secondly, the riot was again representative of the complex relationship between national and local political issues and identities. The thousands

[122] NA, HO 42/122/529, Whitelock to Ryder, 8 April 1812.
[123] Chetham's Library, diary of James Weatherley.
[124] Prentice, *Historical Sketches*, p. 51.

of people who assembled outside the Exchange to protest and in St Ann's Square to give their assent to resolutions calling for parliamentary reform were reacting against local loyalists' representation of a national issue. They challenged the loyalist elite's right to represent the town's opinion to the Prince Regent as much as the actual issue itself: the Prince Regent's choice of Tory government.

John Edward Taylor and his business partner John Shuttleworth were rumoured to be the authors of the handbill 'Now or Never', the most memorable from the many that precipitated the riot. The rhetoric of the handbills emphasized the power of public opinion and the striking language found in them was written by the new generation. 'A Warning Voice', dated 2 April, was one of the most vitriolic in its expression of radical patriotism: 'You behold your country sunk in reputation, degraded in rank and pursuing those measures which will inevitably terminate in irremiable [sic] destruction and misery.' The language of romantic radicalism ran through the broadside, with its idea of corruption endemic to the Pittite state as the root of the problem: 'The Public mind is no longer ignorant of the cause. The cancer-worm of the state in piercing our feelings with agony has at once raised us from a general and unaccountable indifference.'[125] This was a strong theme given more radical inflection by local leaders in response to local circumstances. The language of petitions and handbills may not have expressed the true political beliefs of their writers, nor may it have been entirely shared by all of the general population. It was nevertheless important because it stimulated an excited response which fuelled the riot. It was an extreme way of expressing opposition to government in time of acute economic distress and seemingly perpetual war.

Elements within the wider populace took a more violent attitude towards Pittitism and national events following the Exchange Riot. Food riots broke out in Bolton, Bury, and many other towns and their neighbourhoods. On 20 April, John Holden observed the tumult in Horwich market over the price of potatoes, which escalated into an all-day riot, with arson attacks upon warehouses and the Bolton Rope Walk.[126] Then followed the set-piece Luddite attacks in Middleton and Westhoughton. The climax came when Prime Minister Spencer Perceval was assassinated on 11 May by a Liverpool merchant John Bellingham, disgruntled at the lack of parliamentary redress for his

125 MCL, BR f. 324.942733, Shuttleworth loose leaves, no.4.

126 Holden diaries.

imprisonment for debt. The incident appeared to fulfil the millenarian predictions of both the extremist radical broadsides and the government spies. On 15 May, Colonel Fletcher of Bolton wrote:

> The death of Mr Perceval has filled all good Loyalists with grief—and what is to be particularly lamented is that the *Mob* should have expressed *Joy* on such a melancholy occasion. It would appear as if John Bulls character had experienced a [change] and that he is become [a symbol] for Treason, stratagems and spoils.[127]

The vicar of St Mark's in Liverpool, the church on the street where the assassin Bellingham had lived, preached a sermon on the 'melancholy event'. In response, he received a letter signed by 'Jenkins, Lt de Luddites', which ridiculed his sermon and added: 'had it been in any other place than the church, my pistol would have silenced the blasphemy'. It went on to speak of the 'brave and patriotic Bellingham' and threatened death to 'depraved George the Prince'.[128] Tactics of intimidation like these were isolated and not indicative of any serious revolutionary danger, but they did illustrate how national political figures were by no means unequivocally revered. Threatening letters were sent from Manchester to the Prince Regent and to Nicholas Vansittart, the new Chancellor of the Exchequer.[129] Reported links between Bellingham and the Luddites were quickly proved to be spurious, but this did not lessen the sense that Lancashire was sinking into serious social and political disorder. Rowbottom wrote that in response to the assassination, the authorities in Oldham and neighbouring areas, Crompton, Chadderton, and Royton, enforced the Watch and Ward Act vigorously overnight to prevent any sign of trouble.[130]

The post-war radical activists felt this fear as much as the magistrates and loyalists. They had learnt lessons from what had happened to their predecessors in the 1790s and therefore were keen to separate themselves from the violence of the crowd and extremists. Combining a fear of arrest with desire for respectability, they perhaps also shared some of William Roscoe's suspicion of the 'Burdettite mob' in Westminster whom they may have believed were hampering the reform movement. Samuel Bamford wanted his readers to know that his 'feelings and partialities had

[127] NA, HO 40/1/1/115, Fletcher to Beckett, 15 May 1812.

[128] R. Reid, *Land of Lost Content: the Luddite Revolt, 1812* (London, 1986), p. 159; NA, HO 42/123/101, Blacow to McMahon, 27 May 1812.

[129] K. Binfield, *Writings of the Luddites* (Baltimore, 2004), p. 190.

[130] Rowbottom diaries, 11 May 1812.

hitherto been all on the side of the populace, but I could not witness this cowardly outrage without feelings of indignation and disgust'.[131] Those who organized the opposition to the loyalist authorities' requisition for a meeting withdrew from the proceedings when rioting broke out, to avoid giving any 'appearance of countenance' to acts of violence. John Knight of Saddleworth, the voice of the 'Thirty Eight', wrote: 'These acts of violence induced a number of most respectable gentlemen, who intended to have moved a Counter Address, to decline carrying it forward.' He claimed that the more exclusive meetings of the 'friends of peace and parliamentary reform', that resulted in their arrest, were in fact held in direct consequence of their revulsion against the violence of the crowd.[132] Significantly, William Cowdroy refused to print the resolutions of the Manchester reform meeting of 26 May, in response to the proceedings turning out to be less constitutional than they had seemed.[133] The new generation of radicals had made their mark in a dramatic and somewhat unexpected manner. Though they denigrated the violence, looking towards the more 'respectable' artisanal radicalism of the post-war reform campaign, the experience of the Exchange Riot was nonetheless essential in preparing the ground for the mass platform movement. It demonstrated the possibility of wide popular support, and reinforced the divide between loyalist local elites and radical activists.

Following the suppression of Luddism and the brief sense of relief that arose when the Orders in Council were repealed, the country sunk into depression. The situation in 1813 was bleak. The newspapers recorded not continental victories for the allies but the weekly total amounts of soup given out at soup shops stationed in the centres of most towns. More petitions for parliamentary reform lay for signature in Manchester and Salford.[134] William Rowbottom's reflections on the New Year were despairing:

> with the price of provisions and the lowness of Trade a Genaral Gloom Hung on the Countenances of the poor and the Country in general are in a State of actual Starvation it is impossible to convey to posterity the Lamentable Situation of the Country and there is no very visable Hopes of a Speedy change for the Better.[135]

131 Bamford, *Early Days*, p. 295.

132 *Trial at Full Length of the Thirty Eight*, p. iv.

133 Dinwiddy, 'Luddism and Politics', 54; Prentice, *Historical Sketches*, p. 50; NA, HO 42/124, 2 June 1812; *CMG*, 20 June 1812.

134 *CMG*, 6 February, 6 March 1813.

135 Rowbottom diaries, January 1813.

This was the situation to which Major John Cartwright, legend of the reform movement as he was, began his tours of the north of England.[136] The ground had been prepared by the new generation of home-grown radicals before his arrival, and thus the post-war mass platform was not created by his tours but rather by the succession of petitions and meetings that had occupied the Lancashire populace from 1807. Not all took notice of Cartwright's constitutionalist radicalism propagated in his speeches and in his letters, printed in *Cowdroy's Manchester Gazette* and the *Leeds Mercury*.[137] William Rowbottom himself makes no mention of him or indeed of any reform activity in Oldham or Manchester in 1813–14, preferring to concentrate on the desolation he saw around him. Trade briefly recovered after the overthrow of Bonaparte in October 1813, but as the war continued the situation again worsened and stoked up the discontent, which erupted into the mass meetings and the Blanketeers' attempted procession to parliament after the war.

The symbolism encapsulated in action during the Exchange riots lasted long in popular memory. The new post-war radicals furthermore effectively created a new narrative, pointed by the symbolism of place. The Exchange was crucially commemorated in mass-platform radicalism as the beginning of the new movement: in a procession of 18 January 1819, 'Orator' Henry Hunt deliberately paused outside the Exchange to harangue the loyalist gentlemen inside. The new generation of local radicals nevertheless made a conscious effort to move away from the old tactic of subverting the meaning of loyalist space. They now sought to infuse new, untouched places with radical significance. Having hosted no previous political events, St Peter's Fields and New Cross were adopted by the post-war radicals as central locations alternative to St Ann's Square. The first radical meeting was organized on St Peter's Fields on 4 November 1816.[138]

The boundaries between radicalism, both extreme and constitutionalist, and unionist activities were thinner in Lancashire than in most other regions, although patterns of movement across the membrane are impossible to document. Historians have found it difficult to distinguish radical committees from Luddite and other movements. Nor could contemporaries determine the difference, particularly the spies who infiltrated the meetings. It is likely that there was some overlap

136 Dinwiddy, 'Luddism and Politics', 60.

137 *CMG*, 8 January 1814.

138 Edwards, 'Popular Politics', pp. 164–6.

among radical activists, unionized workers, and Luddite agitators, but much is still hidden under the veil of secrecy and confusion in the magistrates' and spies' reports and distorted witness evidence. The arrest of the 'Thirty-Eight' radicals on 11 June illustrated the mindset of the magistrates, who were eager to associate any political activity with Luddism. In response to the Exchange Riot, the new generation of Manchester radicals, headed by Richard Stamfield and John Knight, decided to meet at the Elephant on 26 May and at the Prince Regent's Arms on 11 June. They drew up a petition to the Commons and an address to the Prince Regent. Joseph Nadin and his men then burst in and arrested the 'Thirty-Eight', resulting in their high-profile trial. The resolutions of the petition exemplified radical patriotism begun by the Friends of Peace, combined with the legacy of Paineite radicalism and a distinct Lancashire tinge. They complained of the tendency of corrupt ministers to 'wantonly plunge' the nation into 'unnecessary and ruinous wars'. The address to the Prince Regent was even more pessimistic about the state of the war: 'We see no prospect of an honourable and successful termination of the contest in which we are engaged, unless conducted in a very different manner.' They retained an anti-Pittite suspicion of politicians, seen as 'so subservient to the minister for the time being' and thus believed nothing would save the country but a thorough reform of parliament.[139]

Lancashire radicalism from 1812 embodied a composite of influences, from traditional constitutionalist arguments to remnants of Paineite republicanism, used according to circumstances. It was furthermore shaped by a distinctive economic outlook, regional identity, and strong belief in Britain's role on the international stage. This was exemplified in the petition to the Commons drawn up by the 'Thirty-Eight'. For them, reform encompassed a wide range of traditional constitutionalist demands, ranging from universal suffrage, peace, equal constituencies, annual elections, and an old Country suspicion of a standing army, to demands that had arisen during the French wars, in particular a minimum wage and repeal of the Combination Acts.[140] It was thus a culmination and consolidation of all the campaigns that had shaken popular politics in Lancashire over the period, though this does not mean that radicals and other activists demanding change were united. Radicals in Lancashire looked up to national leaders such as Burdett and Cartwright, but were organized on the ground by a legion of local radical

139 *Trial at Full Length of the Thirty Eight*, pp. 94–6.

140 *Ibid.*, p. 98.

activists, old and new. Tensions existed among all these individuals and their rhetoric may not have represented all that was thought by the general population who signed the petitions and attended the mass meetings. Yet these tensions were overcome by a shared genuine and active desire for peace and reform, engendered by the pressures of over two decades of war, in the face of local and national elites who appeared to misunderstand their grievances and world-view. This was provincial in the sense of seeking independence from parliamentary intrusion or corruption as well as from Burdettite domination of the reform campaign. It also embodied an outlook upon Britain from the Lancashire perspective, as an arbitrator and trading exchange amongst nations. Lancashire radicalism and loyalism were redefined in the region's own image.

These changes in radicalism in Lancashire between 1807 and 1815 suggest two wider patterns in the nature of popular politics in Britain as a whole. They firstly call into question the decisiveness of the loyalist reaction of the 1790s. Radicalism did survive, and became popular on a much larger scale than immediately after the French Revolution of 1789. Loyalism also evolved, though in an exclusive manner among the (Orange) magistrates, and in tandem with a distinctly neo-Tory Pittite cult among the middle classes, which was to continue against the new forms of radical protest until and beyond the 'Peterloo' conflagration in 1819. Secondly, however, the events of the later half of the Napoleonic War narrowed the ideological gap between loyalists and radicals. Involvement in radicalism may have only been a necessary tool adopted by a large proportion of the general population during dire circumstances.[141] The polarization of the 1790s and closed political atmosphere had been replaced by wider public discussion of politics and a more fluid range of radical positions, that even previously loyalist members of the populace adopted as a result of economic distress or out of a genuine conviction that the government was corrupt and its conduct of the war mistaken. For radical activists, furthermore, the revitalized campaigns marked a genuine, enduring change, and this was especially important in terms of the formative experiences of the new generation of radicals, who became involved in and later led the post-war mass-platform movement.

[141] D. Bythell, *The Handloom Weavers in the Industrial Revolution* (Cambridge, 1969), p. 217.

Conclusion

The Napoleonic War was a formative period for popular politics and the industrializing economy, straddling the old and the new. Political and economic changes affected Lancashire in a distinctive, and probably unique, way. Lancashire responded to the strains of the war and new political ideologies by reshaping loyalism, radicalism, and national identity in its own image.

Popular politics involved processes of definition, contestation, and redefinition. Inhabitants questioned who had the right to represent the region's economic and political identity to the wider nation. The conflation of loyalism with patriotism, and the continuation of elements of 'vulgar conservatism' into new popular patriotic forms in the late 1790s, encouraged loyalist elites to defend their exclusivity in the forms of the Orange movement, Pittite neo-Toryism and Church-and-King loyalism. Though the working classes shared in their employers' economic vision of Britain's future, the trade union activity following the passage of the Combination Acts of 1799 and 1800 manifested their diverging political economies. Luddism was not blindly reactionary, but rather reflected some of this attachment to a more paternalist and protectionist economy and society. The real legacy of Paine's *Rights of Man* lay, as E. P. Thompson argued, in an interest in politics and in social welfare or cooperation among the working classes rather than in a comprehensive adoption of all his tenets. This politicization did not necessarily lead to the formation of a common class-consciousness, though there were certainly incidents of class conflict. Nor did the middle classes gain a united identity. Despite appearances of unity during the invasion scares, many among the middle classes aspired to become gentrified, while also championing sectional economic interests or fighting against radicals within their own ranks.

The wars strengthened the loyalist and patriotic reaction against the French 'other' and enabled a sense of Britishness to flourish. Yet this Britishness was not homogeneous. A regional Britishness was fostered by a variety of events and traditions, from loyalist to radical. Among the loyalists were a 'Country' tradition of suspicion of parliament, together with the volunteer movement, broadside ballads, elections, and other local ways of perceiving and enacting the national situation. Among the middle classes, the campaigns against the Orders in Council and the East India Company presaged the nineteenth-century movement for free trade, while demonstrating the middle classes' commercial mentality and a sense of provincial independence from government. Petitions were shaped by regional economic needs and identity and portrayed a vision of Britain conducting foreign relations upon commercial lines befitting its role as the 'emporium of the world', obviously with Lancashire at its centre.[1] Radical bourgeois intellectuals and artisans meanwhile built the foundations for the post-war working-class struggle for suffrage, thereby shifting the centre of popular politics away from the metropolis to the north.

A strong sense of provincialism and, furthermore, of intra-regional variation had a bearing on the region's relationship with national patterns of politics. The Orange movement was unique to Lancashire, Cheshire, Cumbria, and south-west Scotland. The peace and reform campaigns did not gain popularity as rapidly or easily as in Yorkshire, where the Fitzwilliam influence upon the magistracy and propertied adherents of a Wyvillite tradition were perhaps more sympathetic or acquiescent than the Tory High Church forces of order in Lancashire. Burdettite radicalism and the Westminster elections were inspirational for provincial radicals, but new leaders of the post-war movements consciously maintained their own identities, and the timing of political conflicts depended upon local conditions combining with national events. Britain was and remains a nation of composite allegiances and political identities, tensely held together by a central government and national economy, with provincial influences and demands continually restraining or altering the impact of the centre.

This study of the Lancashire region cannot exist on its own. The region is a vital geographical unit, constantly changing in response to its multifarious connections with other regions and the nation as a whole. J. D. Marshall argued for inter-regional and intra-regional comparisons

[1] W. Roscoe, *Considerations on the Causes, Objects and Consequences of the Present War* (1808), p. 134.

together with studies of contemporary perceptions of regions.[2] Developing this approach would generate a new form of 'national' study, in which the history of the nation is analyzed from the region upwards, rather than, as is usually the case, from the state and high politics downwards.[3] Further study in this vein would indicate whether there was a shared northern or indeed provincial identity defined against the edicts and official national identity propagated by government or the metropolis, whilst keeping particular examples within their specific context and recognizing the distinctiveness of local and regional allegiances within that wider provinciality.

[2] J. D. Marshall, *The Tyranny of the Discrete: A Discussion of the Problems of Local History* (Aldershot, 1997).

[3] P. Clark has attempted this in a looser and less political sense in *The Cambridge Urban History of Britain*, vol. 2, *1540–1840* (Cambridge, 2000).

Bibliography

MANUSCRIPTS

Bolton Archives

ABZ 39/1/2, Bolton Moor enclosure award, 1793.
ZHE 1–8, Heywood papers.
ZZ 530/1, diaries of John Holden of Bolton.

British Library

Add(itional MS) 27798–9, Place papers.
Add 51650, 51566, Holland papers.
Eg 2409, Egerton papers.

Cheshire RO

B/JJ/6/25, Stockport Loyal Volunteers papers, 1798.
DDX 24/23, Lloyd papers, 1808-12.
EDV 7/3–4, Bishop of Chester visitation returns, 1789, 1804, 1811.

Chetham's Library, Manchester

A.2.79, Manchester Pitt Club minutes.
A.3.10, Hay papers.
A.6.30, autobiography of James Weatherley.
A.6.45, Association for the Protection of Constitutional Order and Liberty Against Republicans and Levellers, minute book, 1792–9.
4.C.6-128, St. George's Volunteers papers.
Cambrics scrapbook of broadsides.

Cumbria RO, Barrow-in-Furness

William Fleming diaries and commonplace book, 1800–16.
Soulby broadsides.

Greater Manchester RO

E/Fox/11/D, account book of J. Entwisle.
E4, Egerton diaries and papers.

Harris Library, Preston

Harkness broadside ballads.

Harris Manchester College, Oxford
William Shepherd papers.
Warrington and Manchester College papers.

House of Lords RO
HL/PO/JO/10/3/286/3, Manchester petition against slave trade bill, 1794.
HL/PO/JO/10/3/292/48, petitions for and against Lancashire Sessions Bill, 1798.
HL/PO/JO/10/8, petitions for and against slave trade abolition bill, 1806, and for and against Orders in Council, 1808.

John Rylands Library, University of Manchester
Alexander Kilham correspondence, 1792–1802.
EGR 4/1, Earl of Stamford and Warrington papers, 1758–1819.
Eng MS 989–92, Hibbert-Ware papers.
MCK 3/2/1–2 –4/4/9, McConnel and Kennedy papers.

Lancashire CRO
DDK, Earl of Derby papers.
DDLi 57, Lilford correspondence, 1794–1802.
DDPr 138/76, Preston scrapbook.
DDX 104 acc 7780, Revd William Myers notebook, 1809.
DDX 398/123–5, Yates correspondence.
DDX 760/1, Cragg of Ortner memorandum book, 1698–1816.
LM 1/1, Lieutenancy minutes.
QDS 1/1, Lancashire friendly society bonds and certificates.
QJC 1, Calendar of prisoners, 1805–12.
QSP 2749/12, Report of factories in Ashton-under-Lyne and Salford, 1803.

Liverpool RO
060 LIT 8/1, Liverpool Literary and Philosophical society papers.
252 MIN/COU I, Liverpool town books.
328 PAR, Liverpool parliamentary committee correspondence, 1814.
352 CLE/TRA/2/12, Liverpool town records, 1793–1827.
353 PAR 1/2/1, Liverpool Parish committee and select vestry minutes, 1803–11.
380 AME/1, American Chamber of Commerce minute book.
920 CUR, Currie correspondence.
920 DER (12), 12th Earl of Derby papers.
920 ROS, William Roscoe correspondence, 1796–1813.
M920 TAR, Tarleton papers.

Liverpool University Special Collections

R.P. II, III and V, papers of William Rathbone IV, Hannah Rathbone, and William Rathbone V, 1757–1868.

London School of Economics Special Collections

Webb trade union collection.
Coll Misc 0146, Potter family MS.

Manchester Archives

398.8 B1, Swindells ballads.
BR 329.2 T1, W. R. Hay collection of tracts.
BR f. 324.942733 Sh, Shuttleworth scrapbook.
BR f. 942.7389 Sc 13, Scrapbook of handbills and broadsides.
BR f. 824.04, BA 1, vols. 1–5, ballads.
BR f. 942.72. L15, Manchester broadsides.
BR MS 091 B78, Brotherton scrapbook.
C5/1/8, Samuel Greg papers.
M62/1/2–3, ledgers of William and Thomas Wood of Didsbury, 1791–1838.
M84, Philips family papers.
M9/30/1/1, Manchester police commissioners papers.
M91/16, Voluntary contributions from Manchester and Salford, 1798.
MS BR 21/BR F 356.M12, Committee for General Defence accounts, 1803.

National Archives, Kew

CHES 24/183, Palatinate of Chester, examinations of weavers, 1808.
FS 1/239, 246, 2/4, Friendly societies' rules.
HO 40/1/1, 40/4/1, Home Office correspondence, 1812.
HO 42/46–122, Home Office correspondence, 1798–1812.
HO 42/53–4, Crop returns, 1801.
HO 50/35, 75, 110, 137, 285, Internal defence, Lancaster, 1798–12.
KB 8/90, part 3, King vs John Jackson, 1812.
PC 1/158, Privy Council papers, 1799.
PC 1/3118, evidence of Robert Gray, 1798.
PC 1/42/140, evidence against William Cheetham, 1798.
PC 1/44/A155, 158, evidence on weavers' combinations, 1799.
PL 27/7–9, Palatinate of Lancaster Court deposition rolls; Lancaster Assizes trials, 1799–1812.
PL 28/4, 5, Lancaster Castle Crown Office minutes.
PRO 30/8, Pitt the Younger correspondence, 1798–99.
TS 11/1059/4766, Treasury Solicitor papers, Lancaster Assizes, 22 August 1812.
TS 11/1068, King vs John Joynson, 1808.
TS 11/657/2075, King vs Hanson, 1808.
TS 11/980, Trial of Westhoughton rioters, 1812.

Oldham Local Studies

'Annals of Oldham', MS diary by William Rowbottom of Oldham, 1787–1830.

Stockport Local Studies

B/JJ/6/25, Stockport loyal volunteers papers, 1798.

Warrington Library

MS 11–12, Warrington muster roll and orderly book, 1803–7.

MS 98, 2327, Loyal Warrington Volunteers papers, 1798–1803.

MS 62, Warrington Court Leet proceedings, 1792–1840.

West Yorkshire Archives, Leeds

RAD, Radcliffe correspondence and papers, 1796–1818.

Wigan Archives

D/D Lei C 741–55, Leigh correspondence, 1796–1811.

D/D St C, Standish correspondence, 1793–1812.

D/DZ EHC/32, Anna Walker diary.

PRINTED SOURCES

Newspapers

Blackburn Mail

Cowdroy's Manchester Gazette

Lancaster Gazette

Liverpool Chronicle

Liverpool Mercury

Manchester Herald

Manchester Mercury

Preston Journal

Wheeler's Manchester Chronicle

Official Papers

PP 1803, *Returns of Volunteer Corps in Great Britain.*

PP 1803, III, part 4, *Minutes of Evidence on . . . Petitions Relating to the Act For Settling Disputes between Masters and Servants Engaged in the Cotton Manufacture.*

PP 1803–4, IV (41), *Report of the Select Committee on . . . Petitions Relating to the Act For Settling Disputes between Masters and Servants.*

PP 1806–7, II (107), *Report from the Committee on Petitions of Journeymen Calico Printers.*

PP 1808, II, *Report from the Committee on Petitions of Several Cotton Manufacturers and Journeymen Cotton Weavers.*

PP 1808, X (181), *Report from the Committee on Petitions ... Respecting the Orders in Council.*

PP 1810–11, II, *Report from the Select Committee into the Petitions for Economic Relief.*

PP 1812, III (231), *Minutes of Evidence on ... the Petitions from Liverpool and Manchester ... Respecting the Orders in Council.*

PP 1812, II (309), LIII, *Reports of the Committee of Secrecy.*

PP 1835, XVII, *Select Committee Report on Orange Lodges in Great Britain and the Colonies.*

PP 1836, XXXIV (427), *Select Committee into the Condition of the Irish Poor in Great Britain.*

Pamphlets and Broadsides

At a General Meeting of the Members of the Bolton Pitt Club Held at the Swan Inn in Bolton, Monday 17th May 1813 (Bolton, 1813).

Bancroft, T., *The Chain of Duty, or an Exhortation to Civil and Religious Obedience* (Bolton, 1797).

Canning, G., *Speeches and Public Addresses of the Right Honourable George Canning: during the Late Election in Liverpool, and on a Public Occasion in Manchester* (Liverpool, 1812).

Brougham's Speeches Delivered During the Election at Liverpool in October 1812 (Liverpool, 1813).

A Charge Delivered by William Lord Bishop of Chester to the Clergy of his Diocese (Oxford, 1799).

A Charge Delivered to the Clergy of the Diocese of Chester at the Primary Visitation of that Diocese ... (Chester, 1814).

Cleaver, W., *Two Sermons by William Lord Bishop of Chester Addressed to the Clergy of the Diocese* (Oxford, 1789).

Clegg, W., *Freedom Defended, or the Practice of Despots Exposed* (Manchester, 1798).

A Collection of Addresses, Songs, Squibs etc (Liverpool, 1807).

A Complete Collection of Addresses, Squibs, Songs etc (Preston, 1812).

Dawson, W., *Stockport Flim-Flams* (Manchester, 1807).

A Discourse Delivered in the Catholic Chapel Preston before the Catholic Association for the Relief of the Sick on Monday May 25, 1807, by Rev Joseph Tate (Preston, 1807).

Hanson, J., *Brief Remarks on the Present Volunteer Establishment by Joseph Hanson, Lieutenant-Colonel Commandant of the Manchester, Salford and Independent Rifle Regiment* (Salford, 1805).

History of the Election for Members of Parliament for Liverpool ... (Liverpool, 1806).

An Impartial Collection of the Addresses, Songs, Squibs etc that were Published at Liverpool ... (Liverpool, 1806).

An Impartial Collection of the Addresses, Songs, Squibs etc . . . (Liverpool, 1812).

Nuttall, W., *Orange Miscellany* (Huddersfield, 1815).

Orange Clubs, Dr. Taylor's Speech Delivered to the Liverpool Concentrics at their Quarterly Meeting (Liverpool, 1819).

Philips, J. L. or F., *Travels of Fum Hom* (Stockport, 1804).

Raynes, F. R. *An Appeal to the Public* (1817).

Rigby, J., *An Address to the Roman Catholic Freemen of Lancaster* (1807).

Roby, W., *Civil Magistracy Defended* (Manchester, 1798).

Roscoe, W., *Observations on the Present Relative Situation of Great Britain and France* (1802).

—— *Considerations on the Causes, Objects and Consequences of the Present War* (1808).

—— *Occasional Tracts Relative to the War Between Great Britain and France* (1810).

—— *A Letter to Henry Brougham Esq on the Subject of Reform* (Liverpool, 1811).

—— *A Review of the Speeches of Right Hon George Canning* (Liverpool, 1812).

A Short Sketch or Memoir of the Late Joseph Hanson Esq (Salford, 1811).

A Statement of Facts Relative to the Transfer of Service of the Late Warrington Volunteer Corps into the Local Militia by J. Borron (1809).

Stockdale, J. J., *The Orange Institution: A Slight Sketch* (1813).

Taylor, R., *Letters on the Subject of the Lancashire Riots* (Bolton, 1812).

The Trial at Full Length of the Thirty Eight Men from Manchester, 27 August 1812 (Manchester, 1812).

Trials of the Luddites . . . at Lancaster Assizes (1813).

A Tribute to the Life of Mr William Rathbone of Liverpool (Liverpool, 1809).

Tufnell, H., *Character, Object and Effects of Trade Unions with Some Remarks on the Law Concerning Them* (1834).

Walker, T., *Plebeian Politics or the Principles and Practices of Certain Mole-Eyed Maniacs Vulgarly Called Warrites* (Salford, 1802).

The Whole of the Addresses, Squibs, Songs and Other Papers Circulated During the Time of the Contested Election in Preston (Preston, 1807).

The Whole Proceedings on the Trial . . . Against Thomas Walker and others (Manchester, 1794).

The Whole Proceedings on the Trial of an Indictment Against Joseph Hanson Esq for a Conspiracy to Aid the Weavers of Manchester in Raising their Wages (1809).

Books

The Admission Register of the Manchester School, 3 vols., ed. J. F. Smith, Chetham Society, 73 (Manchester, 1868).

Aikin, J., *A Description of the Country From Thirty to Forty Miles Round Manchester* (Manchester, 1795).

Aspinall, A., *Early English Trade Unions, Documents from the Home Office Papers in the Public Record Office* (Batchworth Press, 1949).
Aston, J., *Lancashire Gazetteer* (Manchester, 1808).
The Autobiography of David Whitehead of Rawtenstall, 1790–1865, ed. S. Chapman (Helmshore: Helmshore LHS, 2001).
Baines, E., *Lancashire*, 2 vols. (Newton Abbot: E. J. Morten, 1968 reprint).
Bamford, S., *The Autobiography of Samuel Bamford: Early Days*, new edn., ed. W. H. Chaloner (Cass, 1967).
Binfield, K. (ed.), *The Writings of the Luddites* (Baltimore: John Hopkins University Press, 2004).
Brown, J., *A Memoir of Robert Blincoe* (Manchester, 1832).
Butterworth, J., *The Antiquities of the Town and a Complete History of the Trade of Manchester* (Manchester, 1822).
Cobbett, W., *Cobbett's Parliamentary Debates* (1798–1804).
Currie, W. W., *Memoir of the Life, Writings and Correspondence of James Currie of Liverpool*, 2 vols. (1831).
The Diaries of Absalom Watkin, a Manchester Man, 1787–1861, ed. M. Goffin (Stroud: Alan Sutton, 1993).
Dickson, R. W., *General View of the Agriculture of Lancashire* (Neeley & Jones, 1815).
Dunn, J. (ed.), *Census of the Catholic Congregation of Preston, 1810 and 1820*, transl. M. Purcell (Blackpool: Ancestral Data Publications, 1993).
Earwaker, J. P., *Court Leet Records of the Manor of Manchester*, vol. 9 (Manchester, 1884).
The Family Records of Benjamin Shaw, Mechanic of Dent, Dolphinholme and Preston, 1772–1841, ed. A. G. Crosby, Lancashire and Cheshire Record Society, 130 (Chester, 1991).
Hansard's Parliamentary Debates, vols. I–XXII (1804–13).
Harland, J., *Ballads and Songs of Lancashire* (Whittaker & Co, 1865).
Hibbert-Ware, Mrs, *Life and Correspondence of Samuel Hibbert-Ware* (Manchester, 1882).
Holt, J., *A General View of the Agriculture in the County of Lancaster* (J. Nicholls, 1795).
Hulbert, C., *Memoirs of Seventy Years of an Eventful Life* (Shrewsbury, 1852).
Percival, T., *Biographical Memoirs of Thomas Butterworth Bayley* (Manchester, 1802).
Prentice, A., *Historical Sketches and Personal Recollections of Manchester, Intended to Illustrate the Progress of Public Opinion from 1792 to 1832*, 2nd edn. (Gilpin, 1851).
Preston, T., *Jubilee Jottings: the Jubilee of George III* (1887).
Roscoe, H., *Life of William Roscoe* (1826).
Thomas Creevey's Papers, 1793–1838, ed. J. Gore (Harmondsworth: Penguin, 1948).

Vicinus, M., *Broadsides of the Industrial North* (Newcastle: Graham, 1975).
Walker, T., *Biographical Memoirs of Thomas Walker Esq of Manchester* (Manchester, 1820).
Wheeler, J., *Manchester, its Political, Social and Commercial History, Ancient and Modern* (1836).
Whitaker, T. D., *An History of the Original Parish of Whalley and the Honour of Clitheroe* (Blackburn, 1801).
Wood, F. and K. (eds.), *A Lancashire Gentleman: The Letters and Journals of Richard Hodgkinson, 1763–1847* (Stroud: Sutton, 1992).

SECONDARY SOURCES NOT CITED IN MAIN TEXT

Place of publication is London unless otherwise stated.

Addy, J., 'Bishop Porteus' Visitation of the Diocese of Chester, 1778', *NH* 13 (1977), 175–98.
Anderson, B. L. and Stoney, P. J. M. (eds.), *Commerce, Industry and Transport: Studies in Economic Change on Merseyside* (Liverpool: Liverpool University Press, 1983).
Anderson, D., 'Blundell's Collieries: Wages, Disputes and Conditions of Work', *THSLC* 117 (1965), 109–43.
Anderson, M., *Family Structure in Nineteenth-Century Lancashire* (Cambridge: Cambridge University Press, 1971).
Archer, J. E., *Social Unrest and Popular Protest in England, 1780–1840* (Cambridge: Cambridge University Press, 2000).
Aspin, C., *The First Industrial Society: Lancashire*, rev. edn. (Preston: Carnegie, 1995).
Bagley, J. J., *The Earls of Derby, 1485–1985* (Sidgwick & Jackson, 1985).
Baker, A. R. H., 'Patterns of Popular Protest', *Journal of Historical Geography*, 1 (1975), 383–7.
—— and Billinge, M., *Geographies of England: The North–South Divide, Material and Imagined* (Cambridge: Cambridge University Press, 2004).
Barker, H., *Newspapers, Politics and Public Opinion in Late Eighteenth-Century England* (Oxford: Clarendon Press, 1998).
Barker, T. C. and Harris, J. R., *A Merseyside Town in the Industrial Revolution: St. Helens, 1750–1900* (Cass, 1959).
Barton, B. T., *Historical Gleanings of Bolton and District*, 3 vols. (Bolton: Daily Chronicle, 1881).
Bayless, J. O. and Crossman, M. J. (eds.), *Biographical Dictionary of Modern British Radicals*, vol. 1, *1770–1830* (Hassocks: Harvester Press, 1979).
Belchem, J., *Popular Politics, Riot and Labour: Essays in Liverpool History, 1790–1840* (Liverpool: Liverpool University Press, 1992).
Bossy, J., *The English Catholic Community, 1570–1850* (Longman & Todd, 1975).

Brooke, A. and Kipling, L., *Liberty or Death: Radicals, Republicans and Luddites, 1793–1823* (Honley: Workers' History Publications, 1993).
Brocklehurst, H. and Phillips, R. (eds.), *History, Nationhood and the Question of Britain* (Basingstoke: Palgrave Macmillan, 2004).
Brown, W. E., *Robert Heywood of Bolton* (Wakefield: East Ardley Publishers, 1970).
Burke, T. (ed.), *Eighteenth Century Labouring Class Poets*, 3 vols. (Pickering & Chatto, 2003).
Burney, L., *Cross Street Chapel* (Didsbury: L. Burney, 1983).
Butterworth, E., *Historical Sketches of Oldham* (Oldham: John Hirst, 1856).
Chaloner, W. H., 'Robert Owen, Peter Drinkwater and the Early Factory Masters in Manchester, 1788–1800', *Bulletin of the JRLUM*, 37 (1954), 78–102.
Checkland, S. G., 'America Versus West Indies Traders in Liverpool, 1793–1815', *Journal of Economic History*, 17 (1958), 141–60.
Clare, D., 'The Local Newspaper Press and Local Politics in Manchester and Liverpool, 1780–1800', *TLCAS* 73–4 (1963–4), 101–23.
Collier, F., *The Family Economy of the Working Classes in the Cotton Industry, 1784–1833* (Manchester: Manchester University Press, 1964).
Cunningham, H., 'The Language of Patriotism, 1750–1914', *History Workshop Journal*, 12 (1981), 8–33.
Curzon, A., *Dr James Currie and the French Prisoners of War in Liverpool, 1800–1801* (Liverpool: E. Howell, 1926).
Davis, H. W. C., 'Lancashire Reformers, 1816–17', *Bulletin of the JRLUM* 10 (1926), 47–79.
Dennis, R., *English Industrial Cities of the Nineteenth Century: a Social Geography* (Cambridge: Cambridge University Press, 1984).
Dickinson, H. T. (ed.), *Britain and the French Revolution, 1789–1815* (Basingstoke: Macmillan, 1989).
Dobson, C. R., *Masters and Journeymen: A Prehistory of Industrial Relations, 1717–1800* (Croom Helm, 1980).
Dobson, W., *History of the Parliamentary Representation of Preston*, 2nd edn. (Preston, 1868).
Dodd, J. P., 'South Lancashire in Transition, a Study of the Crop Returns', *TLCHS* 117 (1965), 89–107.
Dodgshon, R. A. and Butlin, R. A. (eds.), *A Historical Geography of England and Wales*, 2nd edn. (Academic, 1990).
Dozier, R., *For King, Constitution and Country: the English Loyalists and the French Revolution* (Lexington: University Press of Kentucky, 1983).
Duffy, M., *The Englishman and the Foreigner* (Cambridge: Cambridge University Press, 1986).
Eagles, R., *Francophilia in English Society, 1748–1815* (Basingstoke: Macmillan, 2000).

Eastwood, D., *Government and Community in the English Provinces, 1700–1870* (Basingstoke: Macmillan, 1997).

Emsley, C., *British Society and the French Wars, 1793–1815* (Macmillan, 1979).

Evans, E., 'Some Reasons for the Growth of English Rural Anticlericalism, 1750–1830', *P & P* 66 (1975), 84–109.

Farrer, W. and Brownbill, J. (eds.), *The Victoria County History of the County of Lancaster*, 6 vols., reprint (Folkestone: Dawson, 1990–3).

Foster, D., 'Class and County Government in Early Nineteenth Century Lancashire', *NH* 9 (1974), 48–61.

French, G. J., *The Life and Times of Samuel Crompton* (Manchester: Thomas Dinham, 1859).

Garland, D. A., *Methodist Secessions: the Origins of Free Methodism in Three Lancashire Towns*, Chetham Society, 3rd ser., 26 (Manchester: Chetham Society, 1979).

Garratt, M., *Samuel Bamford, Portrait of a Radical* (Littleborough: Kelsall, 1992).

Glen, R., 'Anatomy of a Religious Revival, Stockport Methodism in the 1790s', *MRHR* 10 (1996), 3–13.

Glover, R., *Britain at Bay: Defence Against Bonaparte, 1803–14* (Allen & Unwin, 1973).

Green, P. G., 'Charity, Morality and Social Control, Clerical Attitudes in the Diocese of Chester, 1715–95', *THSLC* 141 (1991), 207–33.

Gregory, D., 'The Production of Regions in England's Industrial Revolution', *Journal of Historical Geography*, 14 (1988), 50–8.

Halley, R., *Lancashire: Its Puritanism and Nonconformity*, 2nd edn. (Manchester: Tubbs & Brook, 1872).

Handforth, P., 'Manchester Radical Politics, 1788–94', *TLCAS* 66 (1956), 87–106.

Hellmuth, E. (ed.), *The Transformation of Political Culture: England and Germany in the Late Eighteenth Century* (Oxford: Oxford University Press, 1990).

Hempton, D., *The Religion of the People: Methodism and Popular Religion, c.1750–1900* (Routledge, 1996).

Hepburn, J., *A Book of Scattered Leaves, Poetry of Poverty in Broadside Ballads in Nineteenth Century England*, vol. 1 (Bucknell University Press, 2000).

Herford, R. T., *Memorials of Stand Chapel* (Prestwich: Allen, 1893).

Hikins, H. (ed.), *Building the Union: Merseyside, 1756–1967* (Liverpool: Toulouse Press, 1973).

Hilton, J. A., *Catholic Lancashire: From Reformation to Renewal, 1559–1991* (Chichester: Phillimore, 1994).

Hindle, G. B., *Provision for the Relief of the Poor in Manchester, 1754–1826*, Chetham Society, 3rd ser., 22 (1975).

Holderness, B. A. and Turner, M., eds., *Land, Labour and Agriculture, 1700–1920* (Hambledon, 1991).

Honeyman, K., *Origins of Enterprise, Business Leadership in the Industrial Revolution* (Manchester: Manchester University Press, 1982).

Hudson, P., *Regions and Industries: a Perspective on the Industrial Revolution in Britain* (Cambridge: Cambridge University Press, 1989).

Hunt, C. J., *The Lead Miners of the Northern Pennines in the Eighteenth and Nineteenth Centuries* (Manchester: Manchester University Press, 1970).

King, P., 'Edward Thompson's Contribution to Eighteenth Century Studies, the Patrician–Plebeian Model Re-examined', *SH* 21 (1996), 215–28.

King, S. and Timmins, G., *Making Sense of the Industrial Revolution* (Manchester: Manchester University Press, 2001).

Knight, F., *The Strange Case of Thomas Walker: Ten Years in the Life of a Manchester Radical* (Lawrence & Wishart, 1957).

Langton, J., 'The Industrial Revolution and the Regional Geography of England', *Transactions of the Institute of British Geographers*, new ser., 9 (1984), 145–67.

Laqueur, T. W., *Religion and Respectability: Sunday Schools and Working Class Culture, 1780–1850* (New Haven: Yale University Press, 1976).

Lewis, J. B., *The Pitt Clubs, A Short Historical Guide* (J. B. Lewis, 1997).

Lock, A. (ed.), *Looking Back at Denton* (Ashton: Tameside MBC, 1985).

—— *Looking Back at Stalybridge* (Tameside: Tameside MBC, 1989).

Lloyd-Jones, R., *Manchester and the Age of the Factory* (Croom Helm, 1988).

Lowton, R., 'Population Trends in Lancashire and Cheshire', *TLCHS* 114 (1962), 189–213.

MacNaughton, D. A., *Roscoe of Liverpool, His Life, Writings and Treasures, 1753–1831* (Birkenhead: Countyvise, 1996).

Makepeace, C. E., *Science and Technology in Manchester, Two Hundred Years of the Lit and Phil* (Manchester: Manchester Lit and Phil, 1984).

Marshall, J. D., *Furness and the Industrial Revolution* (Barrow: J. Milner, 1958).

—— 'The Lancashire Rural Labourer in the Early Nineteenth Century', *TLCAS* 71 (1961), 90–128.

—— 'Proving Ground or the Creation of Regional Identity?' in P. Swan and D. Foster (eds.), *Essays in Regional and Local History* (Beverley: Hutton Press, 1992).

Marshall, L. S., *The Development of Public Opinion in Manchester, 1780–1820* (Syracuse: Syracuse University Press, 1946).

Mather, F. C., 'Georgian Churchmanship Reconsidered, Some Variations in Anglican Public Worship, 1714–1830', *Journal of Ecclesiastical History*, 32 (1985), 255–83.

Menzies, E. M., 'The Freeman Voter in Liverpool, 1802–35', *TLCHS* 124 (1972), 85–105.

Mingay, G. E., *Enclosure and the Small Farmer in the Age of the Industrial Revolution* (Macmillan, 1968).

Muir, R. and Platt, E., *A History of Municipal Government in Liverpool* (Liverpool: University of Liverpool, 1906).

Oldfield, J. R., *Popular Politics and British Anti-Slavery, the Mobilization of Public Opinion Against the Slave Trade, 1787–1807* (Manchester: Manchester University Press, 1995).

Palmer, R., *The Sound of History: Songs and Social Comment* (Oxford: Oxford University Press, 1996).

Phythian-Adams, C. (ed.), *Societies, Cultures and Kinship, 1580–1850: Cultural Provinces and English Local History* (Leicester: Leicester University Press, 1993).

Pooley, C. and Turnbull, J., *Migration and Mobility in Britain Since the Eighteenth Century* (UCL Press, 1998).

Rack, H. D., 'The Providential Moment, Church-Building, Methodism and Evangelical Entryism in Manchester, 1788–1825', *THSLC* 141 (1991), 235–60.

Randall, A. and Charlesworth, A., *Markets, Market Culture and Popular Protest in Eighteenth-Century Britain and Ireland* (Liverpool: Liverpool University Press, 1996).

Read, D., *Peterloo: the Massacre and its Background* (Manchester: Manchester University Press, 1958).

Read, M. and Wells, R. (eds.), *Class, Conflict and Protest in the English Countryside, 1700–1880* (Cass, 1990).

Redford, A., *Labour Migration in England, 1800–50*, 3rd edn. (Manchester: Manchester University Press, 1976).

Rogers, G., 'Custom and Common Right: Waste Land, Enclosure and Social Change in West Lancashire', *Agricultural History Review*, 41 (1993), 137–54.

Royle, E., *Issues of Regional Identity in Honour of John Marshall* (Manchester: Manchester University Press, 1998).

Russell, D., *Looking North: Northern England and the National Imagination* (Manchester: Manchester University Press, 2004).

Salveston, R., *Mill Towns and Moorlands: Rural Themes in Lancashire Working Class Culture* (Salford, University of Salford, 1985).

Samuel, R., ed., *Patriotism: the Making and Unmaking of British National Identity*, vol. 1, *History and Politics* (Routledge, 1989).

Sanderson, M., 'Education and the Factory in Industrial Lancashire, 1780–1840', *Economic History Review*, 20 (1967), 266–79.

Sanderson, P. E., 'The Structure of Politics in Liverpool 1780–1807', *THSLC* 127 (1977), 65–89.

Scholes, J. C., *History of Bolton with Memorials of the Old Parish Church* (Bolton: Daily Chronicle, 1892).

Sellers, I., 'William Roscoe, the Roscoe Circle and Radical Politics in Liverpool, 1789–1807', *TLCHS* 120 (1968), 45–62.

Simpson, C. M., *The British Broadside and its Music* (New Jersey: Rutgers University Press, 1966).

Smelser, N. J., *Social Change in the Industrial Revolution: An Application of Theory to the Lancashire Cotton Industry*, new edn. (Aldershot: Gregg Revivals, 1994).

Snape, M., 'Poverty and the Northern Clergy', *NH* 36 (2000), 83–98.

Snell, K. D. M., *Annals of the Labouring Poor: Social Change and Agrarian England, 1660–1900* (Cambridge: Cambridge University Press, 1985).

Spencer, P., *A Portrait of Samuel Greg, 1758–1834* (Styal: Quarry Bank Mill Trust, 1989).

Stobart, J., *The First Industrial Region: North West England, c.1700–60* (Manchester: Manchester University Press, 2004).

Stufford, W., *Socialism, Radicalism and Nostalgia: Social Criticism in Britain, 1775–1830* (Cambridge: Cambridge University Press, 1987).

Swindells, T., *Manchester Streets and Manchester Men* (Manchester: Cornish, 1906).

Taylor, J. S., *Poverty, Migration and Settlement in the Industrial Revolution: Sojourners' Narratives* (Palo Alto, CA: SPOS, 1989).

Taylor, P., 'A Divided Middle Class, Bolton, 1790–1850', *MRHR* 6 (1992), 3–15.

Thomis, M., *The Luddites: Machine-Breaking in Regency England* (Newton Abbot: David & Charles, 1970).

Timmins, G., *The Last Shift: the Decline of Handloom Weaving in Nineteenth Century Lancashire* (Manchester: Manchester University Press, 1993).

Unwin, G., *Samuel Oldknow and the Arkwrights*, 2nd edn. (Manchester: Manchester University Press, 1968).

Valenze, J. M., *Prophetic Sons and Daughters, Female Preaching and Popular Religion in Industrial England* (Princeton: Princeton University Press, 1985).

Vincent, D., *Bread, Knowledge and Freedom: a Study of Nineteenth Century Working Class Autobiography* (Europa, 1981).

Virgin, P., *The Church in an Age of Negligence* (Cambridge: James Clarke, 1989).

Wahrman, D., *Imagining the Middle Class, the Political Representation of Class in Britain, c.1780–1840* (Cambridge: Cambridge University Press, 1995).

Warnes, A. M., 'Early Separation of Homes From Workplaces and the Urban Structure of Chorley, 1780–1850', *THSLC* 122 (1970), 105–35.

White, A., ed., *A History of Lancaster, 1193–1993* (Keele: Ryburn, 1993).

Index